DIVINE APPOINTMENTS

AN EXTRAORDINARY STORY ABOUT AN ORDINARY COUPLE WHO DARED TO FULLY TRUST GOD

BY

FRED LAWRENCE

ACKNOWLEDGEMENTS

There are a number of wonderful people who contributed in countless ways to my writing this book.

When Jesus filled us with the Holy Spirit He gave my wife, Shirley, some life -defining visions. One was of two burning bushes, representing Shirley and I. Together; we traveled the world sharing the love of Christ with multitudes of people, ministering under the sweet anointing of the Holy Spirit. She was always a strong physical and spiritual support to me, and was the primary partner to me in the miracles we experienced.

Thank you to Debra L. Lupien-Robillard who read my first attempt at writing this book. My writing experience at that time had been learned in engineering school and I was a fairly good technical writer. She lovingly helped me learn to write in a more interesting manner.

Thank you to Dr. Robert Barstow who edited Divine Appointments, and who made important revisions and corrected my typographical errors

Many thanks to our friend and neighbor, computer expert, Joe Comerford , for guiding us from computer illiteracy to the point of meeting the publishers requirements.

Finally, thanks to Rev. Don Yarborough and His

wonderful congregation in Oneonta, as well as to the many others who contributed most of the funds for publishing this book.

FOREWORD

Those who read this autobiography are in for a treat and a treatment. Through episodes that have occurred in the life of one man, Fred Lawrence, a man who dared to take the Lord at His word, you will come to understand more fully that God is no respecter of persons, and that you too can be one who brings His healing and restoration to those in your world

You will smile, and you may shed some tears. You will be uplifted and encouraged. Your hope will be restored, your theology may be challenged. Your faith will be revitalized as you discover for a certainty that the God of Moses, David, and Elijah; and of John and Paul still lives and breathes life into, and works through people today. You will know the comfort of the miracle working power of His active presence in the lives of all who all those who call on Jesus to baptize them in the Holy Spirit. You will learn that you too can experience DIVINE ENCOUNTERS with the Great I AM, the one who rules and reigns forever and ever.

As one who participated in all the Men's Advances and most of the Couples Advances, and thus who witnessed many of these episodes, I can assure you that even though this book in autobiographical, it is really not about Fred

Lawrence and his lovely wife, Shirley

And their family, nor about FGBMFI and BMFUSA, as remarkable as they all may be. But this book is a testimony about the Living God they serve and represent. All glory be to the Father, and to His Son Jesus, and to the Holy Ghost! Amen and Amen!

Dr. Robert Barstow
Chairman of the Arts Department at SUNY Oneonta, NY

CONTENTS

1

DIVINE APPOINTMENTS

Iglanced at my watch for at least the twentieth time that day. In just a few minutes, I would be boarding my plane toward home. The twenty-eight or so hours of flights and airports confronting me between Accra, Ghana and Syracuse seemed small in comparison with the hugs and kisses I'd be getting at the end of the trip. Yes, I was a bit homesick.

My schedule in Ghana and Nigeria had been non-stop for thirty-five days. So I'd have no trouble going to sleep on the plane that night. And it would be that kind of restful sleep that comes at the end of a "mission successfully accomplished," even while sitting upright in my seat.

Just then, "KLM Flight 1242 to Amsterdam now boarding through Gate 2!" came over the loudspeaker.

With a sigh of relief, I picked up my suit bag and carry-on and headed for the gate. A straight-faced official took my ticket and gave me a boarding pass. I strode quickly across the tarmac to our waiting DC-10. What a blessing to find that I was the only passenger in my row of three seats by a window! I'd be able to raise the chair arms, stretch out, and sleep on the long, non-stop night flight to Europe. It pays to fly with God!

Now that my mission was complete, I was anxious for a reunion with my family in Syracuse. My traveling alone on this trip had taken its toll. Shirley and Becky nearly always had been my traveling companions on previous trips. Our nine years of almost daily traveling had prepared us for nearly everything I had encountered in West Africa. And although Shirley would have endured the hardships without complaint, Becky might have had a few problems. Not the least of these would have been dealing with the little green lizards that tried to crawl in bed with you (even though Africans know that they are perfectly harmless), and learning to enjoy eating fufu (an African tuber). In deference to my hosts, I had gotten used to eating their dishes with proper enjoyment!

Once again, I marveled at the sequence of events over the years that had brought me to this point. Most of my life had been a series of divine appointments that directed my steps through life. "DIVINE APPOINTMENTS," I told Shirley, "for they were all scheduled by God." Even more remarkable was my recent discovery that this lifelong dream had been ordained by God before I was born!

As a child, I had always had a strange preoccupation with the people and places of Africa. I could spend hours pouring over any book or article I could find about Africa. One day I found one of my Dad's books about David Livingston, a missionary doctor in Africa during the 1800's. Livingston had heard the noted missionary, Robert Moffat, speak about that great, "dark" continent of Africa.

Moffat spoke eloquently about the Africa he had come to love: "Often, as I look to the north, to the vast plains of the north, I have sometimes in the morning sun seen the smoke of a thousand villages where no missionary has ever been." As these words had gripped the heart of Livingston and of my father, they also gripped me as I grew older.

Livingston was the first white missionary to walk that vast continent from south to north, and from west to east. The paths of his footsteps formed a huge cross, while his tearful prayers bathed that great land with the love of Christ, even though his arm had been severed by a lion. (On a future assignment I would find myself ministering to the businessmen in Kisangani, Zaire, the purported place where Livingston's paths crossed.) His diary contains a prayer of total commitment, a prayer that has become my own: "Lord, send me anywhere, only go with me. Lay any burden on me, only sustain me. Sever any ties but the tie that binds me to Thy service and to Thy heart."

It was that prayer, along with the promise of God, "Lo, I am with you always, even unto the end of the world," (Matt. 28:20b) that sustained and followed him until the morning one of his men found him dead, still on his knees after a night of prayer. It was that prayer and that Scripture that just now had carried me on yet another leg of a journey that had begun before I was even born.

* * * * *

After the death of my father, my Mom shared with me the circumstances surrounding my birth. I then learned of the Divine Appointment my parents had made for me with God. The appointment that they had penciled in over fifty years ago, was the one I just now had confirmed in ink.

Lee William Lawrence was raised on a farm in Wilmington, NY, situated at the foot of Whiteface Mountain. Born the eldest of twelve children, Dad learned early about hard work and strict discipline. According to Mother, Grandpa Lawrence wasn't especially sympathetic to my Dad's dreams and ambitions. He had a farm to run, and his two eldest were my Dad and my Uncle Herb, their father's "un-hired " hands.

One warm, spring day, while plowing and praying in the peaceful solitude of the old "south forty," Dad heard the audible voice of God. He told my Dad, who was then sixteen years of age, to prepare himself to become a missionary to the nation of Swaziland in South Africa. He nearly was overcome with an excitement and purpose for his life that even the grueling work of the farm could not dampen.

Thus, when Dad finished high school, he struck a bargain with Grandpa—he would work a year for one hundred dollars that he then would use for Bible School. However, at the end of the year, Grandpa, not wanting to lose his best farm hand, rescinded and refused to honor the agreement.

Disappointed and discouraged, but very determined, Dad hitched a ride to Allentown, PA. There he found work as a butcher, and enrolled in the Beulah Park Bible Institute, a Wesleyan Methodist Bible School.

Dad was a zealous student, passionately stirred by the Word of God. While still in school, he earned the reputation of being a powerful preacher, and was invited to preach in churches throughout Pennsylvania and New York. It was at one of those preaching engagements in a small Methodist church in Tupper Lake that he was introduced to my mother, Mildred E. Knapp.

At the time, Mildred, who had heard the call of God to be a pastor's wife, was a student at Houghton College in western New York. After a brief courtship, Mom and Dad fell in love and decided to get married. She completed her degree work at Houghton, and then joined Dad at Allentown, where they both began preparing themselves for their mission to Swaziland.

Their first church was in Massena in Upstate New York.

Dad was the happiest he'd ever been in his life. His happiness was compounded when Mother became pregnant with their first child. Little did he realize that this great happiness would challenge his greatest dream.

While pastoring they continued to prepare for their mission to Africa. During the final stages of these preparations my older sister, Bethel Jean, was born. Mother admitted that, "After that, my enthusiasm for Africa gradually diminished." At first, she kept her fears to herself. But as the day of their departure loomed closer, she frantically decided that Swaziland was not the place for them to try to bring up their beautiful baby girl.

"I just can't do it, Lee!" she said, her eyes filling with tears. "You know I love and trust the Lord with all my heart, but I just don't feel any peace with taking Bethel to that terrible place. Every missionary we know has lost children in the wild jungles of Africa. I am so sorry - so very sorry. I don't know what to do."

"It's all right, Millie." Dad said, gently taking her in his arms. "It will be all right. God will show us what to do. I understand."

While Dad did understand, he now was forced to make a decision that would tear him apart. He found himself between the proverbial "rock and a hard place." To fulfill his calling, he would be forced to leave his family behind, even as Livingston had done. He believed that God would somehow make a way for both him and Mom to be obedient. So he put his plans for Africa on hold as they waited on the Lord for an answer to their dilemma.

However, because arrangements already had been made to fill Dad's position at the church, he needed to find another position quickly. With his reputation as a forceful and dynamic preacher, he soon was offered the Pastorate of a Pilgrim Holiness Church located in the Central New York State town of Owasco.

Although convinced he'd been right about staying with Mom and Bethel, Dad still was distraught about not fulfilling God's commission for his life. He and Mother prayed fervently for guidance and for an understanding of what had happened to them. As they prayed and fasted over the next several months, an impression began to form in both their minds. Suddenly they knew how to direct their prayers. Fervently they prayed, "God, please give us a son. We will carefully and prayerfully bring him up to be a man of God. You may then put your calling to the mission field on him." Nine months later, on December 16, 1930, I was born. Coincidence? I don't think so! Mother and Dad had three more children, but I was the only son. I was named Charles Frederick. They called me Frederick or Fred.

In light of what now was happening with me, my thinking about my Father's past brought rather ambivalent feelings. On the one hand, I was sorry my Dad had died without knowing that I indeed had been led of the Lord to carry out the commission he had received in the farm field. On the other, I felt totally satisfied that God had answered their prayer. (What difference would it have made if I had known about all these things as a boy? God knows. Now it was important for me to carry out my own destiny as well as I could.)

My mother chuckled when she heard I was to minister in Africa. "You must admit, my boy, we had good reason to doubt if even God could turn you around when you were young. You had your own agenda, and it wasn't to be a missionary. At least not as we had understood the word!"

As a young boy, I not only began to sense the growing, unasked for pressure of being a "preacher's kid", but also the pressure of being trained by my parents to be a minister of the Gospel. My parents held me to a higher standard of behavior than did the parents of any of my friends. This, in spite of the fact that I hadn't chosen to be the son of a "holiness" minister, nor had I any desire to be a missionary and preacher! These were not vocations I had chosen! So, when either of my parents would push me a little too hard to make me into what they thought God wanted me to be, I stubbornly dug in my heels! However, this paled in comparison to the real spiritual battle that was to begin when I was nine years old, a time during which Dad took a Pastorate at another Holiness Church located in Lake Placid, NY.

At first, I could not believe that as a young boy I could have asked for a more beautiful and exciting place to live than Lake Placid. The changes of seasons provided a wide diversity of sports from skiing and skating, to swimming and fishing. A clear, bubbling stream meandered right through the heart of the downtown and into Chubb Pond, a reservoir formed by an old dam.

Our home on River Street made Chubb Pond an integral part of our backyard, as well as my life. I could lay on the grassy shore and watch the clouds drift lazily along the sky. I could catch a three-pound rainbow trout for our dinner the next day, and at the same time listen to a scrappy old blue jay scold me for intruding into his domain.

At school, however, I once again began to wonder why a group of my classmates insisted on calling me a "holy roller," just as they had at our previous home. I desperately wanted just to blend in and be one of them. Gradually I associated the name with being some sort of religious misfit, because they hurled it at me every time they wanted to make fun of me. One notable exception to this group was Don, a boy who also attended our church. He became one of the greatest things that ever happened to me. A couple years older than I, he became the big brother I always wished for. Mother would send us off to school with a kiss and an admonition to Don, "Keep Frederick under your wing, Don." And he always would! He became a lifelong friend and brother in Christ.

Along with my being called a "holy roller," I also began

to wonder why I had to memorize so many scriptures. At first it was fun, and I was a ready learner. But when I was asked to recite them to my parents, to their Christian friends, or to the whole Church, it ceased to be fun. Being a bashful, shy, boy, I hated to be "put on the stage" for everyone's steady gaze.

On top of that, my boyhood Bible training program began to include piano lessons. Mother was a very accomplished piano teacher, and some of her students became skilled musicians. But little by little, I resisted the pressure to be always just a little bit better than I was. If I could have learned the piano for my own enjoyment, I probably would be a pianist to this day. Eventually, my stomach started drawing into knots every time I got near the piano. Finally, I dropped out of my piano lessons.

Still further, although I seemed to understand everything my teachers taught me in school, I had a strong tendency to write everything I learned backwards. None of my teachers recognized my dyslexia. Maybe there wasn't even a name for it then! But, no matter how hard I studied, I consistently fell short of everyone's expectations, most of all my own. Gradually I learned to write backwards. My schoolwork looked good to everyone—except me!

Somehow, all of these things that were so troubling to me became synonymous with God. No matter what the problem, God always was involved. Each evening after Mother would spend at least an hour teaching me about spiritual things, she would end with a promise: "If you just pray and tell the Lord about your problems, He will straighten things out for you!" But things didn't straighten out! It seemed to me that I failed at just about everything I tried to do. And God invariably played some part in just about everything I did!

When I became more and more a failure, I no longer saw God as my friend, but as a harsh judge. I didn't believe that God answered my prayers. No matter how hard I prayed, I remained a very skinny, pale, kid who wore glasses. By the time I was thirteen, I had become so introverted and anxious that I started sneaking into my favorite Tarzan and Roy Rogers movies. (Movies were a forbidden practice for us Pilgrim Holiness kids. Much too worldly I was told!)

My Father's sermons, seemingly preached specifically to me, proved too difficult for a rebel like me to endure. No tolerance nor forbearance for sin existed in the life of a Christian in a Holiness Church. Rather than change my lifestyle, I became a habitual "backslider." At least once a year an evangelist would come to our church (and home) for a "revival." Usually by the final Saturday night of the revival, he would preach a "hellfire and brimstone" sermon on judgment, and the sinner's eternal destination in hell. Usually I would respond to the invitation, go to the altar and cry and pray my heart out for forgiveness. God would, of course, forgive me and "save" me once again.

During the days that followed, I would gradually fall back into my backsliding habits. But the terrible guilt, the shame, and the conviction of sin became more than I could handle. The persecution I experienced from the "world," my failures to honor my parents, and my lack of success in anything required of me in school—all became unbearable! No one existed for me to talk to about my life. Finally, I decided that there was one thing I might be able to do, and that was to ask God to "get off my case." If He would do that, I knew I would no longer be so burdened by my guilty conscience.

I don't recall the exact words of my prayer, but the essence of it went like this: "God, I love you, but I want you to please leave me alone. Just let me have some peace and be like everyone else." Probably I said some other things, I don't know. But I had the frightful experience that God had left me. I cried out to Him, "Oh God, I'm sorry for what I said. I didn't mean it. Please come back. Please!" But God wasn't there to hear me for the first time in my life. When I tried to pray, it seemed like my voice would echo back to me like speaking into a vacant room. And all of that in answer to my own prayer. (Many years later while studying God's Word, I came to understand that God could withdraw the sense of His presence, while at the same time still being there. Unfortunately for me, I never heard of this distinction. The next seventeen years of my life became hell on earth!)

I began to associate more and more with my school classmates, and was increasingly accepted by them. I did everything to make myself look and act like anyone else. I became a pretty good ski jumper, and enjoyed most of the sports. I lied about my past, telling my friends that I was really just like them. I told them that my real parents died in a car accident, and that those holy roller parents of mine had adopted me. Just about everything I did compounded my sin problem and my guilt!

One night, not long after my fateful encounter with God, I dreamed that Jesus Christ had returned to earth to rapture His followers. My parents and sisters had all gone with Him to heaven, but I was left behind to fend for myself. Fear filled my heart! I knew that I faced eternity without God and that I had no recourse. I believed I had committed the "unpardonable sin." I had sealed my own horrible fate, and would pay for my action eternally in the unquenchable fires of hell. Gradually those dreams became nightmares. As I slid off into that fiery inferno, I could smell the brimstone and could hear the agonized cries of those who had preceded me into that dreadful place.

So, what did it matter what I did with my life? Or how I acted? I tried doing everything my friends were doing to have fun, like drinking beer, swearing, smoking, and fighting. To my dismay, I soon learned that the things my friends were doing weren't that much fun. I even tried to outdo them by doing everything to excess. But that didn't help a bit!

One of my friends was a Roman Catholic girl. I walked her home from school as often as I could arrange it. I thought she was the most beautiful person in the world. And because she was a catholic, I thought that she too would be unable to enjoy heaven when she died. So, knowing that our fates were sealed, I comforted myself that we would go to our eternal reward together. When we went to some movies together, I experienced more fun than anything I had ever done in my life. She quickly became my only close friend and confidant.

Then one day she disappeared—simply and completely disappeared—dropping totally out of sight forever! We were sixteen. I couldn't find out what happened to her, no matter how hard I tried. Gradually, I decided that this was a part of my punishment. Whatever had happened to her was my fault. The little happiness I experienced while we were together was more happiness than I deserved, so God had removed her from my life. Permanently! What did I have to live for? Why should I go on?

One of my responses to these questions was to skip school. Strolling along the street one beautiful Spring morning when I should have been in school, I met a buddy of mine who had become a delinquent from school. I said, "Hi Woody. Where are you going?"

"Hi, Fred. I'm gonna join the Navy. Wanna come with me?" I thought it all over for about ten seconds and replied, "Why sure, Woody! Let's do it." I dropped the two school books I was carrying, turned around and began the process of joining the Navy.

* * * * *

On the day we left on the train for the Great Lakes Naval Training Center, I really believed that in the Navy I'd be able to forget all the things that were so troubling for me at home. "I would be my own man!" But the further that train got away from Lake Placid, and the closer we got to Great Lakes, the more I said to myself: "Fred, you idiot, what are you doing on this train? Why have you done this to yourself? You had so much going for yourself right where you were, why didn't you just stay there and make the best of things? Now, you are really in for it!"

Although they signed the necessary papers giving me the required permission to join the Navy, I could understand why my parent's hearts were broken by my actions. I had broken every rule there was for me to break at home. I had been a total embarrassment to every member of my family. I rationalized that the agony I was causing them a little easier to bear if I no longer constantly battled with them. Also, without their not knowing precisely what I was doing, they now could pray for me from a distance more easily than if I were at home. The chances that I would ever be able to hurt them so much again, would be lessened if I were a thousand miles or more away. So they signed the papers, kissed me good-bye, and I became a sailor, for better or for worse!

2

JOURNEY TO A DISTANT COUNTRY
Luke 15:13

When my Company graduated from boot camp at the Great Lakes Naval Training Center, there was a shortage of Hospital Corpsmen in the Navy. Those of us who met the necessary requirements could volunteer for Hospital Corps School, or become a Seaman (a deck hand). Big choice! So I volunteered to attend the Great Lakes Hospital Corps School.

Somehow the combination of schoolwork, physical training, and strict military discipline all came together for me. I graduated at the top of my naval class. When my parents received my CO's letter informing them of my achievement, they were pleasantly surprised—to say the least!

My next assignment was St. Albans Naval Hospital, St. Albans, Long Island, NY. The training program there was designed to provide each man with experience in every aspect of the work done in a Naval Hospital. My experience at St. Albans, about a 30 minute train ride from downtown Manhattan, included much more than Navy duty. Two days out of three we were free to go where we wished, as long as we were back at the Hospital by eight o'clock the next morning, ready for work. So exploring New York City, the largest, most exciting city in the US, became my first priority. It was a task I could never have completed, but it was certainly a most enjoyable and informative pastime while trying.

Two out of three weekends were also ours to spend any way we wished. So usually one out of three weekends found me hitch-hiking home to Lake Placid. I always had great success getting rides, and the trips themselves usually were pleasant experiences, as well as very inexpensive.

During one of those weekend "liberties," I met a pretty little high school gal named Shirley, from Saranac Lake. We hit it off real well, and soon became quite friendly. Her hobby was dancing, and she knew all the steps. Soon, I made dancing my hobby, and enlisted the able and willing instructorship of my new-found friend. Those were very exciting classes. Shirley and I seemed to have a lot in common, and her company made many of my weekends a real joy.

At the end of my two-year stint at St. Albans, I was considered ready to be assigned to any Naval operation in the world. The Navy assigned me to the USS Midway, CVB-41, one of the largest aircraft carriers in the world. I would serve out the remainder of my four-year enlistment on that magnificent ship. Under other circumstances, I would have loved Navy life. Living on the Aircraft Carrier USS Midway CVB-41 was like living in a small city (the ship had more than 3500 men). And, every few days that little city moved to a different port or country. I was a Third Class Petty Officer Pharmacists Mate, and I worked in the Sick Bay. My work was like that of a civilian operating room/urgent-treatment room nurse. However, our homeport, Norfolk, Virginia, turned out to be not nearly as hospitable as Long Island and New York City had been. Plus, I still was tormented by bad dreams.

The Navy was continuously keeping itself in fighting condition, in order to be ready for combat anywhere in the world at a moment's notice. Numerous medical emergencies and illnesses resulted from the hundreds of daily aircraft flights that took off and landed each day from our flight deck. Our medical department was always being trained to handle the worst kind of injuries, such as burns, gunshot and explosive wounds, etc.. When any of our seven doctors did operations, some of us were always observing or assisting. As a result, in the event emergencies arose when doctors were not around (such as when we were on a much smaller ship or on duty with the Fleet Marines) and worse came to worse, we would be able to do the same operation.

Our ship visited 29 countries on four continents—not bad for a country boy who had never been more than 30 miles from home before joining the Navy! The posters I had seen, "JOIN THE NAVY AND SEE THE WORLD!" were really true. The things I learned and experienced in those four years would fill several books.

In the larger ports near cities like; Rome, Italy; Athens, Greece; Istanbul, Turkey; etc., we were encouraged to take five- or six-day sightseeing tours sponsored by the Navy. They were designed to provide the broadest possible exposure to that part of the world, and I always signed up to participate, at least on my first visit to those places. I found myself thoroughly engrossed in everything I could learn about the places we visited. The history and geography classes that had seemed so dull in high school now came to life for me.

Gradually I learned that most of the important historic sites I visited, especially throughout the Mediterranean region, were originally inspired by the spread of Christianity during the first century and later. Often Christian guides were in charge of the famous places I visited, and provided expert commentary during our visits. My respect for Christianity grew enormously as I got to see the places spoken of in the Bible. God's indelible footprints were apparent wherever we went. Surprise, surprise!

My four Navy years also taught me that a certain freedom comes with the strict military discipline, a freedom that I had never known before. First, I was taught the rules. Then, I learned what the punishment would be if I broke the rules. And I learned that those rules were inviolable, and the subsequent punishment for breaking them certain. So, if living a nice, peaceful life, free of stress was my desire, all I had to do was play by the rules. One Navy Chief explained to me, "In this man's Navy, there's a right way, there's a wrong way, and there's the Navy way. Do it the Navy's way and you'll stay out of trouble." Another important thing I learned was that to be a success, I needed a much better education than I had. I determined that, one way or another, I would further my education after I was discharged from the Navy.

In order to satisfy my desire for greater knowledge about the places I visited, I began to read books again. Some of these were books I bought at the important historical sites we visited, and others came from the rather extensive library aboard the Midway. I often wondered whether my school studies would have made a much more lasting impression on me if they had been mixed with at least some reality.

I would go by myself to old cathedrals and basilicas, including the Vatican, and stay for hours, quietly hoping to feel the presence of God as I once did. Frequently I would have a one-way conversation with God, sometimes telling Him about my great respect for the magnificent Christians I had learned about. At other times I would reflect on the fact that I had joined the Navy to escape from my nightmares, anticipating that somehow I would be able to outrun my spiritual problem. What I began to realize, however, was that I had actually entered right back into my own dreams! Although my family was safely and happily at home with God and each other, I was out in the world, seemingly alone—this, in spite of the fact that the Mediterranean part of the world in which I found myself had God's autograph all over it!

On those occasions when this loneliness would cause me to reminisce about home and the people there that I loved, my pretty little friend, Shirley from Saranac Lake frequently came back to mind. While reading her letters, I often mused that, "The older she gets, while I'm so busy seeing the world, the more attractive she seems to become." Then, just when it seemed like our friendship was elevating into a romance, I wrote a "Dear John" type letter to tell her that I thought both of us were too young to be getting so serious! Why?

Because a steady girlfriend or faithful wife at home could keep an honest sailor from doing many of the things for which they are known while they roam around the seaports of the world. But, of course, I didn't consider myself as being the "one and only" of any one. Nevertheless, as a result of Shirley's sharing with me how she had had a personal visitation with Jesus Christ at the front of St. Agnes Roman Catholic Church, and how He had become her personal friend since early childhood, she now had become an unwanted and unneeded conscience-like little being perched on my shoulder. The majority of the time I wasn't aware of it. But just let me get into any kind of compromising situation, and there she would be! Hey, I wasn't married to that girl, nor were we seriously, romantically involved. Yet, I couldn't get away from her high moral standards nor her Christian "code of conduct". (I now am also very certain that the religious teachings of my parents and their prayers never lost their influence on my life.)

One day after I had been at sea for more than a year, and I had been too busy to write anyone at home for a long time, I went ashore in Palermo, Sicily. Coincidentally, my old buddy, Woody, with whom I joined the Navy, had sailed into port at the same time. It didn't take long for us to locate each other. We had a great time catching up on all we had been doing since we last were together. Woody said, "Fred, I ran into your friend Shirley the last time I was home. When I saw the diamond on her ring finger, I asked her when she and you were getting married. She said it wasn't you, old boy, but a guy from Tupper Lake. Her answer was, 'Soon, I hope.' And, if you ever run into your buddy, Fred, say 'Hi!' to him for me."

Now this Shirley was the same girl who, long before I ever met her, had informed her girl friend that some day she was going to marry me. And while we had become good friends, I had never considered our relationship as anything more than a friendship. Obviously, she had taken my last letter very seriously, and had decided to get on with her life.

Yet, when I got into my bunk that night, all kinds of strange thoughts tumbled through my mind: "What is that girl possibly thinking of, wearing an engagement ring? She's not old enough for such a thing! She seemed to me to be quite satisfied with our casual relationship. Could some guy have just swept her off her feet? What could I do? Here I am, half way around the world, and in no position to talk some sense into her cute little head. Why, she could ruin her whole life if she falls for the smooth line of one of those Tupper Lake Romeo's!"

My troubled imaginings continued to multiply by the minute as the days went by. I fearfully expected each mail call to bring me a wedding announcement stating that she had already tied the knot with that no good scoundrel. "Why was I so concerned?" I thought. "Hadn't I thought of her as just another pretty little girl from Saranac Lake? So what if she did get married? If she did, that was her problem, not mine!"

After a week or so went by, the tension grew to the point where I decided that such a drastic situation deserved a drastic response. I needed to get that little lady's attention before it was too late and she did something foolish that could ruin her young life. A plan began to develop in my troubled mind. If I could do or say something to her that would prevent her from making this horrendous mistake, then I'd better do it. I'd have to fight fire with fire. Now!

My hurried response to the last letter I had received from her a few months before began to take shape. I wrote and rewrote that letter a dozen times. Nothing I said sounded to me like I had enough ammunition to prevent her imminent catastrophe. Finally I wrote: "Dearest Shirley, I wish I were there to speak to you in person about the things that are on my mind. But since I can't do that, I'll just come right out and tell you the truth. I love you. I have wanted to tell you this for quite awhile, but have been a little bit too shy. The more I think about you, the more I realize that I cannot possibly live without you. Will you marry me? I promise to love and cherish you always. Lovingly yours, Fred."

To avoid getting cold feet about the contents of the letter, I immediately sealed and mailed it. Once I dropped it in the mailbox, however, I began to think about the possible consequences of my "good Samaritan" letter. "What have I done? I'm too young to get married and so is she. Oh well, I didn't set any dates. We can be engaged for as many years as it takes for us to grow up. At least I may have been able to get that poor girl's mind off that 'Tupper Lake log roller' for awhile, and to think seriously for a few moments about that tall, dark and handsome sailor, 'moi'! Hopefully my note would at least **get** her attention."

Finally, one beautiful day while in port at Cannes,

France, our company mail clerk called my name. "Lawrence, this letter smells like Channel #5, (and 6,7, and 8)! Hurry up, this is too hot for me to handle!"

"Holy smokes! Could this be what I think it is?" I muttered, as I grabbed the letter and headed for the privacy of my favorite spot on the ship's fantail. Never had I had so many problems getting a letter open. And then, *Voila*, there it was!

"My darling Fred, Thank you for the very nice letter, which was several months overdue. At first glance I thought it was some sort of practical joke. But gradually I realized that you were serious. Why did you change your mind?"

"My answer to your proposal is, Yes! The sooner the better! I have been somewhat surprised that you haven't taken up with one of those French or Italian girls I've heard about. Let me know when you will be arriving home and when we can get married. My bags are almost packed......... Love, Shirley." (And all of that underlined with perfume!) For some reason my mind went back to my scripture-learning days, "Greater love hath no man than this, that a man should lay down his life for a 'girl friend.'" Maybe my impetuosity had finally cooked my goose, or at least landed it in very hot water. Suddenly I had a fiancee who seemed very anxious to have my last name. ASAP!

Thus began my gradual downhill slide toward holy matrimony. She never bothered to tell me that she broke things off with that other fellow on the same day she got my proposal letter. But whenever I had even a thought of suggesting a nice long engagement to her, my lousy conscience would remind me of that diamond I thought she still might have on hand. I wouldn't be back to the States until early December to stake my claim permanently. So all I could do was go along with Shirley's plans for a wedding along about December 16, my birthday! What a present that would be—especially for her!

During the next three months or so, we formulated our wedding plans by mail. My sister, Beulah, and her husband, Al, would be our attendants. My parents, who had relocated to Schenectady, welcomed us to stay with them and get married in their Nazarene Church. After the ceremony, we would travel to the great Capitol of New York State, Albany (only ten miles or so away, at a cost of fifty cents each way on a city bus) and enjoy a fabulous one-night honeymoon in the honeymoon suite at the swanky Iroquois Hotel, at $28 per night! And then, back to the Navy!

Back in Norfolk, and before leaving the base to travel to New York for the wedding, my incredible foresight caused me to make a deposit with a bartender acquaintance for one of his apartments. The apartment was located just a block from the main gate of the Portsmouth Naval Shipyard where my ship would be in dry dock for a few months. As a result, however, I found myself with barely enough funds to hitch-hike home!

The days flew by, and on December 17, we stood before the Pastor of the Church of the Nazarene in Schenectady while he tied the knot for us. My knees were trembling all the way to my teeth. I wondered if something or someone could possibly stop this madness. Talk about fear, I couldn't even look that dear girl in the eyes. And when the Pastor asked if anyone knew any reason why we should not be married, and if so, to speak then or forever hold his peace, dead silence filled the room! Not a word was spoken! I felt like a sailor lost at sea, with no one to rescue him. Then I kissed my bride and we became man and wife, joined together forever in holy matrimony. Only then did I realize my seventeen and a half-year old bride was just as scared as I was. Scared to tears!

Suddenly I knew that now was not a time for fear. This precious little girl wasn't a girl at all, but a very grown-up woman. And she now was my bride. "Wake up, Fred! Get hold of yourself! You got her into this, and you're the only one who can get her through it. Do the right thing, boy! Now!" It was at that second that I finally comprehended the scope of what we had just done. I also knew in my heart that I would try my best to make her dreams come true. From that day to this, more than fifty years later, I've loved her more each day—well almost every day! I not only got married, I became a man. I'd received the most wonderful gift I could have received, and Shirley was the one thing in this world I needed the most. A wonderful gift from the Lord, and He wasn't around for me to thank.

We arrived at the Greyhound Bus Station in Norfolk at 4:00 am, January 2, 1952. My landlord's bar (Salty's Saloon) didn't open until 10:00 that morning, so we sat outside his bar on our suitcases, huddled together to try to keep warm—and waited, and waited, and waited! Later that day, we moved into our two-room apartment with a bath down the hall. The oil space heater didn't work, and there was only a minimum of furniture. We had no linen, bedding nor dishes, and no money to buy any. If our whole situation hadn't been so tragic, we might not have been able to laugh our way through it all. As it was, if we couldn't have laughed, we'd have both broken down into tears. Fortunately, Shirley had some great ideas for making our little apartment into a cozy home. She has always had an uncanny ability to "make do" with whatever was at hand, and that without complaint.

At 6:30 the next morning, I reported back for duty on the Midway, while Shirley sat there in that cold and bare little apartment, wondering what to do next. My dry-docked ship was as high and dry as a beached whale, the workmen spread out over her like bees on honey to give her a total overhaul. The best part of that day was that it was payday. And I had a month's pay coming!

Our first days of trying to be homemakers were sort of

pitiful. First, we learned that every penny we earned was all we had to keep bodies and souls together. The movies we had seen as teenagers of Betty Grable and Lana Turner learning to be married had absolutely nothing to do with reality. We learned how to keep warm (above freezing) at night by wrapping up in our coats and each other. Those were the best of times and the worst of times. But I remembered a favorite saying of my Grandfather Knapp: "And this too shall pass"! We weathered the storm!

I noticed that my bad dreams had nearly stopped, in part because I was so tired by bedtime that I slept like a log. My days couldn't go fast enough for me to get home to my darling wife. My life consisted of just being in Shirley's presence, and the rest of the time just wishing I were with her. What could I have possibly done to deserve such a fantastic answer to the deepest need in my life—the need for a true companion?" I wondered, "Would God see me having so much joy and fun that I didn't deserve, and take her from me?" I couldn't answer that, but one thing I knew with all my heart—I loved a beautiful girl and she loved me, and that our greatest goal in life was to make each other as happy as possible.

When the Midway completed her stay in dry-dock, we sailed out of Portsmouth on a two-month "shakedown cruise" to test out all of the new systems that had just been installed. We anchored for a week in both Guantanamo Bay, Cuba and in Port-Au-Prince, Haiti, spending the rest of the time sailing at sea. During this time, Shirley went to stay with my folks in Schenectady. We could always expect at least one, and sometimes two letters a day from each other.

My ship was frequently in and out of port the rest of that year. And although everything went well, I noticed that the high seas didn't hold the excitement for me it once had. I was due for discharge the following April, and the time couldn't go fast enough for me. Shirley had discovered that she was pregnant, and that our first baby was expected sometime in November. We moved to a Navy housing development in South Norfolk while we awaited this addition to our family. He arrived right on time on November 31.

Charles Frederick, Jr. was a beautiful ten-pound boy who couldn't have been a better baby if he tried. If he was dry, rested, and well fed, he would play with his hands and feet for hours, examining them with great interest. He loved for us to play with him, and then was ready to go back to sleep. We never recall his ever crying. We always knew that Freddy was way above average.

My discharge from the Navy came through for March 25, 1952, a red- letter day in the Lawrence family. I had experienced all the travel I'd ever need by then, so we moved back to Schenectady while I prepared to return to school. Our spiritual lives continued on hold for some future time when we weren't so busy.

I enrolled in Mont Pleasant HS to take some subjects I needed to be accepted at Rensselaer Polytechnic Institute (R.P.I.). While attending Mont Pleasant High, our baby daughter, Nancy, came aboard to increase the size of our family to four. Freddie needed a little playmate, and she fit the bill precisely. A real beauty, she was the baby doll her mother and I had always dreamed of; and just what we thought we all needed to make our lives complete.

My studies at R.P.I. in Troy NY began in September, 1953. I had heard that they required a high level of scholastic achievement there, but I wasn't quite prepared for the large number of daily assignments. Four hours a day of homework was a minimum, but at times I would need to study every hour of the day to keep up with my very smart and unencumbered younger classmates.

To help with expenses, Shirley put her dancing skills to good use as an instructor at the Arthur Murray Dance Studio. Later she learned to be an expert collection agent for a large agency in Troy. We enrolled our children in a Roman Catholic day school. Each day was a supreme challenge for all of us to do everything required to allow me to finish my engineering degree.

Part way through my Junior year at RPI, we were blessed with a second beautiful little daughter. Mildred Elizabeth (Libby) was born prematurely, and had to stay in the hospital several weeks longer than her Mom did. So when she arrived at Georgian Terrace (our home), she was greeted with lots of love and kisses from all of us. She looked a lot like an angel, and added a whole new dimension of love to our home.

In June of 1958, I graduated on the Dean's list from R.P.I. with a BS degree in Architectural Engineering. Three of the most important things I learned in college were that I wasn't perfect, that I didn't have to prove anything to anyone, and that I didn't have to be as smart as my younger classmates. All I needed to do was learn my lessons, get passing grades, and still be a husband and father. Shirley received her "PHT" (Putting Hubby Through) degree, and shared my graduation from "the school of hard knocks" at a beautiful graduation ball.

My career goal in life was to design and build comfortable, affordable housing for everyone who needed it. The owner of a large manufactured-home company in Fairbury, Illinois, who had similar aspirations, put me to work as their Design Engineer. Our long economic dry spell came to an end, and life became something more than the endless struggle for existence. We built a nice home in Fairbury, and were finally on our way to achieving the American dream. As my experience increased in the home-building industry, the design and construction methods I developed gained wider and wider acceptance throughout the Industry.

Our life on the Midwestern plains was great compared with anything we had experienced before that. Shirley and I joined barbershop choruses, took up bowling, and made many new friends along the way. However, Fairbury, Illinois had achieved their reputation as being the "Nation's bread-basket" by being situated on the finest, and flattest, farmland in the world. Corn and soybean fields stretched for as far as you could see in any direction, interrupted only by an occasional hog or beef farm.

It soon became apparent to me that I could pursue my dreams with equal success in a more interesting setting. When a national manufactured homes magazine published an article about my work in Illinois, a New York State home manufacturer became interested and offered me a job. It didn't take us long to pull up stakes in Illinois, and relocate to the big city of Homer, NY, the precise geographical center of New York State. As we drove into the Finger Lakes region of central NY, we all felt like we were coming home. The forests and lakes, the rolling hills and valleys, and the four beautiful seasons, would provide us with endless opportunities to ski and skate, to swim and go camping, and to fish and hunt to our heart's content. As we drove into the picturesque and historic town of Homer, all of us said together, "We're home, we're home!" And so we were!

3

COMING HOME

My new job as Assistant Manager of a medium-sized home manufacturing plant in Homer, NY gave me many opportunities to pursue my dreams, gradually putting into operation the kind of facility which I felt could develop and build the "Home of the Future". Our children successfully picked up their school activities where they left off in Illinois. Shirley began to work her way into becoming fully involved in the social life of our little community.

One beautiful Spring morning while Shirley was doing her housework, she unexpectedly had a very interesting visitor, the Rev. Ed Thorne, pastor of the First Baptist Church of Homer. They quickly became acquainted.

Shirley soon realized that this wasn't just another casual "invitation- to-church "visitation. In fact, as we look back on what happened that day and that week, we've come to realize that it was the beginning of a DIVINE APPOINTMENT. While Shirley had experienced a personal relationship with Jesus Christ during her childhood, having met Him one morning in St. Bernard's R.C. Church, she had gained no understanding of the theology of her beliefs. If asked, she would simply reply, "I've always known and loved Jesus. We are the best of friends." But she never knew there was such a thing as being born again or salvation.

That morning, Pastor Thorne took Shirley, step by step, through God's plan of salvation. He carefully answered her questions as they went along, using scriptures from her own Bible. On several occasions in the past, she had been told that she should get "saved" or "born again" or "converted", but no one had told her how to go about doing that. When she heard the Word of God that day, it ignited her spirit with a desire to know God more intimately.

Shirley was waiting for me when I arrived home from work that afternoon. With a can of beer in one hand and a cigarette in the other, I sat at the kitchen table to hear her story. The things she told me were the last things on earth I expected her to say. But I hung on her every word.

She finished telling me what had happened that morning by stating that "We are going to that church Sunday morning—all of us! It's the big red brick church up on the corner. Only a five-minute walk, at the most!"

Sunday morning, Memorial Day, 1960, was a perfect day. The birds seemed ecstatic about the summer in the air, while the baby green buds and leaves on the trees were reminiscent of a little girl's Easter dress. Everything and everyone seemed to be welcoming the Lawrence's as we entered into that Baptist Church, dressed in our Sunday best.

I ended up sitting directly behind one of the steel balcony support posts—a spot that I'll always remember. We were warmly greeted by the ushers, and each of us were handed a bulletin containing the "Order of Service" and a "First Timer" lapel pin with a "First Timer" card to fill out. As I looked over the bulletin, I recall thinking "All of this looks quite harmless. It'll be a breeze. Stand up when the line on the program is preceded by an asterisk, or stay seated when there is no asterisk. After we're finished here, I can throw my clubs into the car and be on the golf course by two. No problem!"

Pastor Thorne introduced us as "the Lawrence's who live down the street in the big white house on the right. Fred is the new Assistant Manager of Allegany Homes. He is with his wife, Shirley, their son Fred Jr., and their daughters Nancy and Libby. Let's give the Lawrence's a warm Homer Baptist welcome." There was warm applause, lots of smiles and handshakes, and we all felt "home at last!"

Up to that point, nothing had been done or said that was in any way new to us— some announcements, a few hymns, a pastoral prayer, an offering, a number done by the choir, and the sermon. Nothing to "write home about!" It was all nice and harmless, that is, until the New Testament scripture was read. Then I realized the scripture was going right through my ears and head, and straight into my heart like an arrow.

The Pastor read: *"To you who are troubled, rest with us, when the Lord Jesus shall be revealed from heaven with His mighty angels, in flaming fire taking vengeance on them that know not God, and that obey not the gospel of our Lord Jesus Christ; who shall be punished with everlasting destruction from the presence of the Lord, and from the glory of His power. . . ."*(II Thessalonians 1: 7-9)

I doubt if it took more than three seconds for me to know that, although the words were coming from the Pastor's mouth, it was God who was speaking to me. I lost all sense of the presence of the Pastor and of the people. Then as the sermon began, I felt the awesome power of His glory all around me. I shifted the position of my head slightly, believing I could escape the power of those words by putting the balcony post between the Pastor and me.

The post did not help. His words continued to come at me with an irresistible power, making my feelings quite ambivalent. On the one hand, I was experiencing a tremendous relief that the God of Glory whom I had requested to leave me alone as a boy, had chosen after seventeen long years to visit me once again. And for God to so appropriately address me as "troubled" and to invite me to "rest" with that fellowship, was beyond my ability to comprehend.

On the other hand, the convicting power of the Holy Spirit was revealing myself to me. It was not a very pretty picture. My life had become evil, and I abhorred myself.

All of the strength within me could not resist His power. His flaming words penetrated my very soul. What was I going to do? What if the sermon were to be concluded without an invitation for those to whom God was speaking to respond? Where was I to go if I wanted to respond? (When I was a boy, my Dad invited people to come forward to the altar where they could kneel and "pray through" if they wanted to get "saved". But here there was no altar!)

Tears were coursing down my cheeks, and my whole body began to tremble while the sermon continued on relentlessly, seemingly pouring more and more gasoline on the fire within me. I told myself to hold on until the proper time—if I could! But if I couldn't "hold on," I would get myself to the front of that church as fast as I could before God interpreted any delay on my part to be reluctance to His invitation, and then never to reach out to me again. God was giving me one more chance, and after seventeen frightful years, I fully intended to reach out and grab it.

I don't recall when it was that I couldn't hold back any longer. I nearly ran to the front and stood directly before the pastor. It wouldn't have made a bit of difference to me if there were only one other, or a thousand other people in that congregation. As I stood there trembling like a leaf and weeping like a spanked child, I knew I would never leave that building until I had made peace with God—no matter what it cost me, nor what I had to do.

The astonished pastor motioned to the Chairman of the Deacon Board to come and take me to his study for counseling. When we got into the Pastor's Study, I can only remember falling to my knees and crying out to God to please forgive me for the things I had said to him, and the sins I had committed since the last time we talked. Amazingly, I sensed the presence of the Lord Jesus hanging from His cross. His eyes looked down on me with such tender love through his horribly deformed and crucified face. I also felt drops of Jesus' own blood drip off His face onto my head. The result of those drops of His blood, and the look of His eyes changed my life completely, and forever.

I became a child of God in that moment. The tremendous load of guilt that had been accumulating all my life, had become so heavy that the weight of it actually had caused my back to become permanently bent over. The image I had of Atlas carrying the whole world on his shoulders, seemed to portray my condition before Jesus lifted that heavy load of sin from me..

I raised my head to wipe the tears from my face, and my eyes met the eyes of that dear Brother in Christ, the Deacon. I thought he was beautiful, and wanted to throw my arms around his neck. But knowing that to do so would be inappropriate, I looked past his face and through the stained glass window, and began to focus on the most beautiful sight I had ever seen—lilac bushes in total bloom. The colors of those light purple blossoms and fresh green leaves literally exploded with the radiant bright blue sky behind them.

Henry, the Deacon, called my attention back inside, and my eyes were drawn to the grain of the stained oak paneling on the wall. How could something I had seen thousands of times now become so beautiful I couldn't take my eyes from it? A thousand master artists could never paint a picture like I was seeing. A small songbird in the lilac bush began to sing a heavenly perfect little melody to help me in expressing my love and appreciation to God for all he was doing for me. All my senses had become gloriously alive. Never before had I seen through my eyes in the way I was seeing, nor had every sound become like music to my ears! (Later I learned a scripture that explained my condition: *"Therefore if any person is in Christ, the Messiah, he is (a new creature altogether), a new creation: the old (previous moral and spiritual condition) has passed away. Behold, the fresh and new has come."*) (2 Corinthians 5:17, Amplified)

I walked out of the office into the hallway where Shirley; my son, Frederick; and my precious daughters Nancy and Libby were waiting for me. More of those delightful tears streamed down my face as I hugged and kissed my beautiful family. Why had I never really seen them before like they now appeared? Each member of my family seemed to be glowing with the love of Christ. At the same time, I was experiencing a new love for them, a love more deep and real than I had ever known, a pure gift from God. *"Therefore if any man be in Christ, he is a new creature: old things are passed away; behold, all things are become new."* (2 Corinthians 5:17)

That afternoon I took stock of my life as it had become, comparing it with what I now felt it should be. I wanted nothing more to do with anything that might offend my new Lord and Savior. My stock of cigarettes and cigars was the first thing to go. Then my stock of beer and liquor went down the drain, while much of my reading material went up the chimney. I also knew that my vocabulary would have to change. By His grace, the Holy Spirit thoroughly removed those offensive words and thoughts from my mind and mouth.

I never made it to the golf course that Sunday afternoon, so many more important things were happening. Having simple conversations with my family, and even neighbors, had taken on a whole new importance. Phone calls about my experience to members of my extended family were greeted with enthusiasm and joy. And the effects my "new life in Christ" had on our marriage were fantastic.

The next morning, I met Pastor Thorne at the Post Office. He said, "My, Fred, that was a very courageous thing you did yesterday." My instant response was, "Pastor, it would have been a thousand times more courageous for me not to have done what I did." A few days later, I shared my testimony with him so he could understand some of what I had been through, and the dramatic change that had occurred in my life a few days before.

The following Sunday, Shirley responded positively to the Pastor's invitation for salvation. Then, one by one, my children received Christ into their lives. After a one- month series of lessons designed for new believers, we were baptized by immersion in the baptismal pool in the front of our sanctuary. At the same time, we were received as members of the First Baptist Church in Homer, where we have happily remained ever since.

While I had totally quit smoking the day I came back to Christ, I had not lost the powerful craving of smoking 2 to 3 packs of cigarettes a day. The moment I finished my meals, or when I awakened in the morning, I would reach for a cigarette from my nightstand or shirt pocket. Although the cigarettes no longer were there, my craving for them had never lessened in intensity. But at the exact moment I emerged from the baptismal pool, I took a deep breath of the cleanest air I had ever smelled. I had gotten more than wet. I had been set free from my craving for nicotine, and it has never returned. Blessed be the Name of the Lord!

There will never be a DIVINE APPOINTMENT in my lifetime that will surpass my family's salvation experience. This experience closed the door on our past, and opened all kinds of new and exciting doors into the Church of Jesus Christ and the Kingdom of God. If you have never experienced the "New Birth", I can assure you with full authority that God loves you, and desires to have a personal relationship with you. What He did for us, he'll do for you. 1 Corinthians 5:17 says: *"Therefore, if any man be in Christ, he is a new creature; old things are passed away; behold, all things are become new."* You too can receive Him into your heart right now: "Lord Jesus, I confess that I am a sinner. Forgive me of my sin. Come and be Lord of my life." Do it right now and enter into your new life in Christ.

* * * * *

Initially, I often wondered why it seemed necessary to the Lord to let me continue in the debilitating way I had for seventeen years before He saved me. But I soon came to realize how seriously I needed to repent for what I was, and for my sins and my sinful lifestyle, a need that was greatly magnified by the Holy Spirit on that memorable Sunday morning. For me, the appreciation I felt for my salvation was much greater than it would have been if I had just sort of drifted into my new life in Christ. If *"the fear of the Lord is the beginning of wisdom"*, as we are told in Psalms 111:10, then I had become a much wiser man, at least in part because of my fear of God. And that was a very good thing, and an unforgettable DIVINE APPOINTMENT!

4

NEW LIFE WITH JESUS

Our new life in Christ seemed almost idyllic. All of my tensions disappeared. I was free of those horrifying dreams I had experienced while believing I had committed "the unpardonable sin." When that happened, I knew beyond any shadow of a doubt that my wonderful family and I would spend eternity in Heaven together. For the first time in more than seventeen years, I was totally at peace during my waking hours, as well as at night. My depression had gradually diminished until I rarely noticed it anymore.

Those who were closest to me could immediately see the transformation that had taken place in me. Walking in to work the Monday after that life-changing encounter with God, one of my foremen looked into my face and asked, "What happened to you, Fred? Did you get saved?" Apparently my smile had said it all, while I wondered how he knew.

The following months of 1960 were the most remarkable I'd ever known. Relationships within my family and with others improved immensely. The love I felt for everyone and everything was almost overpowering. I had taken great satisfaction in disliking. a man who had deliberately tried to hurt my family and me before Jesus took over our lives. After my salvation experience, I forgot what he had done to me, and counted him as a dear friend.

Prayer became one of the most incredible benefits of our new life. When we prayed together or individually, our prayers were answered almost before we could express them. And the answers to our prayers always exceeded our requests.

Amazingly, I learned that God was so aware of us and of our desires, that often He would answer prayers we hadn't yet uttered. My heart seemed to be an open book to Him.

A few months after we joined the Church, I went for a long walk in the woods during hunting season, just to enjoy the sweet presence of the Lord. With my back against an old apple tree, I sat to rest a bit and drink some coffee. Tears of joy began to run down my cheeks as the love of Christ coursed through me again and again. (One day I would learn that those special encounters with the Master didn't require any response from me except a heart overflowing with love for Him, but each such experience brought me closer to the Lord. I fell more and more in love with Jesus.)

My reaction to the wonder of His marvelous presence that day was to ask Him to do whatever would be required to make me an authentic, bona fide, true-blue Christian. I had had enough of Christians whose love for the Lord seemed only to manifest itself on Sunday morning, while the rest of the time they acted like everyone else.

I had learned about real Christians in the New Testament, and I had come to admire the great Christians mentioned in such accounts as <u>Foxes Book Of Martyrs.</u> These Christians had spent days in the catacombs beneath the city of Rome, as well as many other sites in the Mediterranean region, where they had lived and died under severely adverse conditions.

Other men such as John Huss, Martin Luther, Justin Martyr, David Livingston, Dietrich Bonhoeffer and so many great historical figures had become my heroes. Why should I be held to a lower spiritual standard than they if I now was counted worthy of being named a Christian as they were?

I prayed fervently, "Dear Lord, Whatever it takes, whatever you need to do in me, however long it takes, please do it. I try and try to be obedient, but usually fail." I had been confronted by the Sermon On The Mount (Matt. 5-7), and had learned that I just couldn't be the way Jesus was saying I should be. I desperately wanted to follow every word of Jesus' teachings.

But no matter how hard I tried, I just couldn't pass most of those tests. Some of my fellow Baptists explained, "Fred, just because you were 'born again', doesn't mean you're perfect. Everyone falls short of His glory from time to time." My response was, "Why would God command me to do something, or be some way that I just can't be?"

I also desperately wanted to be a soul winner. Try as I might I could never quite bring someone into the Kingdom, even using all of the Soul Winning handbooks I could find. Often I would be confronted with the words of Jesus, *"Every branch in Me that does not bear fruit, He takes away; and every branch that bears fruit, He prunes it, that it may bear more fruit."* (John 15:2 NAS) I would respond to the Lord's words, "Dear Lord, I try so hard to bear fruit. I'm sure you notice. But I just can't do it. Please don't cut me off." I was determined to continue my search for the answers to the deep questions of my heart until God answered.

During those days between coming to our new life in Christ and finding maturity in the Christian walk, I read Watchman Nee's, The Normal Christian Life, and knew I had a long way to go. I frequently found myself singing a couple little choruses, that were popular in small fellowship groups in those days::

> "Have thine own way, Lord. Have thine own way.
> Thou art the potter, I am the clay.
> Mold me and make me, after thy will,
> While I am waiting, yielded and still."

And another one:

> "Spirit of The Living God, fall afresh on me.
> Spirit of the Living God, fall afresh on me.
> Mold me, melt me, fill me, use me.
> Spirit of the living God, fall afresh on me."

Each of those little choruses and others like them, sung from my heart, were prayers. One day, the Lord spoke to me that to sing those choruses was to yield myself more and more fully to Him. He explained to me that singing in the Spirit is praying as much as any prayer we pray, and I should never sing spiritual songs carelessly. God hears and answers each one. And answer He did!

The teacher of the Senior High girl's class at Church hadn't been feeling well for some time, and had asked to be excused from her position. For some reason the Sunday School Superintendent felt I might be able to do the job, so after visiting the class that Sunday, he asked me to try out for the job. That began an unforgettable experience for me. Five precious senior high girls, trying so hard to live Christian lives while living in an inhospitable world, were my first students. Every Sunday's lesson would take most of my spare time each week to prepare. To this day, I still recall with thanksgiving the feeling that I had found something wonderful I could do to serve God. At least one of those dear girls still attends our Church, and at times we reminisce about the good times we had back then.

The class soon grew to more than 25 girls. Each girl became like a daughter to me

as we learned together the wonderful truths God had for us in His Word. The things of the world became less and less important to us. Our church was very supportive of our enthusiasm, giving us every opportunity to spread our spiritual wings and fly.

Eventually, I also was asked to serve on the Board of Deacons—a daunting task, to say the least. My problem with that assignment was that no one taught me how to "Deac!" I served a standard three-year term, but I will never forget the feelings of embarrassment I had when visiting the sick in the Hospital. Once I left a man's sickbed saying, "Good luck!" I felt like an idiot for days because I hadn't even known how to pray properly for the man. Praying in public also was very difficult for me.

Sometime later I was transferred from the senior girl's class to the Brotherhood class. The Brotherhood consisted of six men, each one over the age of eighty. It was a bittersweet challenge to me, as one by one my students went home to be with the Lord, leaving nobody to replace them. Those dear men taught me an awful lot more than I taught them. And somehow I learned to pray aloud when asked to.

Soon, God presented me with my greatest assignment— an invitation to join the Gideons—and assist in spreading God's Word everywhere. I was privileged to have the State President of the Gideons in our church to mentor me when I became a State officer in that organization. I was required to speak regularly in churches and organization meetings around New York State. And I found it a great blessing to place Bibles in motels, and elsewhere.

"This," I told Shirley, "is the Easy Street I promised you when we were in college." Only neither I nor my education had put us on "Easy Street." The Lord had done it! We sincerely believed that nothing could, or would, disturb our blissfully peaceful new life. I could not have been more wrong!

* * * * *

It now was 1960, and I had become a Senior Engineer with Carrier Corp. in Syracuse. Shirley not only was a housewife and an active church member, but she also donated several hours each day to the Women's Auxiliary of the Cortland Memorial Hospital. She served as den mother of our local Cub Scouts, and was the Founder and President of the successful Cortland Chapter of Sweet Adelines, which she had started in order to continue singing the barbershop harmony she enjoyed so much while we lived in Illinois. She was also very active in my girl's Sunday School Class, dreaming up all kinds of fun activities for the girls, and then seeing to it that the activities went off successfully.

The last thing Shirley felt she had to concern herself with was her health. She had never felt better, nor enjoyed life more than she did then. Her activities were never burdensome to her. When she was doing anything that enriched the lives of our family and others, she was as happy as a clam. However, Shirley had gradually developed what has been called "the silent killer," high blood pressure. I learned later from her doctor that she also was born with a defective suberachnoid vein near the base in her brain.

Christmas this year had been a very happy time for the Lawrence's. It had been a season with almost non-stop activities. We celebrated New Year's eve with the other members of our Adult Sunday School class, skiing, skating, tobogganing, and roasting marshmallows. New Year's Day, 1961, also had the usual flurry of activities with friends and relatives. Before we went to sleep that night, however, Shirley mentioned that she had a headache.

The headache worsened, the excruciating pain awakening

her in the middle of the night. We did everything we could think of to alleviate the pain, all to no avail. The next day, after she had almost completely lost her eyesight, we went to our Homer family doctor. His diagnosis: "It looks like a migraine, resulting from too much Holiday activity!" He prescribed some aspirin and rest. Shirley followed his directions, but she received no relief.

A couple days later I took her to a chiropractor who had been highly recommended by friends. After manipulating Shirley's head and neck, he believed she would be fine by the next day. But unfortunately, she only got worse!

When Shirley began to taste and smell blood, and couldn't walk nor see, I took her to Dr. Peacher, a neurosurgeon in Syracuse. He ordered an emergency angiogram at St. Joseph's Hospital. The test results indicated she had had an aneurysm prior to having a severe brain hemorrhage. Within a short time a doctor came to the waiting room to say, "Mrs. Lawrence has suffered a subarachnoid brain hemorrhage. We wish you could have brought her in when she first noticed the extreme pain. She's in Intensive Care in critical condition Mr. Lawrence. We'll do all we can to save her life."

Only the hand of God, and the skilled care of doctors and nurses in St. Joseph's over a period of four months, prepared her to be moved from Intensive Care to a private room. I was told that no operations were available, and that she would never be free of those excruciating, non-stop headaches.

Being in a Roman Catholic hospital meant that Shirley always had a crucifix on the wall near her bed. As she lay in bed with the intense, burning, head pain as her constant companion, she would meditate on the Cross, on Jesus and His blood, and on His crown of thorns. As a result, she would by faith claw her way back from the dark tunnel of death that seemed to frequently beckon her. She and I would frequently say the 23rd Psalm and other scriptures together, as a means of bringing her added comfort and the courage to go on.

Shirley's optic nerve also had been badly damaged, which made it almost impossible for her to see. The affected area at the base of her brain also controlled her sense of balance, as well as other necessary bodily functions. At the same time, she began to have crippling arthritis, adding the pain of all her joints to that in her head. If those conditions were not bad enough, she became heavily addicted to the pain medicine and sleeping pills the doctors were prescribing for her.

The most excruciating pain came when the doctors did the angiograms that allowed them to examine all of the blood vessels in her brain. The dye burned like fire in her head, a fact made worse by the requirement that she be awake while they did it. This procedure, coupled with her deteriorating arthritic condition, caused her to require increasingly powerful doses of her medications, until they lost all of their effectiveness. When that happened, she would go off all of her medications "cold turkey" for a few days, until they could put her on other pain and sleeping medications.

Needless to say, our happy little family began to turn upside down. We could feel the gradual, yet inexorable, downward pull of the circumstances on our lives. Our Christian friends offered condolences and assistance. But there was nothing anyone could do for us. I managed to visit Shirley almost daily, while the children saw her only on Sundays.

I began to learn an important truth during those difficult days. Absence does not "make the heart grow fonder." As years passed by, the interest in Shirley's illness by our peers in church became less and less. To visit her either in the hospital or at home was not a pleasant experience for them, nor for us. Our need for a home-cooked meal became greater, while the offerings of meals and fellowship dwindled.

Eventually Shirley was allowed to come home, but the

problems never ceased. All of our fun and games were over. Our lives were one long, never-ending series of heartaches, heart-breaks, suffering and pain. Most of the 1960's passed by like a slow agonizing blur, interrupted only by nearly annual, three- or four-month hospitalizations for Shirley to help her live with the pain. She had one remedy that she learned to use with some benefit—she could refuse to live!

Shirley could sleep for days on end without waking up. After two weeks of her deep slumber, I would tell her doctor and she would admit her to a small, private Syracuse hospital called Twin Elms. They specialized in cases like Shirley's. Gradually they would bring her out of her deep sleep, and slowly take her through a three-month process of learning to live with the pain again.

A typical day in Shirley's life then was about like this: I would carry her to the bathroom at 4:30am for her necessary personal needs, including a bath. I had a bed made up for her on our couch where she would spend most of the day. After her AM medications kicked in, I could get her to eat a little breakfast before she would fall back to sleep, groaning in pain. I prepared myself for the day, then awakened and prepared the kids for the day. They ate a hurried breakfast, kissed us good-bye, and off to school they'd go. Then I left for my hour's commute to my work in Syracuse.

Life went on. In 1963, my Dad passed away. In 1964, against all of the doctors orders, Shirley became pregnant. At first we didn't think she could survive a pregnancy. The doctors had warned us that she should never get pregnant. I was left to deal with my own guilt feelings about that. Since her doctors believed she couldn't survive another pregnancy, they urged Shirley to have an abortion.

It would take the agreement and signatures of three doctors to make an abortion legal. Two of them signed the paper, but the third one didn't believe in abortions for any reason. God was still in control of our lives, even though we couldn't seem to feel his nearness as we had in the past. It wasn't God's will for us to abort that baby, no matter what. She belonged to Him, not us.

Delivery day arrived. Shirley went into a nearly three-day labor because of a breach birth. Again Shirley came close to death, but God brought her through it all. Rebekah June came into our lives with a flourish. Her collar bone had been broken during the delivery, but here she was, just waiting to be loved and nourished. She looked all the world like an angel to us. And even though we thought it had all been a mistake, Becky became the light of our lives. She could somehow make us laugh when we needed that the most.

One day Shirley's Doctor told me that he and several other physicians who had been treating her, had conferred about Shirley's case. They decided the humane thing to do for Shirley would be to put her in a State Hospital. There, they could keep her continually in such a heavily sedated, comatose state that she would no longer have to suffer. The only place this type of drug-induced coma could be administered on a permanent basis was the Marcy State Mental Hospital near Utica. I couldn't get myself to do that.

The only alternative was to try to keep on keeping on. The house always seemed to be a mess as the kid's school and social activities took more and more of their time. The work assignments I gave to the kids became more and more burdensome to them, causing me to be less understanding and less patient.

Needing some sort of diversion, I enrolled in a course given by our church that would qualify one to be a lay minister. I finished the work successfully, but never got to take the final test. Another failure, as I saw it!

All this time, my close friend, Rich Davis, had been searching for a deeper walk with the Lord. His quest had led him to an understanding of a work of grace in the Christian life known as the Baptism in the Holy Spirit. We weren't exactly certain why we never learned about this experience at our church. He had learned of it through an organization called the Full Gospel Business Men's Fellowship International (FGBMFI), founded by Demos Shakarian. These were men who had received this Baptism, and had experienced the "speaking in tongues" mentioned in Acts 2 and elsewhere in the New Testament. They were anxious to share their experiences with anyone who would listen.

One day Rich said, "Fred, would you like to learn more about FGBMFI? They believe in divine healing." With some reluctance, I went with him to one of their meetings in Elmira. There I could learn about healing as well as this Holy Spirit Baptism. Just the word 'healing' got my attention. If these were businessmen talking about things they knew to be facts, then they would make quite credible witnesses. Therefore, I wanted to hear what they had to say. (I had learned that a good crisis in a person's life will often tend to correct any false beliefs in his theology.)

"OK, Rich. Let's do it. If it doesn't sound right to me we can get out of there, OK?" Soon we were on our way to Elmira for a most unusual DIVINE APPOINTMENT!

This "Dinner Meeting" had as its speaker a Presbyterian Bible teacher. His name meant nothing to me, but his message was of paramount interest. I sort of wished he was a Baptist whose theology could be expected to be accurate, but I'd be taking notes and could check everything out for accuracy in my Bible when I got home.

The banquet facility was beautiful, with round tables for ten people each. The table settings—sparkling linen cloths with very nice china and silverware—were topped off with linen napkins. I noticed the very nice dress and demeanor of all the people. Several seemingly happy priests were there, which somehow added interest to me. I knew Shirley would have approved of that, even though one of them turned out to be an Episcopalian! Then one of the priests said the blessing over the dinner and the meeting.

For many years I had heard about the emotionalism and fanaticism of Pentecostals. My image of them was of people handling snakes, drinking poisonous potions, and babbling in unintelligible aberrations. I thought they were uneducated, unsophisticated, and without good sense. Suddenly I was seeing well-dressed people of all ages and denominations, priests as well as ordinary people, young and old having a joyous time just praising the Lord. "Could some of my other pre-conceived ideas about these Charismatics be inaccurate, too?" I wondered.

After dinner, the Chairman introduced some of the VIP's at the head table and the music leader. The songs were simple choruses which were easy to learn, yet they dynamically affected everyone. Then a young Jesuit Catholic monk with a big red beard was introduced to share a brief testimony with everyone. His name was Brother David, the Director of the Elmira Jesuit Retreat Center, and he wore a long brown, hooded robe with a sash around his waist.

Brother David's testimony was incredible. A lady who attended one of his retreats had given him a copy of David Wilkerson's book, The Cross and the Switchblade. When he began to read it, he couldn't put it down until he had finished. Then he heard that David Wilkerson would be speaking at the Pentecostal Tabernacle in Elmira. Accompanying him would be a main character in his book, Nicky Cruz.

Each minute until that meeting began had seemed like an hour to Brother David. He could hardly wait. Wearing his civilian clothes in order not to call any special attention to himself, he entered the Tabernacle and found a safe looking pew near an exit in the rear of the auditorium. A lively song and worship service was in progress. It concluded with a prophetic message in tongues, given by an ordinary looking lady in the same pew as Brother David. Being an advanced student of Latin, he understood everything she said. A lady sitting near David gave the interpretation in English, thus confirming to David that the message was of God.

David moved over to the lady and asked, "Madam, where did you learn to speak such beautiful Latin?" Her reply startled him, "Sir, I don't know a word of Latin. I was speaking in tongues!" "Madam, you not only spoke in a beautiful classical Latin, but you also were praising the Lord for the anointed ministry to which He was calling me. Do you know me? How could you have spoken that way?" David's mind was exploding with questions!

When all the preliminaries were completed, the Pastor introduced Dave Wilkerson, author of the best-seller, The Cross And The Switchblade, and his young student, Nicky Cruz. Nicky was a former gang leader in Brooklyn who had come to Christ under David's ministry. His testimony had been included in Wilkerson's book. Nicky's larynx had been injured in a gang fight before he came to Christ. That along with a strong Hispanic accent, made his speech very difficult to understand. As he began to speak the Lord began to heal his vocal chords, and in a few moments he could be easily understood by everyone—an audio miracle, if you will. (Nicky Cruz's ministry as a Spanish/English speaking evangelist has been one of the most productive, soul-winning ministries of his generation.)

An invitation was given for those who would like prayer for anything to come forward. Brother David almost ran down the aisle, wanting everything God could do for him. He had many questions to ask after reading the book and hearing the testimony that night. As he was being prayed for by the church elders, his hands went up in the air and he began to speak in a language he had never learned. In just a few moments, his faith grew enormously. It wasn't a faith based on his knowledge or his broad education, but it was purely spiritual.

When Brother David left the church that night, he was a

new born-again, baptized in the Holy Spirit, and speaking-in-tongues man. These were all the things he had needed so much, but didn't know that he needed them, or how to get them.

Brother David awakened the next morning so full of life and Holy Spirit energy that he hardly knew how to express it. The one thing he did know was what David Wilkerson had written in his book about street ministry to young people. So he headed for downtown Elmira where the kids hung out when they had nothing better to do. All he could think of to say was what he knew about Jesus. Overnight he had become a street preacher, and kids were responding to his words by falling to their knees, weeping and inviting Jesus into their lives. No one knew how many young people and others came to Jesus during that fantastic week, even though he had never knowingly led anyone to Christ before.

Now he was trying to share with us what happened to him, while he was crying and laughing for joy. It was the most power-packed witness I had ever heard. I sat there listening intently and telling God that I could not and would not leave that room until I had what that man was talking about. He was infectious! I don't ever recall wanting something as much as I wanted what that young monk had experienced.

When the main speaker finished his teaching, he gave an invitation for anyone desiring this wonderful Baptism in the Holy Spirit to "Just raise your hand, nice and high." By then the tears were flowing down my cheeks, while my hands were both raised and my eyes were closed, tightly. I knew that if I opened my eyes just then I would see Jesus, standing there in front of me. I was not worthy to look into His beautiful face, but I knew for certain that He was there. *Jesus said, "And when the Comforter comes, whom I will send to you from the Father, that is the Spirit of Truth , who proceeds from the Father, He will bear witness of Me."* (John 15:26 NAS)

Then from behind I felt hands on my head. The power of God was flowing through those hands and into my head. Those hands, which turned out to be Brother David's, began to tremble and became very warm. My head was trembling too, and then my whole body was trembling. Jesus' sweet presence was flooding my soul and spirit with His own Spirit. My lips and tongue were stuttering, although I hadn't expected anything like that. The warmth from his hands left imprints on my head that never left me for several weeks afterward.

As the power of God continued to flow, and while Jesus' lovely presence flooded my being, I began to hear myself speaking in a very rapid, staccato, almost Chinese-like language. My hands went to my face, covering up my lips. After all, I was an educated man, and wouldn't get caught up in any sort of fanaticism. Yet, when the language stopped, I felt like I had stopped worshipping my Lord. So I thought, "I wonder if I can start speaking like that again?" Instantly my lips and tongue began to fully express the incredible flow of love moving through my body again. It felt like a dam had burst within me, and I knew that I was worshipping the Lord in Spirit and in Truth for the first time in my life.

While those strange sounds and syllables flowed from someplace deep within my innermost being and out through my lips, I felt like the words that Jesus spoke to the Samaritan woman at the well were being spoken to me. Somehow, I suddenly knew the meaning of the words of that passage of scripture. The things that were transpiring in my Spirit were more real to me than my own flesh. Jesus said, *"But whoever drinks of the water that I shall give him shall never thirst; but the water that I shall give him shall become in him a well of water springing up to eternal life."* (John 4:14 NAS). Jesus also said, *"If any man is thirsty, let him come to Me, and drink. He who believes in me, as the scripture said, From his innermost being shall flow rivers of living water.' But this He spoke of the Spirit, whom those who believed in Him were to receive; for the Spirit was not yet given, because Jesus was not yet glorified."* (John 7:38-39, NAS) Those words came to my mind, and I knew exactly what they meant.

Eventually, Rich and I got back to our car and started the trip home. I don't recall our conversation. Perhaps words weren't needed for us to understand all that had happened that night. I felt like some sort of invisible seal had been stamped on my inner being, binding me forever to my Master, the Lord Jesus Christ, and to His service. *"In Him, you also after listening to the message of truth, the gospel of your salvation - having also believed, you were sealed in Him with the Holy Spirit of promise.'* (Eph.I:13-14) It seemed that no DIVINE APPOINTMENT I would ever have could surpass that glorious night in Elmira.

When I arrived home, I found Shirley still waiting up for me. For an hour or more I told her about everything that happened that evening, of how the main speaker had shared some teaching about the Baptism in the Holy Spirit, and of physical healing. That was as interesting to her as it had been for me. Suddenly we were full of hope and expectation that God would heal Shirley very soon.

I said, "Sweetheart, there was a young Catholic monk at the meeting tonight that you must meet. I told him about you and your condition. He said that we should meet him on Thursday evening at the Pentecostal Tabernacle in Elmira. Let's plan on going. We'll see what God will do."

Our very eventful evening wasn't quite over yet. When we got into bed I began to feel very uneasy about something. "Shirley, something isn't right. I don't know what it is. Let's pray about it." We got out of bed and kneeled to pray. "Dear Heavenly Father, we thank you so much for all you did for me tonight. Everything was beautiful. But now there seems to be something wrong in this house. Please show me what it is and what I should do about it."

I went to my son's room, and everything seemed OK there. Then as I entered our daughter's room, I knew that that was where the problem was, but didn't know what to do about it. In a few moments the Holy Spirit said, "There are demonic forces in your daughter's closet. Cast them out!"

I looked at the closet and saw through my spiritual eyes three demons leering at me from on top of a stack of games. My mind switched gears for a moment while the Lord reminded me of the words Jesus spoke to the Gadarene demoniac *"Come out of the man, thou unclean spirit!"* (Mark 5:8) I spoke those words with all the force I could. In a few moments, all three demons emitted a plaintive wail as they flew out of the closet and the room. As they went, a ouijah board came tumbling out of the closet along with pieces of the thing scattered around the floor. I picked it all up and threw it out our back door. I thought that was the end of it, but when I got back into bed I still felt uneasy. It wasn't until I threw that game and its pieces into the field behind our property that I felt God's peace again. Since that experience, I've been faithful to share with people to whom we've ministered that ouijah boards are not toys, but are demonic and should never be in a Christian home. Never! The following morning a perfect peace and love emanated from the girl's room in the absence of those demonic forces.

This was the point I had often read in Jesus' great commission in Mark 16: 15 – 18 that seemed to me to be fanatical, something I would never be a part of! Yet Jesus Himself had said, *"Go into all the world and preach the gospel to every creature. He who has believed and has been baptized shall be saved; but he that believeth not shall be damned. And these signs shall follow them that believe; In my name shall they cast out devils; they shall speak with new tongues; they shall take up serpents; and if they drink any deadly thing it shall not hurt them; they will lay hands on the*

sick, and they will recover." Before the Baptism in the Holy
Spirit, I never would have even thought of doing anything
like I had done. I had cast out demons and had spoken in
tongues, both in the same evening. It was all very scriptural,
but had been omitted from the teachings of my Baptist
Church. And the peace that came over my two daughters
after those evil spirits left their room was remarkable.

That concluded one of the greatest days and nights of our
lives, as well as at least two fantastic DIVINE APPOINT-
MENTS. I felt that God had done so much for me that I'd
never have another bad day in my life. Uh!.Oh! Surprise,
surprise! Wrong again!

5

FILLED WITH THE HOLY GHOST AND FIRE
Luke 3:16

Waking up in the morning after the fantastic events of the previous evening was a marvelous experience. Everything about our lives was new again—shiny, gloriously, new! We knew then that we would never be like we were before my Baptism in the Holy Spirit. I shared again with Shirley how Brother David assured me that he would be attending the Thursday evening prayer meeting at the Pentecostal Tabernacle in Elmira, and that he and others would pray that God would heal her at that meeting.

Shirley had heard "speaking in tongues" while listening to a radio broadcast of a Washington, D.C. FGBMFI Convention Meeting. She carefully studied the Word to assure herself that this gift was of the Lord. Although convinced of the reality and the necessity of this gift, she wanted to learn more about it. She could hardly believe that a Catholic monk would be found in a meeting such as I had attended the night before. She was also a bit doubtful that a real Catholic monk would attend a Protestant prayer service in a Pentecostal church. So she could hardly wait for the Thursday evening meeting in Elmira. "I'll have to see that for myself!" she exclaimed.

When we arrived at the church where they were having their midweek service, we were really excited. But when the time came after the worship that the ministry was to begin, Pastor John Bedzyk announced that they would be showing a movie that evening. Shirley whispered to me, "Wouldn't you just know it. We come all the way down here and they're showing a movie!" (The only times a movie was shown in our church was when the pastor needed a rest from his preaching, and the movie served as a filler for him. Therefore, nothing exceptional was ever expected to happen as a result of showing a movie in our church, so I understood Shirley's dismay.)

However, when one goes somewhere to have an encounter with Jesus Christ, He'll be there to meet you. No matter what else was happening, Jesus had come in response to the prayers of Brother David, Shirley and me. After the movie, Sister Bedzyk invited everyone who desired prayer and ministry to come forward and kneel at the altar. Shirley felt a strong force lift her from her seat and propel her forward to kneel on her very painful arthritic knees. (She said, "It felt like two large hands moving me, and I didn't feel any pain when I kneeled at the altar.")

Sister Bedzyk asked, "Ma'am, do you know Jesus Christ as your personal Lord and Savior?" "Oh yes, Jesus is in my heart and He's my Savior." Shirley replied.

Sister Bedzyk continued, "Then I believe I know what you need. You need the Baptism in the Holy Spirit." By then several other people had joined in the prayer for Shirley. "Yes, I think I need that, but I don't know what it means." So the prayer team began to pray that Shirley would receive the Baptism by Jesus, the Baptism in the Holy Spirit.

At first nothing seemed to be happening. I mentioned Shirley's Roman Catholic background, and someone motioned to Brother David to come over from the other side of the auditorium.

Brother David, with his big red beard and his Jesuit robe and sash, made an almost imposing appearance next to Shirley. He recognized me, and recalled our discussion about Shirley at the FGBMFI meeting. He reached out to touch Shirley's forehead, but before he even touched her, she began to sing in the Spirit, something she hadn't heard of before. She remained on her knees while both arms went straight up in the air. (Only Shirley and I knew that it was not possible for her to kneel, nor to raise her arms and her fingers to be extended like they were because of the arthritis in her joints. Thus, our joy and praise were coming from a slightly different viewpoint than the rest of the group.)

Not only was Shirley thoroughly Baptized in the Holy Spirit with the evidence of speaking (or singing) in tongues (the Spirit), but she was being healed of severely deformed joints throughout most of her body. I could hear some of her joints crackling and popping as Jesus immersed her in the Holy Spirit. Everyone was praising Jesus for what He was doing in Shirley's body. Her headache also partially subsided.

One of the ministers asked me if I needed this same experience. I replied, "I'm not too sure. I don't sing when I'm praising the Lord, so maybe I don't yet have it all." That was all they needed to lay hands and pray that I too would receive all God had for me. Almost instantly, I too began to sing in the Spirit along with Shirley. (I don't believe that one can be Baptized in the Spirit more than once, but, like Baptism in Water, one can be immersed as often as they wish, if that makes them feel better. But it isn't scripturally necessary! You may rest assured that once you get a good dose of the Holy Ghost, you will never get all you want of Him!)

The next morning, Shirley was singing in the Spirit as she washed our breakfast dishes. The Lord spoke to her, "Shirley, that is the spiritual language I gave you when you were a little girl in St. Bernard's Church." So, Shirley's Baptism in the Holy Spirit was unique. Jesus had bestowed that beautiful gift on her while still a small child in order to give her the strength she later would need to cope with the very adverse conditions of her family life.

Another aspect of Shirley's singing in the Spirit was that she couldn't seem to stop doing it when we got home, it being such a joyful experience for her. Nearly every time she opened her mouth to say something, she would sing out strongly in her prayer language. Our children wondered what had happened to their parents at that church in Elmira, and some of our neighbors also began looking our way a bit curiously. After nearly a month of this unusual phenomena, we went back to the Tabernacle in Elmira to ask the Pastor what we should do about it.

Pastor Bedzyk, having dealt with this sort of situation before, prayed: "Dear Lord, We thank you for all you are doing in Shirley's life. Now we ask that she speak normally except when she wishes to speak in the Spirit while praying or praising. Please put her to work, Lord. Thank you. Amen". After that, her speaking returned to normal and her headaches continued to diminish, eventually reaching a much more manageable level than before. (However, even now, some thirty years later, the headaches return when she is under any kind of stress. They serve as a warning signal for her to back off those things that may be causing the stress.)

So once again we were rejoicing mightily that all of our troubles and adversity were behind us. Now we would just enjoy life and get back into a normal lifestyle. For at least the second time in my life, I couldn't have been more wrong! Shirley would need every bit of strength and courage that God could give her in the days ahead.

I took a new position as Senior Facilities Engineer for Smith Corona, an office machine manufacturer located in South Cortland. Because our youngest daughter, Becky, continued to require assistance at a baby sitter's home for a few hours in the afternoon, I would drive out past our County Airport to pick her up on my way home from work. It was always a great joy for me to get lots of Becky hugs and kisses every afternoon.

While on my way to pick up Becky one day, I was driving on the State Highway that curves around the north end of the Airport. As I approached the road that turned left into the Terminal, I noticed a line of cars ahead of me slowing down so that the car in front could make a left turn into the airport parking lot. I also noticed a beautiful little blue and white corporate jet coming in for a landing. Just before I came to a complete stop, I heard this big explosion, and then – nothing!

The next thing I recall was waking up about twenty hours later in the hospital. Shirley was stroking my arm, excited and delighted that I was regaining consciousness. I had no knowledge of the accident, whatsoever. A little at a time, I wanted to know more about whatever had happened that put me in the hospital. A doctor examined me and gave Shirley the go-ahead to try to explain the accident to me.

According to the police report, I was struck from behind by a car that was traveling at a speed of forty to forty-five miles an hour. The driver, who had been drinking, also was watching the blue and white airplane. Unfortunately, he hadn't noticed me, nor the others stopped in line ahead of me. Obviously, he also hadn't put on his brakes before the sudden impact that demolished both of our cars. He staggered away from the accident unscathed. I suffered brain concussions, severe whiplash to my neck and back, and other internal injuries that couldn't readily be seen, but which were discovered later.

My neck was swollen to about the same size as my head. However, my major injuries were to my brain, which also swelled up. The doctor kept telling Shirley that if the pressure in my head didn't subside, they would have to take me to Upstate Medical Center where they would surgically relieve the swelling. And that appears to have been what they should have done, but instead, they continued to wait for my brain to return to normal. Gradually the swelling and headache subsided, and I returned home after a week in the hospital.

After three weeks of recuperation, I insisted that I be allowed to return to work. Unfortunately, my brain had been so badly contused that I was left with scar tissue all around my brain. (The doctor explained my condition to me as being somewhat like what happens to a boxer who has been knocked out by blows to the head a few too many times.) As a result, my headaches continued, and I found it difficult to remember names and things that had occurred only moments before. Even simple communication with the people at work became increasingly difficult for me.

I also found it difficult to tell anyone that I still had physical problems, because I had shared widely to others about the wonderful healing power of the Lord Jesus. That I was afflicted again with a condition the doctor couldn't alleviate, was way beyond my comprehension. Even though the Holy Spirit continued to fill me each day, I didn't know how to appropriate that power for the healing of my damaged brain. Even being prayed for and being anointed with oil according to James 5 failed to bring relief.

The work that I was involved with at Smith Corona included increasing amounts of responsibility and workload. Large amounts of production capacity were being transferred from South Cortland to parts of the world where labor costs were substantially less. My job was to coordinate these transfers rapidly and without delays. If I had been in perfect mental health and strength, the pressures would have been challenging enough! As it was, each day found me less and less capable of handling the many aspects of my job, despite my trying desperately to do the best job possible. One day after a lengthy meeting with corporate executives, I left the job in tears of discouragement.

Having failed at something I was highly qualified to do seemed like the end of the world. Depression closed in around me like a black storm cloud. Being in denial about the ill effects the car accident had on me, I refused to seek medical help for my condition. Each day from early morning until late at night I sought other employment. Gradually I couldn't sleep at all, and would go for days without eating.

One morning, I was in Boston to apply for a position for which I was well qualified. I walked out of my motel room to go to my car, and it wasn't where I thought it should be. Standing in the motel parking lot, I didn't have the faintest idea where I was, nor what I was doing there. I sat down on the curb and cried like a baby. A man stopped and asked if I needed help, but I didn't know how to tell him I did.

He led me to the front desk of the motel. The desk clerk recognized me and suggested I go back to my room and rest a bit. He returned my room key and led me back to the room. I fell asleep at last. But when I woke up and realized I had missed the appointment I had wanted so badly, all I could do was cry. Finally I called Shirley. Her soothing voice brought me back to reality, and eventually gave me the strength to find my car and begin the long drive home, even while feeling utterly defeated.

I applied for over 1100 jobs during the period from March to September. For each of these, I was either over-qualified or under-qualified. Then the day came when I couldn't get out of bed. Words cannot explain the feelings that accompany that level of total depression. More than anything else I wanted to be dead, but accomplishing that fatal step was way beyond my ability or strength.

One night during this ordeal, as I once again was lying wide-awake in bed and hoping morning would never come, I heard the audible voice of God. He said, "TRUST ME!" On numerous occasions I had heard God speak to me in "a still, small voice." I also had heard Him speak to me through a prophetic message. And nearly every time I studied God's Word, He spoke to my heart. But this time God spoke to me even as He did to David in the 29th Psalm, verses 3-9 LB *"The voice of the Lord echoes from the clouds. The God of glory thunders through the skies. So powerful is His voice; so full of majesty. It breaks down the cedars. It splits the giant trees of Lebanon. It shakes Mt. Lebanon and Mount Sirion. . .The voice of the Lord thunders through the lightening . . ."* When I heard that mighty voice say, "TRUST ME," I could hardly believe that it hadn't awakened Shirley. It seemed to me that the whole house shook, unlike anything I had ever heard. I had not even the slightest doubt in my mind that it was God speaking to me.

If I had known fully how to be obedient to that amazing command, I would have been able to totally relax and stop scouring the country for a job. All my life I had learned that a man works and supports himself and his family, which I had studied so long and hard to educate myself to do. I was highly employable, with great work experience. Yet, no matter what job I applied for, I was found to be over-qualified or under-qualified and was turned down.

My family's home life became more and more difficult for all of us. Our family altar sort of disintegrated—I suppose for lack of adequate leadership. At first the children would try to talk to me, but gradually they stopped trying, because all I could do was keep apologizing for the horrible mess I had brought about on our formerly happy family.

Becky was three by then, and always had time to chat with me. When I would have one of my migraine headaches, she would put her hands on my head very softly and pray,

"Dear Jesus, Please heal my Daddy, and make him feel better. Thank you, Jesus." Then she would watch for signs that God had heard and answered her prayer. It was never long before Becky and I would have a good time praising the Lord for taking my headache away. She would wipe away my tears with a Kleenex, and run off to play with her doll, having comforted me in a way no one else could.

I continued to contemplate those simple, yet powerful words, *"Trust Me"*, for several days. If I really had known how to "Trust God," I could have taken a leisurely stroll, or enjoyed the morning News with a cup of coffee, or had a nice chat with my neighbor about the weather and other small talk. But I just didn't know how to be "unemployed" and simply "Trust God". (Once again, I had learned all of my life to get up in the morning and go about my personal responsibilities—including work. I could never remain comfortably unemployed on a day when most people were working.)

So the following morning, I was on the road searching for work—all 125 pounds of me. I said, "God you've told me in your Word that, ". . .*if a man doesn't work, he shouldn't eat.* (2 Thess. 3:10). So, I trust you to help me find a job." I couldn't, or wouldn't eat any food. So my very gaunt appearance made my search even more fruitless.

I found that it was easier for me to continue my fruitless efforts than it was for me to do nothing at all except to "Trust God". Oh, the agony I could have saved myself and my family had I done as God had instructed! If I could have found one wise counselor whom I trusted, one who would have told me to relax and to let go of all my fears and concerns, and then would have helped me somehow to just relax and "Trust God," I probably could have made a go of it. But no, I had to keep trying to find work.

The day came in September of 1968 that Shirley had no other choice but to take me to the VA Hospital in Syracuse. I was examined thoroughly, and found to be in an advanced state of deep depression. I also was thought to be suicidal. The officials there had to make a space available for me, so I was told to return the next morning prepared to be hospitalized—for how long, they couldn't tell us!

That evening, someone from church brought us a very nice hot meal. Although I couldn't eat, I was glad for one last opportunity to fellowship with my family before being locked up in a psychiatric ward. However, the most significant thing that happened to me that evening was a response from God addressing one of my inner questions: "How could this be happening to me, one of your Spirit-filled followers? What will my beloved family do without me?" As bad as things seem to be, my wife and children were enjoying dinner, as though I weren't even there.

Suddenly, Becky smiled, looked at me, and with both hands raised said, "Daddy, God does everything with two hands!" It was a most amazing Word from the Lord, spoken to me by my little girl—a word I will remember as long as I live. (We had been teaching Becky to catch and carry things with both hands so she wouldn't drop them. She had seen me catch her ball with one hand, so she wanted to do it that way. So when she assured me that God had everything under control with both hands, in such a uniquely beautiful manner, the words pierced my heart like an arrow.)

The next morning, we put together the few items the people at the hospital said I would need. I kissed my wife and children good-bye, and then got in my car and began the 28-mile drive to Syracuse. God hadn't quite finished trying to assure me that everything would work out someday, somehow. I drove as far as the Rest Area off Rt. 81, between Lafayette and Syracuse, and stopped for a little rest. Trying to get to the Hospital at any appointed time was the least of my concerns. What difference did it make? I was beyond caring about anything.

It was a nice warm day, so my window was open as I sat

there still trying to figure out how all this could be happening to me. I began to hear a hissing sound that seemed to be coming from one of my tires. A closer inspection revealed that I had a good-sized hole in my right front tire. As I put my hand next to the hole, I felt the rapid flow of air escaping from my tire. I already knew that the tire had a bump on it, but I guess I thought it would at least get me to the hospital. A few days before that, I had a flat and had taken the tire to the repair shop. Thus, I didn't have a spare. "So what!" I mumbled. "I am too weak to change the tire anyway, even if my life depended on it! So, I'll drive as far as I can, and when I can't go any farther, I'll pull off the road and sleep for awhile. Who knows? Maybe this is God's way of telling me He didn't want me to go to the hospital. Maybe He'll come up with something He hadn't thought of before."

I don't recall driving the 4 or 5 miles to the hospital from where I was, but I do recall walking from my car in the hospital parking lot to the admission desk and checking myself in as a patient. I had given no further thought to the hole in my tire!

I had been a patient for several days before Shirley came to visit me. A friend had brought her to the hospital to pick up the car sometime after I drove to the hospital. Shirley said, "Fred, you're not going to believe this. But today I stopped at Bill's Sunoco to get gas. While Bill was pumping the gas he heard a hissing sound coming from one of my tires. He said, "Shirley, let me put the car up on my lift so I can take a look at it. I think you have a problem." Bill raised the car up a few feet and said, "Shirley, come take a look! You're not going to believe this! I don't know how you got this car here to the station. I can see right through the hole in it." So Shirley and several other by-standers took a look at the spot where the air was pouring out, and saw that the hole was at least as big as a nickel! Yet, the tire hadn't gone flat! God had to be replacing the air from my leaking tire with an equal amount from His own vast supply of air! Bill put another tire on my right front wheel. But to this day, I wish he hadn't replaced it. Maybe that tire would still be inflated!

* * * * *

The following eight months turned out to be some of the most terrible days of my life, but the miracle of the tire would often come to mind when things really got bad. It seemed to me that if God had taken care of our tire problem so miraculously, then He was well able to bring our family through whatever else might happen during my hospital stay.

6

VETERANS' BENEFITS

My new life as a patient on the 7th Floor of the Syracuse VA Hospital started on September 1, 1969. I was assigned to a locked ward within a larger locked psychiatric ward. My little room was also home for four other patients, all trying to act like we didn't belong there (probably all victims of some VA "screw up," we thought). My roommates were really ticked off that their beds had been scrunched together to make room for me. As a result, the only things they left for me that I could call my own were a bed, a chair, and a ragged pair of GI pajamas. Oh yes, and a Gideon New Testament!

Walking into that ward and being shown to my bed was like a bad dream. The reality of my incarceration finally began to sink into my troubled mind. No, I wouldn't be able to leave that room without a VA escort no matter what I wanted. The VA owned me. I had lost all control of my own life. I fought back the tears until the nurse left, then, with my head under my pillow I wept bitterly—for how long I don't know. If the other four men in that room knew something of how I felt, they never mentioned it.

The thing I remember most during my first week there was that the men in that little ward rarely talked to one another. We slept as much and as often as we could— probably some sort of psychological escape mechanism. We were brought a tray of food and a spoon three times a day. We ate in silence. When we needed to go to the bathroom, we rang a bell. An attendant would accompany us to the bathroom and keep us under observation until we returned to our room.

One of my roomies observed that prison inmates at least were given a minimum amount of an hour a day for R and R outdoors. We didn't even have that.

No partitions separated the showers—privacy was a thing of the past. When we finished our bath in the morning, we were allowed to use the one electric razor provided for the ward, while the attendant watched. I gradually learned that their purpose in keeping us in this kind of situation was to prevent suicides, as well as to closely observe us. Based on these observations, they would release us to a less secure ward as soon as they judged us to be ready.

The day following my admission, a lady doctor came into the room and told me to follow her to her office. She gave me a thorough physical and mental examination. I'd much rather have had a male doctor, because half of the time I didn't have even my pajamas on! When she left the room for a minute, I thought my ordeal was nearly finished. But, then she returned with two SUNY Health Science Center interns! I was their first live specimen on which they would begin to learn how to do physical examinations, compliments of Uncle Sam and me. (They don't tell you when you sign yourself in to a VA Hospital that they are a training hospital, and that you authorize them to use you as a guinea pig for the medical students. If a person has any need for privacy, he'd better not select the VA hospital. You have every reason to rejoice when the whole procedure is behind you.)

Ten days in that little "holding pen" for suspected "suicidals" seemed like a lifetime. "Was this some sort of punishment for being depressed?" I wondered. Something didn't seem right, but in my condition, to whom could I complain? If I make a fuss about something, I might find myself in this room longer than I would if I keep quiet.

During this tenth day (September 10, 1969), I determined that I would put my case before the Lord again, and not move until I got an answer. That night, the lights were turned off at eleven as usual, and each of us was given more than enough medicine to keep us asleep until well into the morning—except that I couldn't sleep, pills or no pills. Fortunately, just enough light came into our room for me to read my New Testament.

About 1:30 am, as I was sitting cross-legged in the middle of my bed, I began to tell the Lord exactly how I felt about things. "Lord," I said, "I might as well be dead. Will you please let me die? Everything in my life is now gone: my health, my strength, my family, my friends, my freedom, and my work. All of my savings, my insurance, and my future are gone. No reason remains for me to live. Please, let me die, now!"

After completing my plea, I finally fell asleep. As I began to dream, God spoke to me again. "Son, you are dead. Now I will live my life through you." I trembled, and tears rolled down my cheeks as the incredible pathos of this experience penetrated my soul. I didn't know how, but once again I knew my life would never be the same. DIVINE APPOINTMENTS are like that.

The scene then shifted, and I found myself looking down on a funeral parlor at a funeral service. My family and friends were all there. The casket was surrounded by flowers. I was dressed in my blue suit, and had been fixed up to look quite contented. My pastor began by reading Philippians 2:5-11, "Have this same mind in you which was also in Christ Jesus. . . who took upon Himself the form of a servant, and became obedient unto death, even death on the cross." As he read those words, he wasn't speaking only to the mourners, he was speaking to me through my own funeral sermon.

God was revealing my life to me. Paul said, "I am crucified with Christ. Nevertheless I live. Yet not I but Christ liveth in me." (Gal. 2:20) I too was being "crucified" with Christ. It was no longer I who would be living, but Christ would be living in me. The final scripture used by my pastor that day for my funeral service was from 1 Peter 4:1-2. "Therefore, since Christ suffered in His Body, arm yourselves also with the same attitude. As a result, He does not live the rest of His earthly life for evil human desires, but rather for the will of God." Somehow I knew then that I had been separated unto a sanctified life in Christ. I was dead to this world, to my own dreams and ambitions; dead to other people and their opinions, and alive unto Christ Jesus.

I don't recall waking up again until morning. For a while I lay there looking at the ceiling, recalling the things I had experienced the night before. Gradually I realized that I felt free, free of all the influences on my life that dictated unnecessary actions, beliefs, behavior, or state of being that had not been put there by God. At the same time, I realized that much of my life had been devoted to making myself look good to others.

The next morning my doctor came to my room and asked me to follow her to her office. After a brief comment about the weather, she began, "Mr. Lawrence, We've discussed your case this morning, and have decided to move you to the eighth floor. It is an open ward, so you may come and go as you please. You may wear your own casual street clothes. You will receive further instructions from the eighth-floor nurse. Your medications will remain the same for the time being, and you will continue to see me twice or three times each week. Any questions?" "No, Ma'am," I replied. She gave me no time to tell her about my experience the night before, but I planned to do so as soon as an occasion arose.

Later that day, Shirley came for a visit. We both detected a difference in my demeanor. While still deeply depressed, I wasn't embarrassed about being a psychiatric patient, nor did I have as a first priority my obtaining a discharge from the hospital. I didn't seem to care what anyone thought about my situation. If anyone had ever come to visit me, I wouldn't have been ashamed of my condition, nor of any stigma that might result from my hospitalization. My concerns no longer were about myself, but rather about Shirley and the kids.

My Whole Family was in God's hands

On Shirley's next visit, she brought me some important news. She only shared a part of all that had happened, but even the part she shared with me was difficult for me to take. We had received a check for $500 from some unknown source. Having prayed fervently for the badly needed funds, we knew that ultimately it was God who provided us with the money. But when Shirley deposited it in the bank, the money was credited to the account of another "C.F. Lawrence" who lived in our area. By the time she learned of the bank's mistake, she had written checks for most of the money. Needless to say, the checks were bouncing all over the place! Even the bank teller, who was a friend of ours, couldn't recall Shirley's bank transaction the day she deposited the $500.

Shirley nearly flew home to take her most recent problem to the Lord. While Becky played with her dolls, her Mom opened her breaking heart to the Master. How often we had wondered why God had seen the whole matter, yet hadn't seemed to intervene. Now, because He understood the circumstances even better than Shirley, He waited for her to finish her story, then ministered peace to her troubled soul. Before she got up from her knees, she had a clear picture of what her next move should be. She was to go to the Cortland Memorial Hospital and apply for a job God already had prepared for her.

Although Shirley had no training for any of the jobs to be found in a hospital, she went into the employment office with the assurance in her heart that a job was there for her. She was told to fill out an application, and she would be informed if any jobs opened up. After applying for her new job as she had been instructed to do, she told the hospital official that God had told her that a job would be available at the hospital, so she expected to hear from them shortly. She left the lady a complimentary copy of David Wilkerson's book, The Cross and the Switchblade, and assured her that she would see her soon.

That night Shirley had a dream, one of her more exciting DIVINE APPOINTMENTS. The dream began with Shirley feeling herself rising from her body, and then moving from our home to the Hospital. She was looking down on Private Medical, a critical-care facility. She saw that double-wing facility with the central nursing station, exactly as it looked in the evenings after the patients had been put to bed. She even saw certain people with whom she would be working

Then, as she returned to her body, she felt the power of the Holy Spirit moving up and down her body, with a warm, rippling feeling that seemed to pour relaxation and strength into her physically and emotionally exhausted body. Before she went to sleep, she was still concerned about getting an appropriate baby-sitter for Becky. As she drifted off into a peaceful sleep, God assured her that He had the perfect sitter for her and that

To this day, she can totally recall each detail of that dream.) she would meet her the next day. (Shirley's spiritual dreams always occur in vivid Technicolor and with stereophonic sound! Her dream that night was no exception.

In the morning, Shirley received a call from the Chief Nurse at the hospital. "Mrs. Lawrence, would you be able to come in and see me today? I believe we have the job you are looking for."

"Why certainly, Mrs. Smith, I was expecting your call. I'll be there to see you at eleven." Shirley replied. Then the phone call came informing her of the baby-sitter the Lord had already prepared for Becky.

At the hospital, Shirley learned that the average time between a job application and the first day of work was from ten days to two weeks. However, the urgency of the hospital's need for her was so great that they were able to do the tests and check her references, etc., all in less than a day. She was given her uniforms and was told to report to work on "Private Medical" the next day at 3:00 PM. Her job? A nurse's aide! By the time Shirley got to tell me about her new job, she already had been working two days.

"Shirley, how can you do that kind of work with the terrible headaches you have?" I asked. Although some of Shirley's afflictions had been healed, she still lived with constant, excruciating headaches. "Fred, I know the Lord gave this job to me, and I'm confident He will give me the strength I'll need to do the things required of me. Just continue to pray for me." She continued to take a strong pain medication.

At first Shirley was motivated to succeed at her work for financial reasons. But gradually, as God took care of the financial crisis, Shirley's love and concern for her very ill patients became uppermost in her mind and prayers. She prayed one basic prayer before she went to work each day, and as often as needed during the day: "Dear Lord, I can't do the things being required of me. Please take Shirley out of Shirley, and replace her with Jesus Christ. Put a smile on my face that I may be a blessing to everyone with whom I come in contact today."

The third or fourth day on the job, while Shirley was moving a male patient in a wheelchair, a wheel of the chair rolled over her toes. She winced from the pain, but continued her task and returned the patient to his bed. By the time she was able to go to the ladies room and remove her shoe, her foot already was swelling and turning black. She discovered she now had a broken toe to add to her misery.

(Rarely did Shirley inform me of the anguish she was experiencing. Only in the years since then have I learned most of the full extent of the agonizing pain she lived with during her ordeal. Dealing with adversity was becoming a daily part of her life and mine. It had to be God's love and mercy enabled her to continue without complaint, and to minister to her patients as before.)

It also was God's special grace that equipped Shirley to care for her very ill patients in unique ways. When she gave a patient a backrub, the power of God flowed freely through her hands. Many of them would be fast asleep before she finished preparing them for the night. Usually she would sing softly in the Spirit as she went about her duties. Not only did that bring strength and anointing to her, but also to many of her "thought to be terminally ill" patients who were getting better and going home. Both doctors and nurses would ask Shirley where she had "trained" to learn the amazing nursing skill she demonstrated. Her reply could only be, "It's not me, but God who works through me who does what He does. Do you know that Jesus loves you very much too?"

One of Shirley's patients was an elderly man who was dying of liver and kidney disease. He suffered from severe DT's (Delirium Tremens), and would beg her for pain medicine. She began to talk to him about the love of Christ, and of His wonderful power to heal the sick. To her amazement, the man began to quote scriptures he had learned years before. He told her that his wife was divorcing him. As Shirley began to rub his back, praying fervently in the Spirit, his body completely relaxed and he fell asleep.

The next afternoon when Shirley arrived at work, she was told that her patient had shown remarkable improvement. Throughout that week he had many questions to ask her, and indicated that for the first time in many years, he wanted to live again. On the second or third day, the man's wife came in to see him once more before he died. She was shocked to find him like the man she had married many years before. By the end of the week, he was transferred off the critical care ward.

On another day, a nurse came to Shirley and told her that one of the patients on another wing had requested her to go and pray for her. She was in the final stages of abdominal cancer. When it was time for Shirley's coffee break, she went to pray with the sick lady.

As usual, Shirley stopped outside of the door, prayed for wisdom and the anointing to meet the need of the person, and also to let her face glow with a smile. Then she went in to pray in the Spirit for that very sick lady. Shirley laid her hands on the lady's abdomen and began to pray fervently in the Spirit. In a few moments, the lady also began to pray in the Spirit, and her arms went straight up in the air, praising the Lord. Shirley never saw that lady again. However, a few weeks later, after returning from being taken for a car ride and feeling better than she had in many years, she wrote Shirley a beautiful letter about the glorious healing she had received.

* * * * *

We came to understand that the Spirit of God had Shirley in His School of the Spirit in a most unusual manner. She was assigned to minister to the most seriously ill. As she took care of their bodily needs, the Lord was touching them spiritually. One after another of her patients responded to her strong, gentle, loving touch in Jesus' name. Often, with tears streaming down her cheeks as she interceded for her patients in the Spirit, she would feel a warm flow of the healing virtue of the Lord Jesus moving through her hands into their hopelessly ill bodies. Some of them passed on after Shirley went off duty, while others improved enough to be transferred to a less critical care unit. But all of them responded positively to the healing touch of the Lord Jesus through Shirley's "First Grade" in the School of the Spirit.

Another characteristic of the new healing ministry God was developing in Shirley was that her hands would shake when God's healing power began to flow thru them.

Initially she wondered about it, but since she was ministering to the sick in private, it didn't pose a problem. Later, however, when God began to minister healing to the sick in public, people began to ask questions about her shaking hands. To allay their fears, Shirley would inform people ahead of time that it would happen, and that they need not be concerned. Only God knows the number of critically ill patients that Shirley ministered to during the year she spent at Cortland Memorial. But in just a few months, her reputation had spread throughout the hospital and beyond

Most of us have heard reports of those who claim to have a healing ministry. In contrast, Shirley never claimed to have any such ministry. She simply was doing her best to make those people for whom she was responsible, feel a little better during their dying days. That was her job. Anything beyond that had to be God, for which she took no responsibility or credit.

In addition to her work at the Hospital, Shirley took care of her responsibilities at home; found time to visit me several times a week; do the things I would have done if I had been at home; and be a good Mother to our four children. She did all these things while suffering a continually severe headache caused by her hemorrhage. God was building a foundation for ministry in Shirley that went far beyond her previous knowledge and experience.

We both took great comfort in scriptures such as 2 Corinthians, 12: 9 (LB): *Paul said , "Three times I begged God to make me well again. Each time He said, "No, but I am with you, that is all you need. My power shows up best in weak people. Now I am glad to boast about how weak I am. I am glad to be a living demonstration of Christ's power and abilities. Since I know it is all for Christ's good. I am quite happy about "the thorn," and about the insults and hardships, persecutions and difficulties; for when I am weak, then I am strong - the less I have, the more I depend on Him."*

Then in Hebrews (LB), after God tells us about the training and discipline He brings upon us, He says in vs. *12: "So take a new grip with your tired hands, stand firm on your shaky legs, and mark out a straight path for your feet so that those who follow you, though weak and lame, will not fall and hurt themselves, but become strong."*

P.S. Many years later, while Shirley was giving the part of her testimony that included these experiences, one of my fellow International Directors and his wife said to me, "Fred, your testimonies don't glorify the Lord. Only the devil is out to 'kill, steal, and destroy,' the way he did in your lives. God is only glorified by healing and health!" So not everyone agrees that suffering can be a part of the life of one of His children.

7

LEARNING TO WALK IN THE SPIRIT

My occupational therapy as a psychiatric patient at the Syracuse VA Hospital turned out to be pushing patients around the hospital each day in wheelchairs or gurneys. I would report to the "Wheelchair Brigade" at 8:00 am. When a nurse anywhere in the hospital needed someone to take a patient to the lab, to X-ray, or elsewhere, they would call our department, and one of us would answer the call. What began as somewhat uninteresting tasks, turned out to be one of my greatest blessings. I had enrolled in God's Servant Ministry 101, (Philippians 2:5-8 NAS) *"Have this attitude in yourselves, which was also in Christ Jesus, who although He existed in the form of God, did not regard equality with God a thing to be grasped, but emptied Himself, taking the form of a bond-servant, and being made in the likeness of men, He humbled Himself by becoming obedient to the point of death, even death on a cross."* These tasks, assigned to me as therapy, began my servant/disciple life, a life God had called me to in a vision he had given me about two weeks before.

I don't recall ever being a true servant to anyone before then. I was more used to being a supervisor. My previous attempts at being a servant had always contained a tinge of self-serving. As I gained access to the hospital wards that housed men who were really suffering, I began to pray fervently for them in the Spirit. These wards contained hopelessly wounded men: severe burn victims, paraplegics, quadruple amputees, etc., who had been hospitalized for years—some since World War I. Soon I began seeing these men with the "mind of Christ," as His great compassion for these fellows began to flow over me like a flood. I doubt if a person who simply wishes to be more compassionate could attain real Christ-like compassion apart from direct contact with, and daily service to, those who are truly suffering.

My first day pushing wheel chairs wasn't my greatest. I had only enough strength to make one trip. But gradually I regained my strength, and learned to love what I was doing like nothing I had ever done before. I learned to stop praying for myself, and to pray fervently for these men who were far worse off than me. They became more important to me than any building I had ever designed or built. Then God made it even easier by giving me the ability to see the face of Jesus in each of those patients. He has continued that same gift up to the present time as I minister to men everywhere, even to men who aren't especially lovable! But God sees beneath their looks, and sees His original purpose for that man's life. When Christ judges the nations according to Matthew 25:31-46 (KJV) *He will separate the "sheep" from the "goats" on the basis of whether or not we have ministered to the sick, the imprisoned, the hungry and thirsty, etc.* Now I was beginning to learn precisely what that scripture meant.

Weeks went by without any change in my mental condition. Much of the time I was unable to hold any kind of conversation without weeping (another symptom of depression and the brain damage I had incurred.). It was especially difficult for my family to see me like that. All I could do was tearfully and continually pray for them. At the same time, I learned that the men I was transporting in wheelchairs were becoming my friends. They would often request that I be the one to push them wherever they had to go. For some reason, a few of them just seemed to enjoy having me push them around.

I discovered that I could sort of lay hands on them by putting my thumbs very lightly on their shoulders, and pray in the Spirit very softly or silently as I pushed their wheelchairs or gurneys. As I did this, the Lord would ease their suffering. My inability to talk with them became a blessing, because nothing I said ever seemed to help any of them anyway. That it wasn't necessary for me to do anything for these men but to be with them for awhile and touch them with the compassion of the Lord, was an important principle that I could have learned only by experience. To just be there and convey the precious love of Christ to them was enough to make a big difference in their lives.

One day God showed me what St. Paul meant when he said in 1 Corinthians 9:22, *"To the weak I became weak, to win the weak."* And in 2 Cor.12:9, *"My strength is made perfect in weakness."* The most important thing for me to do for God at any given moment was to be obedient to Him and serve these men.

If I could have found a way to get myself to some foreign mission field instead of where I was, I would have been totally out of His will for me at that time. I asked myself the question, "Is this place any less a mission field than anywhere else God might send me?" I never encountered anyone else, even from any of the more than five hundred churches in the Syracuse area doing any sort of ministry at the VA Hospital. Of course a hospital chaplain visited there, but I was there all the time for more than eight months. I, like most others, had learned the meaning of religious terms such as "mission field" from folks who had never served people who had no hope, no joy, no love. I discovered that most mission fields exist not far from where we are.

I suppose some will find these remarks to be symptomatic of the condition that put me in that place, both spiritually and physically. But I wouldn't exchange the things I went through for the best day in my life before then. My work had become my calling. The men I pushed in those wheelchairs allowed me to become, at least in part, the very personification of Jesus. He knew and loved those veterans so much. As I prayed for them, I seldom had a dry eye. But those tears were cleansing me, and purging me, and were becoming my strength.

All this time insomnia continued to be a problem, even though sleeping pills were prescribed for me. I finally opted not to take them and have a fuzzy brain all the next day. So with permission from my supervisor, I would sit out in the day room at night, read my Bible, and listen to the CBN Radio Nightwatch program. I especially enjoyed Henry Harrison, widely known as "The Apostle of Love," or "Second Fiddle" of PTL Club fame, who hosted this all-night call-in program. Along with the Christian music and inspirational testimonies, God ministered life to me through Henry's words of tender, loving encouragement.

Sometimes one of our night nurses, a regally beautiful black woman, would come in and enjoy Nightwatch with me after she had caught up on her work. Often after she had returned to her duties, I would sit and be amazed at the effect of both her and Henry's ministering to me at the same time. "Could she be an angel?" I wondered. (Before being discharged from the hospital, I inquired about her in order that I might tell her how much I appreciated her ministry to me. No one seemed to know to whom I was referring! I have met only a very few Christian people who could counsel and minister to people like me with the wisdom and loving maturity that she had.)

In contrast, I recalled the times I had spoken with Christian friends and relatives about some of my difficulties. They always seemed to have a quick scriptural (and sometimes not so scriptural) answer to my every problem or question. They usually told me about someone they knew who had gone through something like I was going through. Many times they would finish my sentences before I knew how I wanted to express myself. I asked the Lord what He thought of all this. His reply was, *"He who gives an answer before he hears, it is folly and shame to him."* (Proverbs 18:13)

As a result of going through the above "Christian Counseling 101" course, my advice for would-be counselors is: be joyful, but not boisterous; be slow to speak, but quick to listen; and, finish with a thoughtful Spirit-filled prayer, a hug, and an early departure. Then make return visits as often as you can. Your sick friend will recuperate more rapidly, and you will be glad you came to visit. (All that wisdom for you at no charge!)

In addition to my fellow patients, one of my doctors confided in me that he had studied theology near his home in Germany. After receiving his ThD, he became a pastor of a church near his home. To his dismay, he learned that he wasn't sure of the reality of the things he taught and preached, even the reality of God Himself. So he left the ministry, and started the long road toward his MD in Psychiatry. When speaking with me, he would inquire about my Christian beliefs, listening very thoughtfully and carefully to everything I said. And, unlike my Christian "friends," he never finished a sentence for me, or even tried to analyze anything I said—at least not out loud!

My fine German doctor also had a doctorate in music,

and was a world-renowned organist who often gave recitals in Crouse Auditorium at Syracuse University. On two occasions, he invited Shirley and I to attend his recitals. We were thoroughly blessed and impressed by each one. His rendition of Handel's Messiah nearly lifted us from our seats.

One day I shared with my doctor what I had seen and experienced in the Washington, DC Convention (See Chapter 8). He was very interested. God was revealing to him that the very things he doubted about Christianity were perhaps true after all. I saw a man in agony of spirit unlike any I had ever seen before. Should he explore the things I was telling him, or should he finish his residency in Psychiatry at Upstate Medical Center? A few days later, I received word that I was being assigned to a new doctor. Apparently, a psychiatrist must never get emotionally involved in any way with a patient!

Some time later, my ex-doctor and I met in the corridor. He said, "Fred, I'm glad to see you. I've wanted to say, 'May God bless you. I believe God has something very important for you to do someday.'" Then we continued on our ways.

Central New York was having an especially severe winter that year. I was usually quite concerned about Shirley's driving the thirty miles to the hospital, especially because she frequently seemed so tired by the time she arrived. One day she was anxious to tell me about the experience she had had driving home from her last visit.

She had fallen asleep at the wheel of our car just as she was entering Homer. When she awakened, she and the car were sitting on top of a five- or six-foot snow bank on the side of the road, with the car turned in the opposite direction! She had done at least a 180-degree spin before climbing the bank.

"What am I doing on top of this snow bank? How did I get up here, and how am I ever going to get down? " No sooner had the questions come than a car stopped next to her. A man got out of his car, took a tow chain from his trunk, hooked our car to his, and very gently began to pull Shirley and the car off that bank and safely onto the road again. The "man" unhooked the chain, returned it to his trunk, and drove away. He never said a word, and didn't even give Shirley a chance to thank him.

After she told me about the event, we both asked, "Was it an angel?" Whether it was or not isn't as important as the fact that God had arranged the rescue. It was just one more DIVINE APPOINTMENT showing the loving hand of God taking care of us, no matter what our need, and no matter how serious our other circumstances were at the time. Once again, we praised the Lord!

* * * * *

The human mind is so complex, and the range of mental problems so complicated that very few people are able to cope daily with the mentally ill over any extended period like psychiatrists and psychologists do. In spite of this, for some reason many of the Christian ministers I've heard not uncommonly refer to them as "Shrinks," at least in their private conversations. But I came to respect and appreciate both as special people who had studied and worked very hard for many years in order to help people with mental illnesses or conditions. Mine always treated me with utmost care and thoughtfulness.

I firmly believe that when these professionals acknowledge and incorporate Jesus Christ into their lives and their practices, they can successfully treat even greater multitudes of mentally ill people. I also believe that most of the ministers mentioned above could benefit greatly by the advice and counsel of good, Spirit-filled psychiatrists or psychologists. Perhaps fewer controversies would occur among

Christian ministers if that were the case!

* * * * *

The Thanksgiving/Christmas/New Year season arrived too soon for me. As children, we learn to look forward to that special time of the year. But then, as some of us grow older, our expectations for those special events like Christmas never quite live up to the actual holiday celebrations. Some folks even find themselves glad when these holidays are over!

I was allowed to spend a couple days home during Christmas, something I had prayed for. But I was a disappointment to everyone, especially me. Summing up the whole matter, I'd have to admit that I was glad to return to the safety of the VA Hospital just before New Year's Day.

JIM

On January 2 of the New Year (1970), Jim was admitted to my ward and was assigned to the bed next to mine. He wasn't catatonic, but he seldom, if ever, spoke to anyone. For hours at a time, he could be found walking along with his hands clasped behind his back and his eyes looking at the floor. On occasion he would stop, and for several minutes he would look intently at some spot on the floor, or at some object. At those times, I assumed that he somehow was escaping from the reality of where he was and what he had become, and was secluding himself into a more hospitable world within his own mind.

One evening, the night nurse gave me a little of his background. A dentist from downstate NY, he recently had gone through a painfully difficult divorce, and had been granted only limited access to his three children whom he dearly loved. Tragically, he also still loved his wife as well.

He had begun to drink during the divorce proceedings, and as a result, daily had gone from bad to worse emotionally.

Concerned, I often would walk in silence with Jim. At other times I would sit next to him, sometimes reading, sometimes just sitting quietly in prayer. At night he would lie on his back with his hands behind his head, looking intently at the ceiling. He would often get up in the night and walk, until someone guided him back to bed.

One night, I returned to the ward around 2:00 am, and Jim was nowhere to be found. Upon entering our room, I saw him sitting cross-legged on the floor between our beds. He was silently and slowly tracing the outlines of the floor tiles with his finger.

As I got into bed and began to pray for Jim, I heard the sweet voice of the Holy Spirit ask, "Why don't you join him in what he is doing?" So I sat down across from Jim, crossed my legs, and began to trace the outline of the floor tiles along with him. He didn't seem to notice even though the ward was totally silent except for a few snores here and there.

I sat there with him for fifteen minutes or so before I noticed tears from Jim's eyes dripping onto the floor. He had started to cry with just a whimper at first. Then he gave way to great, gulping sobs. I brought him a box of tissues and sat back down. In a few more minutes, he got up, got in his bed, and went to sleep.

I went out to the nurse's station and described what had just taken place. The nurse made a full report, and then told me that they had never before observed Jim crying like that. The next morning, our doctor came and spent quite awhile with Jim. When I later saw the doctor, she mentioned that Jim was making progress, and suggested that I continue to do whatever it was I'd been doing!

Valentines Day was a big day for Jim. Although none of his family actually visited him that day (or any other day), he did receive a Valentine, a picture, and a note from his children. From that time on, those treasures were always in his pocket or close by him. One day he told me his children's names as he showed them to me for the umpteenth time. Then he shared with me that he expected to be discharged from the hospital the next day. He thanked me for being there when he really needed someone. Then he left to take care of some other business. The following day Jim walked out of that ward with my New Testament under his arm, and he never looked back.

One day my doctor mentioned Jim, having heard he was continuing to progress at home. "You were pretty good friends, weren't you, Fred? I think you helped him. Mind telling me what you did?"

"I didn't do anything, doctor. Oh yes, I prayed for him every day. And we sort of became friends." That was all I could think of at the moment. However, I believe there are important lessons to be learned from the result of such seemingly insignificant activities.

* * * * *

Apart from my association with Jim, the months of January, February, and March were relatively uneventful. No end to the despair, the loneliness and the heartache in my own life, nor to the horrible circumstances that my family was enduring, seemed in sight. My only solace during those long and dark winter days came as I read the Psalms, in particular Psalms 88 and 142.

Although David was King, yet he was courageous enough to write about his deeply depressing thoughts. Obviously God had approved, because He included those thoughts and others like them in His Bible. Like so much of the Word, these and other Psalms previously had had little, if any, meaning for me. Now, however, these words gave me strength, if for no other reason than by reading that a man such as David could have the same kinds of feelings I was having. God had put me in a place where these words became life for me. I saw that King David, that noble and brave warrior for God, had been there before me and had successfully recovered.

Parts of the Book of Lamentations also became almost daily comrades of mine, as the Holy Spirit ministered hope to me when there seemed to be no hope. I came to love Lamentations 3:18-24. *All hope is gone, my strength has turned to water, for the Lord has left me. Oh, remember the bitterness and suffering you have dealt to me! For I can never forget these awful years, always my soul will live in utter shame. Yet there is one ray of hope. His compassion never ends. It is only the Lord's mercies that have kept us from complete destruction. Great is Thy Faithfulness, His loving kindness begins afresh each day."* The great hymn, GREAT IS THY FAITHFULNESS became a constant companion of mine, and still remains my favorite hymn. From His Word and this hymn, and from the reports I had read of our soldiers who had spent years in North Vietnamese prison camps, and how they were well served by portions of scripture that they had "hidden in their hearts" long before they underwent the cruel torture of their captors, I learned that God is so thoughtful and gracious to those who suffer.

After these first three months, I was assigned to an additional type of occupational therapy. At first glance, it looked like a few guys sitting around doing arts and crafts. But it really was more than that, and the choices we could make about different projects were seemingly endless. My first choice was to try leatherwork. I started with a belt, thinking that perhaps some day I could create a beautiful horse saddle. Well, I never made a saddle, but one day I did give Shirley a hand-carved leather purse I had made.

This experience helped set me free from my erroneous

belief that I had to accomplish great things for God for Him to be satisfied with me. I learned that I wasn't required to do things to please God, but rather, just to be what He wanted me to be in whatever circumstances I found myself. Each day He led me to do things I had never done before. If I just did what I was instructed to do, God was happy, I was happy, and others seemed quite satisfied. I believe that the greatest lesson I learned during my stay in the Hospital was that GOD LOVED ME, as is! His love didn't depend on anything I did or didn't do, or where I happened to be. It was just a fact that stood completely alone.

The things I did for other men around me in the hospital afforded me with great joy and satisfaction . But, it wasn't doing something for just anyone. On the contrary, I found that God had His own itinerary for me. He would lead me to minister to someone in greater need than anyone else, as I simply waited on Him for direction. I also learned that He would teach me how to do what was needed to ease the suffering of someone. God taught me to walk in the Spirit in my Christian life.

Once I joined in a nine-ball pool tournament put on for the patients. I had always excelled at pool, and began to get the "feel" after just a few games. Willy, one of the men on my ward who had been a drug addict and alcoholic, also joined the tournament and did quite well. He was very competitive, and would moan and groan when he missed a shot. The day came when all of the players were eliminated except Willy and me. Quite an audience gathered to watch, and shouted or clapped as we made or missed a shot. Finally, we were down to the last ball and I was up. Willy had left me with a pretty easy set-up. However, I had been witnessing to Willy about the Love of Christ. I began to ask myself, "Should I, or shouldn't I sink the shot?" I decided to miss! Willy won the tournament and the grand prize, both of which were obviously very important to him. A few days later he spoke to me very quietly and said, "Fred, you missed that final shot on purpose didn't you. You let me win." I guess it had been pretty obvious, but I was glad I did it. Soon after that, he joined with me in saying a sinner's prayer. And we've remained friends ever since. I guess you could say I won by losing!

In addition to the Psalms and the passage from Lamentations, I've always loved II Corinth. 5:17, *"If any man be in Christ, he is a new person, old things have passed away, and behold, all things have become new."* I had pondered that scripture a lot in light of my own circumstances. If indeed everything had become new in my life when Christ came in, then why was I going through such mental and emotional distress? Did I have some hidden sins in my life that prevented me from receiving total health? Or was my faith in God's power to heal me just too weak? By then, I was trying to memorize Kenneth Hagin's booklets on faith and healing. From those readings, it seemed to me that most people who had incurable or chronic illnesses either lacked faith, or had some unconfessed sin.

Hebrews 5:8 says that *"Although He (Jesus) was a son, he learned obedience from what he suffered."* It was a wonderful day when I learned that nothing less would be required to bring me to a place of total brokenness and obedience to my Lord, and that neither a lack of faith nor sin in my life caused my circumstances. Rather, God had used the condition I was in to teach me lessons I could never have learned in any other way. These weren't lessons I could have learned from a book, but were principles that became integral parts of my being as I lived my life under these unusual conditions.

Equally important, it wasn't necessary for me or anyone else to totally understand why God, in any way, would cause or even allow one of His own, Spirit-filled disciples to undergo the adversity and hardships that we were going through. My VA hospital was nothing less than a DIVINE APPOINTMENT with the Master Teacher of the universe.

8

A MIRACLE IN WASHINGTON

"Would you like to go to a FGBMFI Convention at the Washington Hilton next month?" my good friend Rich Davis asked me. He might as well have asked me if I'd like to fly to the moon. He knew I had been a patient in the VA Hospital in Syracuse for more than seven months, and that I wasn't expected to be discharged anytime soon. I didn't have money enough to make such a trip, even if I weren't in the hospital. But I explained my situation anyway. "You'd have to take responsibility for me, and clear it with the Hospital Administrator and my doctor—in person!" He did exactly that!

Soon, we were on our way to D.C. for some DIVINE APPOINTMENTS I'd never forget. As we were unloading our bags at the hotel entrance, a Greyhound bus pulled up behind us. I couldn't help but notice that only one man, an Army Colonel, got off the bus. The driver took his bag, and they went into the lobby. No one else was on the bus, which seemed unusual to me.

We had been trying all day to arrive at the hotel in time

for the Kathryn Kuhlman meeting that evening, but were a couple hours late. We checked into our room, unpacked our bags, and went downstairs to see if anything was still going on. After we literally squeezed our way into the packed-out auditorium that night, I saw things I'd never dreamed of before. Miss Kuhlman was announcing to the more than a thousand people in attendance that God was healing people of various kinds of illnesses (the gift of the Word of Knowledge). I had never experienced a stronger feeling of the presence of God in my life.

I had heard about these kinds of meetings, but never could quite believe what I heard. Now I was actually experiencing it! Miss Kuhlman would announce that God was healing someone of such and such disease or condition. Sometimes it was one, and sometimes it was more than one who would stand up and declare they had received their healings. Usually they were ushered up to the platform where she would talk with them about what had just happened to them. She spoke sweetly to them about what God had done, and they would tell some of the most incredible stories about their sicknesses and their healings that I'd ever heard. Then she would touch them on the forehead, and the power of God would cause them to fall backwards like a ton of bricks! (Miss Kuhlman had a very experienced crew of people working with her, so they were never injured by their fall.)

God even allowed me to see a few of the healings happen right before my eyes! Then, she told us that someone was being healed of a scoliosis of the spine. She pointed in our direction and probably six people stood up in front of us, praising the Lord, touching their toes and claiming their healings. I was so happy for them that I forgot that I, too, had a 7 cm spinal curvature or scoliosis, which was documented in my Navy records. I didn't feel anything unusual, and nobody touched me or spoke to me.

When we got up to our room, I began taking my tie off

in front of a mirror. For the first time in my memory, my head was straight up and down instead of being cocked off to my right. I asked Rich if he could see anything that might be a curvature of my spine, to which he replied, "It looks OK to me." I had received a healing, and hadn't even realized it until then.

Another amazing thing that happened was that, for the first time in years, I slept peacefully and soundly all night. My back wasn't especially bothersome, but it was the cause of many headaches that interfered with my sleep. Although I had some other major problems that were not healed, I knew that the "clay" doesn't argue with the "potter" about whether he'd rather be shaped some other way. I was a very happy man the next morning!

That Thursday morning, we went to our first FGBMFI Breakfast Meeting. We sat at round tables with ten to twelve other folks, all from different parts of the country. I don't remember the exact sequence of events, but sometime after we had finished eating, a lady at our table stood up and gave a message in tongues, and another lady at our table gave the interpretation. The ladies sat down, and everyone continued as before except me. (How could I sit, when every atom of my being felt amazingly energized?)

Because of my limited knowledge, I had thought that "tongues and interpretation" were meant for the whole audience. But in this case, it was directed specifically to me. God had spoken very clearly to me. He not only related exactly about all the incredibly painful days I had been spending in the hospital, but also for a long time before that. He assured me that He had chosen this time and this place to lift me out of my deep, dark valley, and to set my way on a higher plain so that He could begin to use me in ways I had never even thought of before. He reminded me of the years of loneliness and isolation I had been through, and that He was now going to surround me with many brothers. He also said that through all my tribulations, I had never blamed Him for my problems. Can you believe that God spoke other things to me that morning that I can't even remember? If Shirley had been with me, she'd have remembered every word. Unfortunately, He hasn't repeated Himself, so I'll never know all that was said to me. (If you ever think you might get a "word from the Lord," try to have your tape recorder turned on. You'll want to play it over again and again.)

When the main speaker was introduced, I said, "Rich, that's the man we saw getting off the bus last night." The man was Army Col. Merlin Carruthers, a chaplain whose life had been transformed by the Baptism in the Holy Spirit. God had revealed to him that when he prayed, he should remember that God knew about all his needs even better than he knew them. So rather than ask, he should abundantly praise God for already meeting the need.

The speaker then used what had happened to him the night before to illustrate his point. He had been trying to get to the Convention early enough to attend the Kuhlman meeting. The person who was supposed to meet him at the Washington National Airport and take him to the hotel wasn't anywhere to be found. So, Merlin just stood in the Terminal and praised the Lord for all the great things He was doing for him. As he was praising, a uniformed man walked up and asked him if he was going to the Washington Hilton. When Merlin said he was, the man took his bag, and led him outside to his waiting Greyhound bus. And with Merlin as his only passenger, the driver took him directly to the hotel and let him off right in front of us. Colonel Carruthers went through the hotel lobby and directly to the head table of the Kuhlman Meeting. What a great God we serve

By the end of that Breakfast meeting, I thought that everything else that would follow would be sort of anticlimactic. How could anything be greater than what we'd already seen and heard?

From the meeting room, we wandered around the lobby and book room. As we wandered, it seemed like everyone I met wanted to hug me and tell me how much they loved me—I mean just about everyone! Do you know just how healing those hugs can be? There was no way these people knew me, nor what I had been through. It had to be God. All I could do was praise the Lord, which I had just learned to do a few minutes earlier in the Carruthers meeting. I also had people come to me with words of personal prophecy that seemed to corroborate the earlier prophecy the ladies had given to me. I began to understand that not only could God speak to the whole body through prophecy, but also that He could speak to anyone, at any time, in any way he wished.

That afternoon we received a wonderful Bible teaching, and after dinner we were off to the big evening fellowship meeting. As excited as I was, I didn't expect another "barn burner!" After the worship time, the emcee introduced Demos Shakarian, a very successful businessman who founded and served as President of FGBMFI. All during his talk, I felt like I was on fire. He shared his vision of FGBMFI, which included how God took him like a space ship on a couple of trips around the earth. The first time around, he saw millions of men in every nation and mode of dress standing shoulder-to-shoulder, Each of them appeared to be in a state of spiritual death, their arms folded, their heads bowed in hopelessness and despair. Then he said that God sent him around the world a second time. Only by this time, Demos' wife, Rose, had entered the room and was seated at the piano. She gave forth a message in tongues and the interpretation that went something like, "My son, you are in my will. Look not to the left or the right, but follow in the way I am leading you. The things you are seeing will shortly come to pass." (The complete scenario is beautifully told in detail in Demos and Roses' book, The Happiest People On Earth.)

As Demos related this vision, the miracle for me was

that I was seeing almost the same thing in my own soul or spirit. I don't know yet how to explain it, but it was supernatural, and it would always be indelibly impressed on me. (As I look back on the last twenty five years and on the things God did through me, I know without a shadow of a doubt that that vision God gave to Demos was the power behind the things I did. I would read that story over and over and let God show me more and more all the things He had in mind when He gave that vision to Demos.)

* * * * *

I returned to the hospital, which had actually become my home by then. I tried to tell my doctor the things I had experienced at the Convention. What could she say? My treatment now was two one-hour sessions each week with my psychiatrist-insight therapy, I believe they called it. I was totally free to say anything I wanted to say to her, so I would ask the Lord to show me something nice for the doctor. After about two weeks, she told me that a doctor must never become emotionally involved with a patient, so she had asked that she be excused from my case. I don't know what her problem was.

* * * * *

Shirley and I heard about a healing evangelist coming to Syracuse and decided to attend a meeting. Roxanne Brant was a young medical student at Harvard when she had a dramatic encounter with Christ. She transferred from Harvard to Gordon-Conwell Seminary, where she not only became a doctor of theology, but also received the Baptism in the Holy Spirit. As the Lord led her step by step into a public ministry of Teaching, she also began to move into the gifts of prophecy, word of wisdom, word of knowledge, and finally into a full-blown healing ministry very much like that of Kathryn Kuhlman. Boy! Was I a good candidate for her ministry!

Much like the Kuhlman meeting, the Brant meeting progressed from a beautifully anointed worship service and a prophetic teaching ministry into signs and miracles (wonders). At one point, she informed us that God was healing someone of brain damage caused by a car accident. And, someone was being delivered of migraine headaches. She put her hand on my shoulder and said, "Brother, God is healing you, just receive it in Jesus' name." I felt as though something lifted from my brain and off the top of my head.

From that day to this, I've never had another migraine. It appeared to me that I had received a deliverance rather than a healing, for at the same time, I was set free from fear, depression, and other spirits that I don't recall. I wish I could fully explain what it felt like. Suddenly, I could laugh again. I was free at last! Praise God! "Jesus Christ, the same yesterday, today and forever." (Hebrews 13:8)

I returned to the Hospital on Monday morning, feeling better than I had felt in years. I spoke with my doctor that morning, telling him every detail I could remember of the healing service, and of my deliverance and healing. It was no coincidence that I was speaking to a man who desperately needed to hear that God was alive and well, and that He was doing miracles today. I believe that some day I will hear for sure that he returned to his former ministry, only with the assurance that he served a risen Savior who was in the world today, doing miracles for His people.

RELEASE FROM THE HOSPITAL

Later that week I spoke with several other doctors who obviously had put their heads together at a staff meeting and decided that something indeed had happened that had been very beneficial to me. The following week, I was discharged from the Hospital.

When an experience as serious as mine happens in the life of a believer, I believe that he benefits immensely. I cannot look as objectively at myself as others can. But, I can see clearly that even these hospital events worked together for my good, according to Romans 8:28. When I came completely to the end of myself, to the end of my self-sufficiency, to the end of anything in myself on which I could ever rely, to being totally destitute, I then was able to receive all that my Lord Jesus had for me. My life now was based on Jesus Christ alone, and on the precious work of the Holy Spirit in my life.

It was to my great advantage that all of those months I spent in the solitude of my own mind had brought me into an intimate relationship with Jesus. Rejection by my friends and others had allowed me to enter into the sufferings of Christ in a way I never could have done otherwise. Jesus was "despised and rejected by men, a man of sorrows, and familiar with suffering. Like one from whom men hide their faces...." (Isa. 53:3) God had allowed me to enter into a similar experience. 1 Peter 4:12 (LB) assures us, *"Dear friends, do not be surprised at the painful trial you are suffering as though something strange were happening to you. But rejoice that you participate in the sufferings of Christ, so that you may be overjoyed when His glory is revealed."*

Oswald Chambers sheds some light on these truths, in his Devotional for January 15, in MY UTMOST FOR HIS HIGHEST, 9, entitled, "Do You Walk In White?")

According to him, no one experiences complete sanctification without going through a "white funeral," the burial of the old life. If you have never experienced this crucial moment of change through spiritual death, sanctification will never be more than an elusive dream. A "white funeral" must take place, a baptism into His death (Rom 6:3), a death with only one resurrection into the life of Jesus Christ. Nothing can defeat a life like this. It has oneness with God for only one purpose—to be a witness/disciple for Him. (I believe these words accurately describe my experience of October 10, 1969, at 12:30 am, when I made my agreement with God.)

Have you had your "white funeral"? Has there been a point in your life **that** you now mark as your last day? Is there a place in your life to which you go back in memory with humility and overwhelming gratitude, so that you can honestly proclaim, "Yes, it was then, at my 'white funeral', that I made an agreement with God?"

"This is the will of God, your sanctification. . . ." (1 Thess. 4:3). Once you truly realize this is God's will, you will enter into the process of sanctification as a natural response. Are you willing to experience that "white funeral" now? Will you agree with Him that this is your last day on earth? The moment of agreement depends on you."

Reading these words brought to my remembrance that, as a boy, I had heard (and rejected) my Dad preach so powerfully about sanctification. I had come to believe that my family had rejected the Doctrine of the Baptism in the Holy Spirit, and had substituted the Doctrine of Sanctification for it. Now, I see very clearly that all of these things are a part of God's Word, and that they are a part of the normal Christian life.

My discharge from the Hospital in March of 1970 began a whole new chapter in my life and in the life of my family. It was a joyful occasion leaving the VA after eight months, yet I had made many friends of both patients and staff who had become like another family to me. So leaving them was a bit sad in some cases, yet I was very anxious to get on with life at home again.

8B

THE REFINERS FIRE

(Author unknown)

He sat by a furnace of sevenfold heat,
As He watched by the precious ore,
And closer He bent with a searching gaze
As He heated it more and more.

He knew He had ore that could stand the test,
And He wanted the finest gold
To mold as a crown for the King to wear,
Set with gems of price untold.

So He laid our gold in the burning fire,
Though we fain would say to Him, "Nay";
And watched the dross that we had not seen
As it melted and passed away.

And the gold grew brighter and yet more bright,
But our eyes were dim with tears;
We saw but the fire - not the Master's hand -
And questioned with anxious fears.

Yet our gold shown out with a richer glow
As it mirrored a Form above
That bent o'er the fire, though unseen by us,
With a look of ineffable love.

Can we think it pleases His loving heart
To cause us a moment's pain?
Ah, no! but He sees through the present cross
The bliss of eternal gain.

So He waited there with a watchful eye,
With a love that is strong and sure,
And His gold did not suffer a bit more heat
Than was needed to make it pure.

9

RETURN HOME TO A NEW LIFE IN CHRIST

My homecoming was a very happy occasion. Relatives, friends and neighbors gathered around to welcome me home. It didn't take me long to get back into the swing of things around the house. And it didn't take God long to let me know how serious He had been when He said "TRUST ME" so many months before.

The Lord seemed to almost go overboard to rebuild my confidence and trust in Him. My home and family became more beautiful to me than ever before. I had a whole new outlook on life, and a relaxation into Christ's plan for my life that made it pure joy just to be alive. (Perhaps a good dose of depression can be a good thing, in light of God's promise in Romans 8:28 *"And we know that all that happens to us is working for our good, if we love God and are fitting in to his plans."*)

The second day after I returned home, I got a phone call that went something like this, "Mr. Lawrence, this is Bill

Wright with Lapeer, Wright, and Simon (a fictitious name) Architects and Engineers in Syracuse. Our firm is very busy, and we are expanding our work force. We need a Chief Specifications Writer. I understand you have extensive education and experience in the architectural and construction field. I thought that perhaps you would be interested in a position with our company"

My immediate response was, "Why yes, Mr. Wright, I would be interested. When would it be convenient for you to discuss this further with me?" "I'm glad to hear that, Mr. Lawrence. Would you be able to come in tomorrow at 11:00, and we can talk more about this?" "Yes sir," I replied, "I'll see you in the morning."

After previously spending over a year and a half submitting applications to more than 1100 companies—without any success—I would have crawled all the way to Syracuse and back just to hear what this man was talking about. I was shouting, "Hallelujah, Praise the Lord!" all over the house. I didn't know anything about this Mr. Wright or his company, nor could he have known me. I kept wondering, "How could this be happening? I just don't understand." I said, "Shirley, with my VA disability pension and social security, we make just enough for us to live on. But if this man is on the level and will offer me 5 cents an hour more than we're making now, I'll accept his offer. I want to go back to work more than you'll ever know." The next morning at 11:00 sharp, I was knocking on his door.

"Mr. Lawrence, I'm glad to meet you. My name is Bill. May I call you Fred? I believe we met while we were studying at R.P.I. You were a year ahead of me there. I've taken the liberty to look into your work background a bit, and I know what you learned in school. We think you are just the man we've been looking for." I said, "Bill, I've been a psychiatric patient for the last eight months at the VA Hospital here in Syracuse. While I'm feeling well now, I'm sure this would have some bearing on your decision here." He replied, "Fred, I don't care where you've been, I only care about what you know. We are prepared to have you spend the next 8 or 9 months getting up-to-speed with what we are doing, before you take full responsibility for our Specifications Dept." He added that they had 75 architects, draftsmen and engineers and other staff members then, and that they would rapidly expand by at least another 50 per cent. I tried not to seem too excited, but I quickly accepted his offer.

Bill then said, "Fred, if you could start work for us at—and he offered 3 times as much as the minimum I would have accepted—we'll be able to double that amount as soon as you're ready to assume full responsibility for our Specifications Department." I suspect my jaw must have dropped to my knees as I said, "Yes!" to his salary offer, and began thanking the Lord for another DIVINE APPOINTMENT

One day, while I was "getting up to speed" as he put it, he called me into his office and asked if I'd be willing to spend some time doing graduate work in Specifications Writing at the University of Wisconsin, work that would prepare me to do the very most modern procedures in my field. Of course, I jumped at the chance!

I enjoyed a most satisfying semester at the University, studying Specification Writing and Technical Writing—all expenses paid! Words cannot fully express just how happy I was with my new position with such a prestigious Architectural/Engineering firm. Here I was, working along with some of the finest men in the business, doing what I loved to do best, and making more money than I had ever made before. God was so, so good to me! We could never thank and praise him enough. (My experiences working with those professionals also turned out to be great training for the ministry God was preparing for me—working with men.)

A condition one must cope with in Upstate New York is

the intense cold and snow in the wintertime. My work required a 35-mile commute each day, come rain or shine or snowstorms. However, the time this drive allowed me to spend with the Lord was so precious that I looked forward to each trip. The Lord even reminded me one morning that He enjoyed my fellowship too!

Usually the TV Weathermen are quite accurate, so on one cold winter night I was quite apprehensive about the severity of the storm predicted for that night and the next day. I woke up about 5 am, and spent my usual time fellowshipping with the Lord. He had been teaching me about faith for several weeks, and had helped me understand that there is a big difference between the faith we experience when we get saved and for other basic needs, ". . . *the measure of faith God has dealt to every man.*" (Romans 12:3), and the faith and power that Stephen had in Acts 6:8 when he went about doing "*great wonders and miracles among the people,*" *i.e.* "The Gift of Faith" spoken of in 1 Corinthians 12:9. So I was about to get a lesson in the latter. (Both kinds of faith are necessary for the Lord's servants.)

At 6 am that morning, all the roads in Central New York were declared closed because of a heavy snowstorm, including those between Homer and Syracuse. I had just finished thanking God for the wonderful job He had given me. It just didn't seem possible that He would give me work that I couldn't get to because of His weather. (The gift of faith began to rise up within me like springs of living water from a fountain.)

I ate my breakfast, kissed my family goodbye, and walked into my garage as I always did. When I opened my garage door, I saw that five or more feet of snow had drifted into my driveway. I said, "Lord Jesus, you gave me this job, and I know you expect me to work eight hours each day. Therefore, since you are the God who calms the wind and the rain, I believe you are the Lord of this storm. I am your servant and unless the roads are impassable, I will go to Syracuse as usual."

I wish I could adequately relate the exact feelings I was having as I backed my car out of my driveway and onto the street. I was in the midst of a very special DIVINE APPOINTMENT. Remember now that the snow was at least five feet deep, with drifts much higher. Snow was falling at an incredible rate of several inches per hour. Yet I was driving down my street on a bare road. I turned onto State Rte.281, and then onto 81N. As far as I could tell, the road was bare at least thirty feet in front of me and several feet behind me. No snow was falling on my car. It was like being in a large cocoon, inside of which the weather was perfect, and outside of which a wall of snow surrounded me.

Mine was the only car moving on the road, although several cars were abandoned by the side of the road or had slid into the ditch. No one appeared to be in any of those cars or I would have stopped to give them a ride. My speed was a steady forty miles per hour all the way into Syracuse, although I could have driven faster. I was having my usual fellowship with the Lord. I drove through the city to Ridings Rd. on the north side of the city without having to stop for any reason. I drove into my company parking lot and parked just as my boss was arriving at the office on his cross-country skis. So he watched me make my entrance, just as I would have on any other day of the year. He began to question me as to where I had spent the night, how I had traveled across town when even the snowplows weren't able to move.

My boss knew of my strong love for the Lord and of my deep faith in God. But what he was hearing and had witnessed went far beyond his current understanding of faith. This was purely supernatural, and there was no other way to explain it. So, even though the office was closed for the day, we opened it and went to our desks to work. I overheard him making some phone calls, but it sounded to me like the folks he was calling about my amazing miracle weren't buying his story. (Who'd have blamed them?)

I worked that morning like I would have any other day, except I didn't have a secretary to type my work. Just before noon, my boss suggested we give up and try to get back home. "You'd be welcome to spend the night with me and my family, since the roads were still all closed," he added. I shared with him how God had helped me solve a difficult engineering problem that I'd been working on that morning. Then I assured him that I would be just fine, and that I'd return home the same way I got there. In the meanwhile, I would slowly drive in front of him until he got to his home on his skis—and then watch him in my rear-view mirror with his mouth wide open in astonishment as I drove out of sight.

Again, I drove steadily across town in my protective cocoon. I entered Rte. I-81S from Rte 690, and then journeyed on home to Homer, 40 mph all the way. I sat for a few minutes in my garage trying to put everything into perspective, and trying to figure out a way to explain it all to my family. Shirley opened the door to the garage with all kinds of questions about my miraculous trip to and from Syracuse. I said "Shirley, get in the car. I want to show you a miracle. She put on her coat and got into the car. The garage door opened to a wall of snow almost to the top of the door. I started to back up my car, seemingly with all the faith I had used so effectively just moments before, but that wall of snow just began to cave in into my garage. So, I had to shovel it out before I could shut the door again. My fervent prayer was to no avail this time.

The Lord's response to my questions about all of these things was indeed that He had divided the Red Sea to allow His children to cross over on dry land. Then when some of them began to grumble about things in the desert and wanted to return to Egypt, God had no intentions of dividing it again to let them go back. Nor did He have any intentions of showing off for me or my family! Shirley knew that I had been in Syracuse that day, because she had spoken on the phone several times to my boss. He couldn't explain things for her any more than I could, but he knew that he had seen what he saw. And now that I was safely home, he could only mumble a few words before hanging up his phone when he called us later that evening. (You won't be alone if you find it difficult to believe this testimony, but it all happened just like I've told it—a true DIVINE APPOINTMENT.)

* * * * *

Give Thanks for Everything Eph 5:20

Another time, Shirley and I (with Becky along) were to speak at a Friday evening chapter meeting in the Finger Lakes Region of Central New York State. It was a typical winter night, with heavy snow being forecast for much of the weekend. Only once in more than twenty years had we ever been hindered from our work by the weather, so we weren't alarmed by the weathermen, nor by their prognostications.

The meeting went very well, and we slept like babies that night in our motel room. We woke up earlier the next morning than we intended, and for some reason we just couldn't go back to sleep (one of my roomies intimated that my snoring was preventing them from getting their beauty sleep)! So, about 6:00 am we got up and headed for home. While we were stopped to eat breakfast, we heard on the restaurant radio an up-to-date—but not very encouraging— weather forecast that a storm was approaching from the west. We decided that since we were getting an early start, we would attempt to outrun it.

We traveled south and east on Rte. 17 through Corning, and then turned north on Rte. 13 to take us through Ithaca and on to our cozy little home in the big city of Homer.

Hopefully, we would beat the storm home.

The first part of the trip saw the predicted weather growing steadily worse, with the main problem being heavy wet snow falling at probably 3 or 4 inches an hour. As we approached Ithaca the visibility was close to zero. We had been traveling as fast as the conditions would allow, hoping to get home before the roads were closed. But as we drove through Ithaca, our progress slowed almost to a stop. No, this time there was no cocoon!

As we were passing through Ithaca our car's engine began to act up. It would run a few seconds and then stall. I turned off the main highway onto a side street so I could get "Old Faithful" running again. As I did, we heard the radio announcer say that Rte. 13 had been closed until further notice. (By then there was probably 24 to 30 inches of new snow on the road—not especially cold, but heavy, wet snow.)

After wrapping up Shirley and Becky in a blanket, I started off to the auto parts store to get some ether spray that would help me start the car again. On the way, I happened to see a telephone and decided to call the Assembly of God pastor to see if he had any mechanics in his church that could help us. He couldn't think of anyone, but he thought he could get to us in his four-wheel drive vehicle. He would swing by while he was on his way to do some banking and other errands and take Shirley and Becky to his home until the storm let up. We praised the Lord for always having His people on hand to help wherever one goes. At the same time, God was setting the stage for another delightful DIVINE APPOINTMENT.

At the time I called, the pastor was just leaving his apartment located on the second floor of his church. His wife, who was a night-duty nurse in the city hospital, was asleep in the front bedroom. Their small son was asleep in his bedroom. A Cornell student who also lived there, was finishing up her laundry before leaving for school. The

Pastor informed me that his business would probably take at least an hour.

By the time the Pastor arrived where we were, the storm was becoming even more intense. He felt he first should take Shirley and Becky back to his home, because by then they were shivering with the cold. So we slowly went back across town, even though by now the streets were closed to all public traffic. We waded through snow higher than our knees to get to the rear door of the church, which was also the entrance for the parsonage We entered the parsonage, being careful not to make any noise that might awaken the mother and son. Instantly, the pastor ran for the laundry that was located some forty feet from where we were entering. He was greeted by flames shooting up the wall from the dryer. Apparently, the girl's clothes had caught fire after she left for school, and the flames were now eating away at the wall and ceiling. Another two or three minutes and the parsonage would have been engulfed in flames, trapping the pastor's wife and son in their bedrooms. Fortunately, the pastor quickly put out the fire with his extinguisher, losing only the girl's clothing, some paint on his laundry wall and ceiling, and the clothes dryer itself.

Later, we all sat around the kitchen table rehearsing the events of the morning. What if the pastor had not received our call and had gone to take care of his business and errands in town? These would have taken at least an hour and perhaps much more, because the roads were closed shortly after his departure. Even if someone had seen the smoke and fire and called the Fire Department, the snow would have severely delayed, if not made impossible, their arrival. Mom and baby probably would not have survived. Last but not least, the Ithaca Assembly of God Church also would have been engulfed in the fire. These things I'm saying here were not just suppositions. They would have happened just as I've related them.

The storm tapered off and the pastor and I went over to see if we could get my car started again. Just before we started to leave, we joined hands in prayer and thanksgiving. When I prayed I thanked the Lord for causing my car to stall, and that as long as the emergency seemed to be over, then the car had no further reason for not taking us home, without further problems. The car did indeed start perfectly and soon we were back on the road to Homer.

Would you just stop for a moment, and praise and thank our Dear Lord Jesus for preventing this horrendous tragedy from ever taking place: all because God woke us up early, and had taken us through that storm the sixty or so miles to the city of Ithaca, had caused me to call that dear Pastor within seconds of his leaving his home for an hour's worth of business? And had saved the lives of that mother and son, as well as the apartment and church. Isn't God fantastic! Thank you, Lord Jesus for another DIVINE APPOINT-MENT. And Jesus said, *"The things which are impossible with men are possible with God."* Luke 18:27.

Matt. 19:26 says that, *"with God all things are possible."* The Bible also tells us that when Peter saw Jesus walking on the water, he had some difficulty believing what he saw. But, in order to get to Jesus, Peter had to get out of the boat. His walk on the water went fine as long as Peter kept his eyes on the Lord. But when he "looked around at the high waves, he was terrified and began to sink. "Save me Lord!" he cried. *"And immediately Jesus stretched forth His hand, and rescued him, and said to him, "O man of little faith why did you doubt me?" And when they climbed back into the boat, the wind stopped.* (Matt.14:29-34 LB)

I've shared my testimony many times, but rarely have I shared this part of it. Most people would think I belonged back in the mental hospital to say such things. But I can't leave this out of DIVINE APPOINTMENTS, because God did it and I give Him all the glory and praise for it.

I must also say that, in spite of the many storms we drove through to get to our ministry destinations, God never provided another cocoon. Once we were to speak on a Saturday morning meeting in Buffalo. A heavy storm was predicted, but we felt that if we were scheduled to be there, that we should at least give it our best shot. When we got about half way, we heard on the radio that the Thruway was closed just west of Rochester. When we arrived at that exit, a barricade blocked the road. So we went into Rochester and spent the night. I called the men in Buffalo to inform them of our situation. They said that they had cancelled their meeting. (So, God had no reason to deliver us through that storm in some miraculous way!)

After a few phone calls to my Rochester friends, we were provided with some great fellowship, a nice place to spend the night, and an invitation to speak in one of the finest Churches in Rochester. (That experience deserves its own chapter, but will have to wait for another time.) The Church called us later that same week asking if we could come back and spend a week ministering to the children and teachers of their school. When we returned for that engagement, we experienced marvelous miracles of healing that we had never seen before. The whole situation became a superb DIVINE APPOINTMENT that we will never forget.

* * * * *

LIVING BY FAITH

That Spring I spent a great weekend at my boss's camp on Skaneateles Lake with the men of the Syracuse Chapter. We swam and ate, and fished and ate, and talked and prayed and ate, and relaxed until early afternoon on Saturday. I decided to take my Bible and wander alone along the Lake until I found a great spot to sit, read, and pray awhile. Ever since my hospital days it was easy for me to feel the sweet presence of the Lord. In fact, most of the time I stayed permanently in his lovely presence, and He just stayed with me.

I told him how much I appreciated all he did for me day by day. But I was having a problem finding enough time in the day to take care of my business, and also to do all I was expected to do as Convention Chairman and as Vice President of the large Syracuse Chapter. "Dear Lord, I'd give anything if I had more time to do your work. I'm spending a lot of time trying to satisfy the needs of my clients—so much that often I don't have time for the ministry you've called me to, or even time for my family.

The answer I got was almost instantaneous and one I never expected, *"Would you be willing to give me everything?"* Even though I owed Him my life and everything He had done for me and my family, I had to take some time to answer Him. I knew that my everything and His everything were not the same! His everything would mean each and every aspect of my life. How I wished that Shirley had been with me to help me think this whole thing through before proceeding further. The thought that crossed my mind was that it was to be my decision and mine alone, and that Shirley was the kind of person who, knowing all the circumstances, would go along with me whichever way I decided to go.

For more than an hour I counted the cost of saying "Yes!" to Jesus. My job and profession probably would be the first to go. What about my five years of college after the four years I spent in the Navy? Would they be part of the deal? Didn't the Lord like my large tithes and offerings, which might have to be reduced drastically if He were to have my everything. He also gave me some of the costs that would be involved in fully serving Him: adversity, persecution, illness, and a few others that really didn't seem like living the abundant life He had promised all of his children.

The ball was in my end of the court, and He wasn't about to discuss the matter further with me. My experiences with the Lord while I was in the hospital made my decision easier for me. What did I have that He hadn't given me? I really didn't have a choice, even though I knew I could say "No!" I thought it was so loving and generous of the Lord to allow me to decide this incredibly life-changing matter. At the same time, I was sweating profusely and trembling with emotion. Finally, I could hold back no longer. I said, "Yes Lord, I give you everything." I knew that God promises to meet all of our needs according to His riches in glory, went without my saying it again. Instantly, I had perfect peace. It almost seemed like my experience had been surreal—like a dream. I then rejoined my brothers on the Lakefront and finished the afternoon with them.

Of course, I was anxious to share my incredible experience with Shirley. And the children would eventually have to know what had happened. We talked at length when I got home. At that point I had no way of knowing just what the Lord had in mind for us. But we had learned to TRUST HIM in every area of our lives, so all we could do was wait and see.

On Monday, Shirley had to go with me to Syracuse in order to take the car and do some errands while I was at work. I kissed her goodbye before entering my office, and she left. The phone in my office was ringing when I walked in. The first call was one of my clients who told me that because of certain decisions by the Zoning Board, he would be unable to continue the project we were working on together. We parted company amicably and I answered the next call, which was remarkably like the first one. Then a few more calls came in, and soon I was essentially out of business. If I had wanted to close my business down, it would have taken me months to do what the Lord did in a few minutes. By 11AM, I had gathered my belongings, had spoken with the people whose office I had occupied, and was on my own again with the Lord. (The Lord does not fool around. His "No" means "No!" And His "Yes" means "Yes!" God had a DIVINE APPOINTMENT all ready for me as soon as I totally yielded to Him.)

Immediately I had a lot more time on my hands, which is what I had asked for. Now I would just go ahead and do all the things for which I previously hadn't had time. We were totally at peace about our life. All I had to do was thank Him each day for his direction and guidance, without any feeling that I was malingering, and let Him show me what He wanted me to do. All I had to do each day was to "Deny myself, and take up my cross and follow Jesus." (Matt. 16:24)

A nice lady from Blodgett Mills had a large farm, a part of which she offered me to plant a garden. Soon I was laying out a wonderful plan for all the vegetables we'd be able to use that summer and Fall. It was beautiful, rich soil, so all I needed to do was have it plowed up and tilled, and put together all the seeds and plants I'd need to plant my garden. I soon learned that this kind of work required muscles I'd forgotten I even had. Within a few weeks, I was feeling much stronger and more full of energy than I had in years. And my planting project went ahead beautifully. Before I put any seeds into the ground, I anointed them with oil, which, incidentally, kept them free of bugs all summer. Then I planted them in long beautiful rows, thanking God all the while for the bountiful crop we soon would have. Every few days the Lord sent rain to help the plants in our heavenly project peek their little heads up toward the sun, which usually would shine the next day.

Across the street from my garden, my dear Brother in Christ, Dale Hunter, the Pastor of the McGraw Full Gospel Church, was doing the same things on another section of the land. We prayed, and laughed, and enjoyed our aching muscles almost every day. There was no end to the spiritual lessons to be learned while farming. Perhaps I was learning things my Dad had learned on the family farm in Wilmington years before. Of course, my new project wasn't producing any income, but since God had promised to *"supply all our needs from His riches in glory, because of what Christ Jesus has done for us."* Phil. 4:19, all I needed to do was remind the Lord of what we needed, and leave the rest to Him. And that applied to each day from then on. Praise the Lord!

One morning I had to stop at the bank and tell them I needed a little more time to make my mortgage payment. While I stood in line to speak to the Bank teller, a stranger came up to me, handed me an envelope, and then disappeared into the crowd. Upon opening the envelope, I discovered there was not only enough money to make my payment, but also enough for my tithe and an additional amount to buy some necessary items on my way back home. I'll bet I was the happiest customer that teller saw all day. Naturally, that DIVINE APPOINTMENT gave me an opportunity to share with her how God was meeting our needs, and how wonderful it was to serve Jesus.

Now, getting back to our lovely garden, It grew and grew until we had more than enough for ourselves, our family, and every one in our Church that needed fresh vegetables. People were amazed at how beautiful my garden was. Finally, I put up a notice that anyone who needed anything they saw there was welcome to help themselves, compliments of the Lord. Another DIVINE APPOINT-MENT for which to praise the Lord!

GOD'S CARS

Although my car was a bit on the old side, it ran beautifully. However, my tires were wearing a little thin, so I reminded the Lord that the police had been checking on tires lately. One day while praising the Lord with a dear Brother in Christ, he paused by my car and said, "Fred, it looks like you'd better do something about those tires soon. The police have been setting up roadblocks to check for illegal tires. I replied that I agreed with him, and that we'd take care of it as soon as I could. A short time later, my tire dealer from out on Tompkins street called, telling me that I would need to come over there and have my new tires installed. He added that they were all paid for. I didn't need a second invitation to follow instructions, and away I went for my new tires.

Within a few minutes my new tires were on my car, and I was driving over to McGraw to share my good fortune with my dear Brother Dale, the Pastor. On my way, I had to pass under a bridge that crosses Rt., 81, and guess what? There was the road block! The policemen gave me the "go ahead" after checking me out. He admired my tires, and remarked that the labels were still on them. Of course, that gave me a golden opportunity to tell him how God had just provided them for us.

I also must share how the tire dealer and his mechanics were astounded at the more than 125,000 miles I had driven on my old tires. He said, "Fred I can hardly believe that those are the same tires we put on for you over a year ago." Then I had a great chance to testify how God had provided those tires and took good care of them for all those miles, including trips to St. Louis, and just about everywhere in New York State.

* * * * *

As the time for our trip to Miami for the Annual World Convention became shorter and shorter, I reminded the Lord that one of my responsibilities as an International Director was to attend these events. The engine in our car (with over

225,000 miles) began making some loud knocking sounds. My approach to such circumstances was that this was the Lord's business, and if my car wasn't up to such a long trip, then I could safely assume I wasn't supposed to go. (No! We didn't pray for a better car. The Lord had given us this car, and I was perfectly satisfied with it if that was His decision.)

One morning we got a call from Brother Bruce Bowen, Chapter President of the Henrietta chapter in Rochester. The conversation went something like this: "Bro. Fred, you'll never be able to guess what just happened here. I had decided to buy a company car for my work. Edie and I prayed that God would show us what to do with our light blue GM station wagon, since we didn't need two cars. After I got to work, I began my day, as usual, with prayer. At the end of my prayer I said, 'By the way, Lord, what am I to do with my blue car?' His immediate response was, 'Give it to the Lawrences.'"

"I called Edie to tell her what the Lord had just told me. She said, 'Bruce, before you tell me why you called, I was praying after you left for work. The Lord spoke very clearly to me that we were to give our car to the Lawrences. Isn't that wonderful! Now, what was it you were calling me about?'" Bruce gulped and said, "Edie, I was praying and the Lord told me to give the car to the Lawrences." They had a real hallelujah time, and then called us on a conference call to relate the whole story to us. We rejoiced and gave the Lord a lot of thanks for His divine direction.

Bruce continued, "Fred, I'd like to take the car to the dealer and have them go over it, and maybe replace the brakes and tires and anything else it may need. On Saturday, we will drive to your house and deliver your new car. We should be there about noon."

By then I had two cars, one almost new and the other on its last legs. It probably would be difficult to dispose of our old car because it sounded and looked so bad. Nevertheless,

I parked it on my front lawn.

On Saturday, Bruce and Edie drove their two cars into my driveway, and we had a hallelujah, shouting, praise meeting on our front lawn. Shirley had lunch all prepared, so when we got over our excitement, we sat down to eat. We had just thanked the Lord for the food and the car, when a young fellow rang our doorbell. He said, "Sir, do you know who owns that car in your front yard? And do you know if he'd like to sell it?" I told him it was mine, that I'd like to sell it, but that it had some engine problems." He took it for a drive, but hardly seemed to notice any defects it may have had. He told me that he and his Dad were looking for a car like that because they enjoyed taking cars apart and making them run like new. Then the father asked me if I would take $250 for it. (I didn't tell him, but I would have let him have it for much less.) So we made the deal, he father paid in cash, and they drove it away. I returned to the table and finished lunch, and had another rejoicing spell. There's really no way to express the joy for such an occasion, but it certainly was a DIVINE APPOINTMENT of the first order. Two days later, we were merrily off to Miami!

* * * * *

(I will be sharing more of these fine experiences as I go along, but I feel led to stop here and give a few admonitions about the subject of "living by faith"! Rom.I:19.LB says, *"The man who finds life will find it through trusting God." Rom. 1"19.* When we are sharing the experiences we've had during our Christian life, it is very important to realize that these experiences are in response to God's promises for our lives. We can't put our faith in experiences. But we can allow God to bring us to a place in Him where, in order to fulfill our calling in Him, He does things we call miracles to accomplish His purposes. From the day I started speaking publicly, the promotional flyers always said that I was an Architectural Engineer—which I am—but never mentioned that we "lived by Faith." A real temptation exists to tell people that you have no income except what God gives you, so that they will help you. There simply is no place in a walk of faith for sympathy or other emotional feelings. Our priorities must be God first, God second, and God last. When our personal lives work their way into the equation, then God steps back and lets us do it our own way. We then learn that we have surrendered God's best for us with what we think God's best is. But God's way is far superior and He must be acknowledged as the author of everything we do, or have, or hope to accomplish.

My ministry to men has always been an acknowledgement that the farmer, or the engineer, or the doctor, who has put his trust fully in the Lord, is every bit as much a faith walker as me or anyone else. In my case, God called me to be fully available to Him to do His bidding at any time of the day or night, to any place in the world, to minister either to one or a thousand, and in any capacity. So that is why I warn you that you'd better not try to quit your job to do something nice for God, and think that you can trust the Lord the same way He called me to do. You'll starve to death! But if God calls you to a certain ministry for Him and you yield to His calling, then he will make a way for you to carry out that calling with or without any help from anyone. He will even train you for the work you are called to do. Thus, the reason for this book is to encourage those whom God is calling to do something for Him, to relax and He will make a way for you to do it and provide for all your needs in the process.

* * * * *

I planned to bring this chapter to a close, but Shirley reminded me of another DIVINE APPOINTMENT we had at the Blodgett Mills farm garden that is certainly noteworthy.

On the side of the mountain above the garden is a wooded area with gorgeous blackberries covering the ground in several places. Those bushes had been there for many years, so they were mixed in with hay and all kinds of underbrush you find in wooded areas. One day Becky and I went up to the blackberry patch, rejoicing in the Lord for the beauty of the place, and praying that we wouldn't get too scratched up from the thorns on the bushes that towered way over my head. We had to move very cautiously through that heavy underbrush to find the beautiful huge berries. After about half the day, we decided that enough was enough, and left for home.

I had taken off my regular eyeglasses, put them in my shirt pocket, and put on my sunglasses. When we arrived home, we were greeted with lots of "oos and ahhs" about our bounteous supply of blackberries. Then, when I walked into our house and reached into my pocket for my glasses, they were nowhere to be found. I sheepishly explained that I had carelessly put them in my shirt pocket, and that I didn't have the vaguest idea of where I might have lost them. But I assured them that finding them would be absolutely impossible in that two- or three-acre field of the most dense wild berry patches that I had ever seen.

Without any hesitation, Shirley announced to the whole family that they were to dress with long-sleeved shirts and pants and get ready. We were going up and find Dad's glasses, in spite of my warnings that it would be a big waste of time. Shirley told all of us that God knew precisely where those glasses were and that *"The steps of a good man are ordered by the Lord."* (Psalm 37:23) He knew exactly where I was when those glasses fell out of my pocket, and He would lead us directly to them. "Come on, let's go before it gets dark." And away we went!

When the kids, including my skeptical son-in-law, saw

that blackberry patch, they were about flabbergasted to think we would even try to find those glasses. I mean, you couldn't even see your shoes in that mess, to say nothing about finding a pair of glasses. But Shirley's instructions for us to spread out and carefully walk around until we found them were not to be denied. She gathered us together for a word of prayer, reminding us and God that "they were not Fred's glasses, but rather that they were God's glasses, and He knew right where I dropped them. "He would direct our paths to them, so let's get busy and stop moaning about it all," she admonished.

I think it was about a half hour before I happened to look down and see my glasses. I had almost stepped on them. They were probably only 90 feet from the edge of the field. By this time the kids were all stuffing themselves with blackberries, and having a pretty good laugh at Shirley's positive feelings about the whole matter. But when I shouted that I had found them, they all shouted out with joy, and just a little apology for making fun of Shirley's absurd faith. We all had a good laugh, and headed back down the mountain, having experienced another one of our DIVINE APPOINTMENTS! (My dear buddy, Cliff Gillis, appropriately called it God's lost and found department! If you ever lose something, perhaps you will recall this and believe God for a successful outcome for yourself. Jesus never fails! Only believe!)

10

.......EVEN THE WIND AND THE SEA OBEY HIM MATT:4:41

During the months following my desert experience at the VA Hospital in Syracuse, the Lord seemed to go overboard to build my confidence and trust in Him in every area of my life. Often I wouldn't realize I was in the midst of one of these faith building experiences, or it would be all over before I realized I had had a Divine Appointment. A couple of these experiences were especially memorable.

When I was released from the Hospital in Syracuse the Lord immediately put me to work in a very fine architectural firm in Syracuse. (see Chapter 9) I loved that job more than any I had ever had, because so many of those men I worked with came to know Jesus while I was there.

One aspect of living in Upstate New York is the intense cold and snow in the wintertime. My work required a 32 mile drive each way come rain or shine or snowstorms. However the time I had to spend with the Lord was so precious during my daily commute that I looked forward to each trip. The Lord often reminded me that He enjoyed my fellowship too.

The TV weatherman is quite accurate at times, so on one particular day I was just a bit apprehensive about the severity of the storm he predicted. I woke up about five AM and spent my usual time fellowshipping with the Lord. He'd been teaching me about faith for several weeks, and I had become aware that there was a difference between faith in God for salvation and other basic needs, and faith for moving mountains. Both kinds of faith are very necessary for the Lord's servant.

At 6 am all of the roads in Central New York were declared closed, including those to and from Syracuse, as well as within those cities. I had just finished thanking God for the wonderful job he had provided for us. I couldn't see how God could provide a great job for me and then allow me to be prevented from going to work by the weather. A gift of faith had risen up within me. From my innermost being springs of living water were springing up like a fountain.

I ate my breakfast, kissed my family good-by and walked into my garage without the slightest hesitation. When I opened my garage door there appeared to be several feet (five or six) of snow drifted into my driveway. My response was, "Lord, you gave me this job. You expect me to fulfill my obligation to work eight hours per day. Therefore, since you are the God who calms the wind and the rain, I believe you are the Lord of this storm. I am your servant and unless the roads are impassable I will go to work as usual."

I wish I could adequately relate the exact feelings I was having as I backed my car out of my driveway and onto the street. I was having a Divine Appointment to beat all Divine Appointments. Remember now that the snow was four or five feet deep in the street, with drifts much higher. Snow was falling at an incredible rate of inches per hour. Yet I was driving down my street on a bare road. I turned out onto State Rte. 281, then onto 81 N. As far as I could tell the road was bare for at least thirty feet in front of me and several feet in back of me. No snow was falling on my car. It was like being in a large cocoon, inside of which the weather was perfect, and outside of which there was a wall of snow surrounding me.

Mine was the only car on the road, although several cars had been abandoned by the side of the road or had slid off the road into the ditch. No one appeared to be in any of the cars I passed. My speed was a steady forty miles an hour all the way into Syracuse, although I could have driven faster, I believe. I drove through the city to Ridings Road on the north side of the city, without once having to stop for any reason. I drove into my company parking lot and parked just as one of my bosses was also arriving at the office on cross country skis. So he saw me make my entrance, just as I would any other time of the year.

My boss began to question me as to where I had spent the night, how I had traveled across town when even the snow plows weren't able to move. He already knew of my strong love for the Lord and of my deep faith in God. But what he was hearing and had witnessed went very far beyond his understanding of what faith in God really meant. This was supernatural and there was no other way to explain it. So even though the office was closed for the day, my boss and I opened the office and went to work.

I worked that morning like I would any other day except, of course, I didn't have a secretary or any other fellow employees. At almost noon my dear boss suggested that we give up and try to go home. He lived a short distance from the office and I would be welcome to spend the night with him and his family, since, of course, all of the roads were still closed only more so by then. I thanked him and told him that I would return home the same way I came. I also shared with him how God had shown me how to solve a difficult engineering problem I had been working on. It was beautiful; simply beautiful.

As we walked out the door the deep snow around the entrance of our office building was instantly cleared of snow. I got into my car and suggested I drive slowly ahead of him so he could get home on his skis. As we passed his house I waved and proceeded on my way. My boss was standing there with his mouth open in astonishment until I drove out of sight.

Again, I drove steadily across town, in my protective cocoon. I entered Rte. I-81 South from I-690, then south to my little town of Homer- forty mph all the way. Up West Main to Burgett Drive and into my garage. I was sitting in the car trying to put everything into proper perspective and figuring out how I was going to explain the things I had experienced that day. Shirley opened the door to the garage, with a hundred questions to ask me. I said, "Shirley get in the car. I want to show you a miracle. She put on a coat and got into the car. The garage door opened to a wall of snow that was five to six feet high. As I backed toward it, seemingly with the same faith I had earlier, that wall of snow didn't budge. I tried prayer, fervent prayer, but to no avail. The Lord's response to my questions was that He hadn't opened the Red Sea to allow his Israelites to return from whence they came and I was not to try to tempt Him to do something like that.

But Shirley knew I had been to Syracuse that day because my boss had called her to say I arrived OK and that he couldn't explain it but that I appeared to be returning home OK too. A DIVINE APPOINTMENT of the first order.

I have shared my testimony hundreds of times but I've never shared that one with anyone except my wife. Who would have believed me? I could scarcely believe myself what I had experienced. But this one thing I know is that Jesus is still in control of the elements. And he can make adjustments in a few natural laws as He pleases, to accomplish his purposes. Yes, "Jesus Christ is the same yesterday, and today, and for ever" Heb. 13:8.

In order for God to do wonderful miracles in our lives we have to be totally dependent on Him , whether it is financial, material, health related, or what-have-you. We have been taught by our family, teachers, and society in general that we must learn to depend on ourselves - to be self-reliant, so we rob ourselves of opportunities for God to do miracles in our lives. God won't need to do a financial miracle for you if you have a pocket full of money.

Give Thanks for Everything Eph 5:20

Another time, Shirley and I (and Becky) were speaking at a Friday evening chapter meeting in the Finger Lakes Region of Central New York State. It was a typical winter night, with heavy snow being forecast for that weekend. Only once in more than twenty years had we ever been hindered from our work by the weather, so we weren't alarmed by the weather men, nor by their prognostications.

The meeting went very well, and we slept like baby's that night in our motel room. When we woke up early in the morning we just couldn't go back to sleep. (One of my roomies intimated that my snoring was preventing them from getting their beauty sleep.) So we headed for home at about 6:00 am. While we were eating breakfast we heard an up-to-date, and not very encouraging weather forecast on the restaurant radio. So it was good that we were getting an early start. The storm was approaching from the west so we would attempt to outrun it.

We traveled south and east on Rte. 17, through Corning, and then north on Rte. 13, which would take us through

Ithaca and then on to our cozy little home in the big city of Homer. Hopefully, we would beat the storm home.

The first part of the trip saw the predicted weather growing steadily worse, with the main problem being heavy wet snow falling at probably 3 or 4 inches an hour. As we approached Ithaca the visibility was close to zero. We had been traveling as fast as the conditions would allow, hoping to get home before the main storm closed the roads. But then our progress slowed almost to a stop as we drove through Ithaca. No, this time there was no cocoon.

As we were passing through Ithaca our car's engine began to act up. It would run a few seconds and then stall. I turned off the main highway onto a side street so I could get "Old Faithful" running again. That was about the time when we heard the radio announcer say that Rte. 13 had been closed until further notice. By then there was probably 24 to 30 inches of new snow on the road - not especially cold, but heavy, wet snow.

We got Shirley and Beck's wrapped up in a blanket while I went to the auto parts store to get some ether spray that would help me start the car again. Then I saw a telephone and decided to call the Assembly of God pastor to see if he had any mechanics in his church that could help us. Just off hand he couldn't think of anyone, but he thought he could get to us in his four wheel drive vehicle. He would take Shirley and Becky to his home until the storm let up. He had to go out anyway to do some banking and a few other things while he could still get around on the city streets. W e praised the Lord for always having His people on hand to help wherever one goes.

Now God had set the stage for a delightful DIVINE APPOINTMENT. .When I spoke to the pastor he was just leaving his home when my call came in. He estimated his business would take at least an hour. His wife, who was a night-duty nurse in the city hospital was asleep in the front bedroom. Their small son was also asleep in his bedroom. The pastor's apartment was on the second floor of his church. One other person lived there, a Cornell student, who was finishing up her laundry before leaving for school.

The pastor made his way to where we were. The storm was getting even more intense. He felt he should take Shirley and Becky back to his home because they were shivering with the cold by then. So we went slowly back across town, even though by now the streets were closed to all public traffic. We got to the rear door of the church which was also the entrance for the parsonage, by wading in snow past our knees.

Recall the scenario just once more. If we hadn't called for help, the pastor would have left home to do his errands . That would have taken at least an hour and perhaps much more because the roads were closed after he would have left. His wife and son were asleep in the upstairs apartment. And the student had left for school with her clothes in the dryer. Only this time the scenario changed.

We entered the parsonage being careful not to make any noise to disturb the mother and son's sleep. Instantly, the pastor ran for the laundry, perhaps some forty feet from the rear door. He was greeted by flames shooting up the wall from the clothes dryer. The girl's clothes had caught fire after she left for school, and the flames were now eating away at the wall and ceiling. Within two or three minutes the parsonage would have been engulfed in flames, and the pastor's wife and son would have been trapped in their bedrooms. The pastor put out the fire with his extinguisher. The greatest loss was the girl's clothing and some paint on his laundry wall and ceiling, and perhaps the clothes dryer

The pastor and his wife and we sat around the kitchen table going over the events of the morning. What if the pastor had not received our call and had gone about his business in town ? Perhaps someone would have seen the smoke and flames and called the Fire Department. But it would have been either impossible or very slow and difficult for the Firemen to get through the storm with their equipment. Probably Mom and baby would not have survived, and last but not least, the Ithaca Assembly of God Church would have also been engulfed in the fire. These things I'm saying here were not just suppositions. They would have happened just as I've related them.

The storm tapered off and the pastor and I went over to see if we could get my car started again. Just before we started to leave we joined hands in prayer and thanksgiving. When I prayed I thanked the Lord for causing my car to stall, and that as long as the emergency seemed to be over then the car had no further reason for not taking us home, without further problems. The car did indeed start perfectly and soon we were back on the road to Homer.

Would you just stop for a moment, and praise and thank our Dear Lord Jesus for preventing this horrendous tragedy from ever taking place: all because God woke us up early, and had taken us through that storm the sixty or so miles to the city of Ithaca, had caused me to call that dear Pastor within seconds of his leaving his home for an hours worth of business? And had saved the lives of that mother and son, as well as the apartment and church. Isn't God fantastic! Thank you, Lord Jesus for another DIVINE APPOINT-MENT. And Jesus said, *"The things which are impossible with men are possible with God"* Luke 18:27.

11

"PRIESTS OF THE KING" (1 Peter 2:9)

After my trials and tribulations of the 1970's, God began to train me for the ministry to which he had called me- a ministry primarily to men. I learned so much from my experiences as a construction manager and with the veterans in the hospital. Then I learned more about business men while employed at the Engineering firm, the professional architects and engineers, how they act and react, how devoted they are to their work, and how important they become in the Kingdom of God when they turn their lives over to Jesus. God does not prefer one gender over another, but it goes without saying that He made men and women different from each other. If one is to reach out primarily to men, then He needs to learn about those differences and use that knowledge more effectively to reach men with the glorious Gospel of Jesus Christ. A highly respected theologian told me one day after I had received the Baptism in The Holy Spirit that I should look around and find a church or organization where the men are winning souls to Jesus and "Get on board!" It became increasingly apparent that God had called me to the Full Gospel Business Men's Fellowship (FGBMFI). It was an International Ministry of Spirit-filled men reaching out to other men in every corner of the world with the Gospel of Christ. St. Peter put it this way: "He has made us Kings and priests of the King, holy and pure, God's very own, all this so that we may show to others how God called us out of darkness into His wonderful light !" (I Peter 2:9)

We learn to do this by sharing with other men our personal testimonies of what God has done in our lives, rather than by preaching to them. We say, "This is the way I used to be. This is how I received Christ into my life as Lord and Savior, and this is the way I am now. It is a magnificently powerful method of leading people to the Lord. One doesn't have to be a theologian to tell people what God has done in their lives. I suppose we all become theologians after He has filled us with the Holy Spirit because we all spend so much time studying the Word of God.

Of course, not all churches see things exactly alike. But the basic tenets of the Faith are the same in all Spirit-filled Churches. One thing never changes, and that is what God has done in our own lives, and that is always the truth. God is universally true and unchanging, and what he does in the lives of people is nearly always very similar.

This non-denominational nature of the Fellowship was very appealing to us. I had been brought up in a fundamental "Holiness" church. Shirley was Roman Catholic. We were married in a Nazarene Church, and have attended a Baptist Church since we got saved there in 1960. So when we joined with FGBMFI, we found ourselves fellowshipping with all of these kinds of Christians plus a lot more. I can't think of any denominational churches where we haven't spoken and ministered. Our personal theological beliefs just never came up in our meetings, which we believe is the way things will be when we all get to heaven. We keep our personal beliefs to ourselves while we are witnessing for Christ, and use His Holy Word while explaining the way of salvation, the Baptism in the Holy Spirit, and God's Healing power.

When people have heard and positively responded to God's wonderful calling to follow Jesus, we encourage them to ask God to show them the right Church where they can be discipled and taught the Word of God. Their continued fellowship with our organization helps them to learn to be soul-winners, and to spread the Gospel around the world. We say," His banner over us in LOVE," and that is what we do, love each other and everyone else.

The longer we worked in this great organization, the more it became a part of our lives. I had served as Vice President of the Syracuse Chapter, and had become the Chairman of the Central New York Regional Convention. We met more and more beautiful Christian people from the Central New York area because of the well-known speakers we had for our Chapter Meetings and for our Conventions. We also attended Conventions in Washington, DC, Toronto, and New York City, and elsewhere. We couldn't get enough of these exciting programs and the people we met.

One day I got a phone call from our International Director from New York City, Simon Vikse. The Vikses and we had become closer and closer at the many meetings we attended. He said, "Brother Fred, Demos (Shakarian) and I had a talk while we were at a Board meeting in Chicago. We think that you are the man we've been looking for to be the Director of our Upstate New York Chapters. Would you consider that?" my response was, "Simon, I don't think I would qualify for such an important position. There are a lot of men in the New York State Chapters who've been in the Fellowship far longer than I have, and know a lot more about FGBMFI business than I do. Have you considered any of these older, more experienced, men than me? I also think that a few of those brothers would be very hurt if I got promoted ahead of them." Simon responded, "Fred we've been observing you in the Syracuse Conventions and elsewhere, and we see that the people think very highly of you and Shirley. We've talked it over at length and believe that you are the right man for the job. Would you at least pray about it and get back to me as soon as possible?" "Simon, I'll pray about it, and get back to you." I said.

I talked the whole matter over with Shirley; with my dear friend, Frank Hummel, President of the Syracuse Chapter; with my pastor; and with a number of other close friends. Each of them agreed with Simon. After considerable prayer and fasting, I called Simon back and told him somewhat reluctantly I'd do it. (I didn't know it then, but it was truly a DIVINE APPOINTMENT.) I still doubted if I'd be able to win such an important election, and I had serious questions as to how the other men in the State would take the news. However, each chapter was invited to attend the annual convention where they could nominate anyone they chose to be elected to the Board, and they all had a vote in all the elections.

Soon I found myself on the International Board of the largest men's Christian organization in the world. It would open doors for us to minister that we hadn't even heard of. But my concerns about some of the other men in the State (and beyond) soon proved to be "right on". Many of them were less than excited about my promotion to the Office of International Director. Fortunately, the Lord solved the problems, helped me to forgive, and even to forget most of that. I have always believed that God allows these things to strengthen us and increase our spiritual endurance, and that Romans 8:28 applies to these situations as well.

Retreat NO, Advances YES

The Pastor of the Canisteo Baptist Church invited me to share at their Couple's Retreat at the Watson Homestead Retreat Center near Corning, NY. We had a great time together. On Saturday evening after a precious time of fellowship and communion, everyone went to bed except me. I couldn't get the problems I was having in my new work off my mind. When I am really in a serious situation, I prostrate myself on the floor and with real tears cry out my needs to the Lord. My prayers went something like this, "Dear Lord, you know I didn't ask for this position on the Board of Directors. I let myself get pulled into it because of who was doing the pulling (Demos Shakarian, etc.). Now most of the men in the State suddenly dislike me, and don't accept me as their leader at all." After telling God all the things He already knew about my case, He began to talk to me. *"No, Demos and the other Board members didn't influence you into this position. I did! Now if you follow my instructions, everything will turn out fine. Have I not told you that I came not to bring peace to the world! No, rather a sword! A man's enemies will be right in His own home. If you refuse to take up your cross daily and follow Me, you are not worthy of being Mine."* (Matt. 10:34-38)

Then God gave me some clear instructions. As soon as I could get an appointment with the Director of Watson Homestead, I should find out when the next weekend would be available for a FGBMFI event. My meeting went real well until I asked for the whole place—275 spaces—with a minimum of 200 beds and meals. I replied, "That is what God told me to do just last night." I signed a contract with them for the second week of April the following year.

That was the beginning of an exciting year. At first I thought of it as a Men's Spiritual Retreat. Then it came to me that we should be advancing, not retreating. So the name of it became the Empire State Men's Advance. I spoke to my friend, Tommy Ashcraft, about these developments. After considering it, he said, "Go ahead, Fred. I'll be there, and I'll talk with Demos and I'm quite sure He'll want to attend as well."

I began asking men to work with me, but only one dear Brother agreed to help. Nate Caldwell, a banker in Syracuse, offered to handle the finances. I would trust the Lord to help me do everything else.

Together Nate and I put together a flyer, stating the name, place, time, purpose, cost, speakers, and a warm invitation to attend this life changing event, which no one had ever heard of before. My sales abilities were really put to the test and found wanting. I put Ads in local newspapers, radio stations, and Church bulletins, and talked to men about the Advance until even I got tired of hearing about it. At times I wondered if it was really God who had put these ideas in my head.

One week before the Advance I had 60 men signed up. Many of them I had invited to come as our guests because they weren't familiar with our organization. So, with a heavy heart I went back to Watson Homestead with my sad story. They were quite gentle with me while showing me my signature on the bottom of the contract, as well as some fine print that I hadn't bothered to read before. Then he sweetly said, "Mr. Lawrence, I believe you said God told you to do this. Do you think He changed His mind?" (Thanks a lot, I really needed that remark!) I left there trying to figure out what my mortgage would look like if we had to pay for room and board for over 100 men.

On my way home that day I had to pass by Connecticut Hill where the CBN Radio Station was located. I decided to stop there and ask my dear Brother Bill Freeman to pray for me. Between songs and news programs I shared my hard luck story with him, and we prayed together. Then Bill said,

"Fred, you know about our afternoon call-in/talk show which starts at 1 o'clock. Why don't you wait around and I'll talk with our listening audience about the Advance. You realize that most of our listeners are women whose husbands are at work, but we'll just talk about it and see what God does. At 1 pm Bill opened the program and told his listeners that there would be a very special guest with him on the show that day, Mr. Fred Lawrence, the International Director of Full Gospel Business Men's Fellowship International (a real mouth full to be sure). After such an auspicious introduction, he began to ask me questions about the big Men's Advance to be taking place that weekend. We discussed all the what, where's, who's , costs, etc.. Then I said something like this, " Bill, the men who will be attending this great event would be getting saved, filled with the Holy Spirit and the joy of the Lord. They would be going home better men, better husbands, and better fathers—new men, excited about Jesus. Our speakers were considered to be some of the best in the world, and Watson Homestead was one of the most beautiful places on earth." Someone asked me later if I wasn't exaggerating a bit, but I could only say that that is what the Lord seemed to be telling me to say. I left Brother Bill that day feeling greatly encouraged.

When I walked into our house that afternoon, Shirley was talking on the phone to a lady about the Advance. She had told Shirley that her husband wasn't a believer and if she could talk him into attending, would we be doing anything that might embarrass him. Shirley told her what a beautiful place it was, and that if her husband didn't enjoy the meetings he'd be more than welcome to wander around the mountain trails, swim in the pool, and join us only for the meals. The lady immediately signed up her husband, a high power electrical lineman from Buffalo. After Shirley finished talking, she left the phone off the hook to show me the list of men whose wives had signed them up since the radio broadcast. It was pure excitement around our house the rest of the week. The Lord had arranged for me to talk to precisely the right audience on that wonderful Christian Radio Station. The men, however doubtful they may have been, felt compelled to go to the Advance because their wives had already paid their dues. By Thursday, 200-plus men were registered.

Nate and I went to Watson Homestead on Thursday to set up for all those men. We were rejoicing all over the place. We were very happy to inform the Watson Homestead people that indeed it had been God who started the whole thing, and that they should get enough food on hand for even more than 200 men. Some of the fellows came on Thursday evening, giving us a nice opportunity to sit around the big fireplace and fellowship together. Early Friday morning our guest speakers and another 27 men arrived in time for the Friday AM opening meeting.

Time and space will not allow me to share all the wonderful things that happened that weekend, but to this day I get blessed to even reminisce about that first Advance. The man from Buffalo was quite reticent about attending the meetings, so at the Friday morning meeting he sat in a back seat near an exit so he could make a quick getaway if need be. But on Friday afternoon he came to me and told me this story: When the invitation for salvation was given Friday morning, the speaker asked those who wished to be born again to raise their hand. He told me that while he had no intention of raising his hand, nevertheless his hand went up. So, being next to the door he ran out to deal with his feelings. He was about in the middle of the parking lot when he fell to his knees weeping. He prayed for forgiveness for his sins and for God to please bless him and his family. He went to a phone and called his wife to tell her what had just happened to him. With tears of joy they praised the Lord together for a whole new beginning to a very rocky marriage situation. It was a beautiful testimony and one that he shared with all the men that evening. At least another thirty-five men came forward that morning for prayer for salvation. And fifty or sixty men came forward for the Baptism in The Holy Spirit, as well as several others for various kinds of healings. It was a glorious evening for all of us. On Saturday afternoon, a local pastor baptized those new believers and others by immersion in the swimming pool. Things could hardly have been better as many more exciting things continued to happen during each passing moment.

That evening after Demos had shared his testimony, everyone wanted him to pray for them. That is how it was where ever he went around the world. As the men came up for ministry, Tommy had the men who already had been prayed for stand next to Demos and him so that they too could pray for the next man. Soon the whole front of that room became a double row of men praying for the next ones as they came through what Demos called a "tunnel of love". There were men all over the floor "resting in the Spirit," unlike anything any of us had ever experienced.

At some point I looked up in amazement to see a thin layer of flames going across the room just above the heads of the men. It seemed like they hit one wall and then went back over us again and again. I doubted if any of us would ever be surprised again by any manifestation of the Holy Spirit we might experience. God has always punctuated His appearances with unforgettable spiritual manifestations, but none of us had ever even heard of what we saw that night, and we'll never be the same again.

The next morning after breakfast we gathered in the chapel for a worship and communion service. A Spirit of Praise came upon our group with tremendous power. At some point we noticed that it seemed to be raining, even though we were inside the building. It was sort of like the launching of a ship. Instead of someone breaking a champagne bottle over the bow of the ship before it sailed out to sea, the Lord had broken His bottle of anointing on all of us and on Men's Advances. We weren't getting wet, but we sure got blessed. I wish I could explain all these things more clearly, but this is the best I can do. The Lord had certainly put His stamp of approval on our gathering and on similar men's fellowship meetings

I repeatedly have said that I take no credit for any of these things. I was as stunned as everyone else by the whole matter. My reward has been the great success that men have had holding Men's Advances all over the world. Now, many churches have the same kinds of weekends. Of all the DIVINE APPOINTMENTS we've experienced, none can duplicate the first Advance we had at Watson Homestead, nor any of them we've had since then.

The following year we had more than 275 men at our second Advance, which was the limit for Watson Homestead. Highlighting this Advance was the heart-warming incident of "Little Boy Lost." The complete story, printed up in an issue of VOICE MAGAZINE, has blessed many around the world.

The third year we moved the Advances to Keuka College, which had a capacity of five hundred men. After two years there, we had to search for larger quarters. The Lord led us to the Silver Bay YMCA Christian Conference Center on Lake George in the Adirondack Mountains, where we've been ever since. After two years there, we outgrew that place. In order to accommodate the increased numbers, we decided to have two weekends in a row at that facility, using the same speakers and program each week. Our attendance had grown to more than 1500 men. The last time Demos Shakarian attended one of our Silver Bay Advances, he told me that we had all seen God do a miracle there that he had never witnessed before. I was so glad that he had worked with us from the beginning, returning at least every other year, and being such a blessing to all of us. Tommy Ashcraft was another man who had been a tremendous blessing to us at least every other year. His unique teachings on Chapter Operations were masterful, and helped each of our chapters to be more effective each year.

Then we moved to the YMCA Christian Conference Center on Lake George in the Adirondack Mountains. It was designed for 1000 people, but within two years we outgrew that place too. Since we couldn't find a bigger or more appropriate place, we held the Advances two weekends in a row. Each one was a little different, but we never changed our basic format. The power of God never diminished. The testimonies of the men never ceased to bless us.

As a result of the men's enthusiasm, their wives began to plead with us to have an Advance where they could get in on the great things their husbands were telling them about. So we started the Empire State Couples Advances in 1982. We also completely filled Silver Bay with our first Couple's Advance. So for the second Couple's Advance, we had to have two weekends in a row like we had had for the men. There were times when we not only filled Silver Bay, but also all the motels within a fifteen-mile radius. In addition, we needed some of the gracious people in the area to take some of our couples into their private homes for the weekend.

The meetings for both groups were some of the most glorious events we had ever experienced, and we continued to give all the glory and credit to the Lord Jesus. The praise and worship in that big auditorium was out of this world. We just prayed that it could go on forever. In one of the meetings while Big John Hall was leading us in the very rhythmic song, "Blow The Trumpet In Zion," the Executive Director of Silver Bay called me to the back of the auditorium to observe how the whole building was shaking up and down because all of the thousand or more people were jumping up and down to the same beat. He said, "Fred, this building wasn't built to handle this. You'll have to calm things down right now before this whole building collapses!" Although it wasn't easy to quiet them down, we complied, and everything went back to some semblance of order. On Saturday afternoons, as many as forty people would come to be baptized by immersion in the cool Lake George water.

During the Sunday morning meetings, many couple's marriages were renewed, and some marriages were saved from divorce. Sometimes Shirley and I would wonder just how many marriages were brought back from the brink of divorce (a few of them had already gone over the brink, but came back). But it's probably a good thing we didn't know, because knowing those things sometimes causes pride to creep in, like when King David counted his people. The Lord knew, and that is all that was necessary. But it was certainly a phenomenon we will never forget, nor for which we will stop thanking and praising the Lord.

Now you may begin to see a little bit why I had to write about these DIVINE APPOINTMENTS that God made for us! We, again, give the Lord all the glory and honor for these wonderful things. Thank you, JESUS!!!!!

12

A BOUNTIFUL HARVEST
John 15:8

When God created Advances, He did wonders for us here in New York State and beyond. The Fellowship, which at that time had only 16 chapters in N.Y., seemed to catch on fire. Close to the end of the first Advance that was held at Watson Homestead, I asked if there were any men who lived in towns or cities that didn't have one of our chapters. I then asked those men who didn't, but who would like to have us help them organize a chapter to please come forward. Incredibly, about thirty men came forward. We prayed over them, took their names and phone numbers, and I gave them a sheet of preliminary instructions to follow. Soon after we got home, I spoke to each of them to begin to form a plan to get all those chapters organized. They were spread over most of N.Y. State and even into Vermont.

Armed with all the information I had gathered at Chapter Operations Seminars around the country, I started our campaign to start all those new chapters. I would pack enough clothes and personal items to last me a couple weeks and head for the cities **to** which God first directed me. I spent a lot of time praying over each city, and seeking God's direction for me at each place. If a brother invited me to stay in his home for a few days, I'd accept, wanting to get fully acquainted with him and his family. It would always be a blessing to hear him tell his family and friends about the things he experienced at the Advance. His testimony of what he had been through at Watson Homestead was infectious because He began to visualize all the people in his town or city experiencing the things he had just experienced. We would go out and talk to pastors, Christian bookstore owners, and other Christian men whom he believed would make good members. It didn't take me long to realize I had taken on a full-time occupation, and in effect had become a missionary in my own State.

As soon as we could get a group of interested men, we would get them together for an introductory meeting at a local restaurant. We explained to the Pastors that, because we were a non-denominational laymen's organization, we never met in churches nor could Pastors serve as officers of the chapter. At the same time, we were always happy to have the Pastor's full cooperation and participation because we wanted our new members to have a home church in which they could continue to grow and develop. I always had plenty of VOICE magazines and other literature for the men, and God's anointing was always evident. I loved what I was doing more than anything I had ever done in my life, and was beginning to get accustomed to public speaking, while still having a long way to go in that field. But it became evident to me that part of the secret to public speaking is having a subject that you are really zealous and excited about (and a gift of love to energize the whole talk).

The exact procedures for organizing new chapters were well documented by our home office, so explaining things was a joy. I also could write all night here about the advantages of having a good chapter in your town or city. They are all a gift from God and something to be cherished and sought for.

"Just how many chapters were actually started?" The list for N.Y. is as follows: Amsterdam, Auburn, Auburn Convicts for Christ, Binghamton (Endwell), Bath, Buffalo-Mid-towns, Canandaigua, Corning, Cortland, Ellicottville (Valleys View), Elmira II, Fredonia, Fulton, Gates-Chili, Glens Falls, Geneseo, Greece, Greene, Sidney ,Germantown, Hamilton The New York City Executive Chapter, Henrietta, Indian Lake, Jamestown, Johnstown, Kingston, Lake Placid, Lowville, Mt. Kisco, Niagara Falls, Ogdensburg, Olean, Ossining, Owego, Palmyra, Cheektowaga, Plattsburg Champlain Area, and Plattsburg #2, Port Jervis, Potsdam, Rochester Downtown, and Rochester South, Rome, Seneca Falls, Troy, Warsaw, Watkins Glen, Waverly, Wellsville, White Plains, Geneva, Albion, Malone, Oneida, Pawling, Penn Yan, Stamford, and Norwich. I should add Bennington, Vt. for good measure.

After that, we organized Full Gospel chapters in many of the Central/Eastern New York Correctional Facilities (both State and Federal). Then during the 1980's, we reached out to nations around the world, starting new chapters wherever the Lord led me. Most of these were in West and Central Africa, with a few in the former Yugoslavian nations of Slovenia and Serbia.

We'll stop right here and give all the glory and credit to the Lord for each one of these chapters. It was God's idea from the beginning. He shared each one with me, but I was never smart enough to start even one of them. I am very glad to have worked along with God in this important work. I am still their servant and God is their leader. Each of those chapters were DIVINE APPOINTMENTS for us.

This chapter is written in honor of the many men across

New York State and beyond who worked so hard with me to organize these chapters. We couldn't have done it without them. (If you would like to know more about starting a new chapter in your area, you should contact me. I either have the answers, or I know where to find them.)

NEW CHAPTER CHARTERS

When new chapters were organized, it was my responsibility and privilege to present them with a Chapter Charter at a special Charter Banquet. It was a very important time for the chapter, but also was especially gratifying to me. As much as we had tried to teach the new men how to operate their chapter well, it was still necessary for me to explain to all the members and their guests about the vision of FGBMFI. While I was preparing my remarks and praying about the first charter presentation, the Holy Spirit showed me that the Fellowship did not really begin with Demos Shakarian, but that I should read St.Luke 5:27-32 (NIV): *"After this, Jesus went out and saw a tax collector by the name of Levi sitting at his tax booth. "Follow Me." Jesus said to him, and Levi got up, left everything and followed him. Then Levi held a great banquet at his house and a large crowd of tax collectors and others were eating with them. But the Pharisees and the teachers of the law who belonged to their sect complained to his disciples, "Why do you eat and drink with tax collectors and sinners?" Jesus answered them, It is not the healthy who need a doctor, but the sick. I have not come to call the righteous, but sinners to repentance.*

The chapters and their guests needed to learn the many principles that are contained in this passage of scripture. None of this great event took place in a church. Jesus met Levi on the street. Levi was not one of Jesus' band of followers, nor was he even a believer as far as we can tell.

But God had directed Jesus to invite Levi to "Follow him" (John 5:19).

Tax collectors were noted to be crooked in all of their dealings with the people. After they collected the taxes from the people according to the Roman laws, they then collected however much more the traffic would bear for themselves. They became very wealthy, and were hated by one and all. It is important for us to remember that Jesus loved them anyway, and that Levi would soon become St. Matthew. We also need to be reminded that it's the business/professional men in our towns that Jesus calls us to invite to our meetings.

Not only did Levi immediately rise up and begin to follow Jesus, but he also went to his spacious home and put on a reception for Jesus. He invited his friends, fellow tax collectors and other acquaintances (both men and women) to come to his banquet so he could introduce them to the Lord. (This passage from Luke 5 beautifully illustrates the vision of FGBMFI and/or BMFUSA. Several times Demos spoke to me about my approach and agreed that it was perfectly proper.)

It was especially important to remind the new men that their meetings were receptions for Jesus, and that their guests were there to meet Him. It was not to be a church service, but a Meal, with Jesus as the guest of honor. There also were no Bible teachers at Levi's reception. But Levi's testimony, of how he met the Lord and what that had meant to him, was the main program. And, of course, Jesus was there to invite all of Levi's friends (and others) to follow Him, too.

Occasionally our methods were questioned by some religious leaders who also wondered why we didn't make them more a part our program, or why we didn't meet in their church. But this passage of scripture make it crystal clear that *"It is not the healthy who need a doctor, but the sick.* A banquet or other type of meeting in a public place will attract more sinners than churches will. That was not to say that we disagreed with the necessity of the Church of Jesus Christ. On the contrary, as soon as our friends and guests got saved, we suggested they get fully involved in a Bible-believing Church, as well as become members of our Fellowship. We always encouraged our members to become the best Churchmen possible.

The Advance Work Continues

The format for each subsequent Advance always remained the same as God planned for that first one. One speaker (like Demos Shakarian) would excel in spiritual matters, while another one (like Tommy Ashcraft) would be an expert in starting and operating chapters. Although we promoted this very successful plan, some men who came forward to start new chapters in their towns decided that they didn't need regular chapter workshops to keep their men focused on the purpose and procedures of the meetings. Almost always those chapters seemed to dwindle away, little by little.

Although our numbers now are less than they were in those early days, we continue to see the Lord do great things at the Empire State Advances. Many of the people who used to come to Silver Bay now attend Advances in Western New York and Vermont, which makes it easier for more to attend because of the shorter distances they must travel.

We had so many Divine Appointments that all I can do here is call Advances one huge DIVINE APPOINTMENT with national, and even international significance.

Not only have Advances been held by FGBMFI and BMFUSA, but also by many other Men's Organizations and Churches around the world.

13

THE LEAST OF THESE MY BRETHREN
Matthew 25:31 - 36

Jesus warns each Believer that, *"When the Son of Man comes in all His glory, and all the angels with Him, then He will sit on His glorious throne. And all the nations will be gathered before Him: and He will separate them from one another, as the shepherd separates the sheep from the goats; and He will put the sheep on His right, and the goats on the left. Then the King will say to those on His right, 'Come, you who are blessed of my Father, inherit the kingdom prepared for you from the foundation of the world. For I was hungry, and you gave me something to eat; I was thirsty, and you gave me drink; I was a stranger, and you invited Me in; naked and you clothed Me; I was in prison and you came to me.'"*

"Then the righteous will answer Him, saying, 'Lord when did we see you hungry, and feed You, or thirsty and give you drink? And when did we see You a stranger, and

invite You in? or naked and clothe you? And when did we see You sick or in prison and come to you?' And the King will answer and say to them, 'Truly I say to you, to the extent that you did it to one of these brothers of Mine, even the least of them, you did it to Me.'"

*"Then He will also say to those on His left, 'Depart from Me, accursed ones, into the eternal fire which has been prepared for the devil and his angels; for I was hungry and you gave me nothing to eat; I was thirsty and you gave Me nothing to drink; I was a stranger, and you did not invite Me in; naked and you did not clothe Me; sick, and in prison, and did not visit Me?' Then they themselves also will answer, saying, 'Lord, when did we see you hungry, or thirsty, or a stranger, or naked, or sick, or in prison, and did not take care of you?' Then He will answer them, saying, 'truly I say to you, to the extent that you did not do it to one of these, you did not do it unto Me. And these will go away into eternal punishment, but the righteous into eternal life'"*No matter how I tried to get around the details of this passage of scripture, I couldn't do it. It was plaguing me, day and night. I knew I couldn't pass the test because I had never even been to a prison. Prior to our 1979 Men's Advance at Keuka College, these words were going round and round in my spirit. I thought, "I haven't been called to a prison ministry." Yet even my own thoughts convicted me. I thank the Lord that He emphasizes those things to us so we can prepare for the day that we will stand before Him without excuse for failing this test, no matter how we try. My understanding of the Word is that God calls us to follow Him, rather than to a particular ministry. We bring our own talents and gifts into the equation, which leads us to the ministry we enter.

As a leader/servant of Christian men, I also was made aware of the fact that God would judge me by how I influenced His brothers with my own life. It was a problem for me that God had never given Full Gospel Business Men any responsibilities in prisons! Or had He? Doesn't this scripture apply to one and all? And if so, and if the rules and regulations of our Fellowship did not specify where chapters should be formed, why not in prisons?

On Sunday morning, Dr. Doug Fowler, a physician and International Director from Georgia, was ministering to the men who had just gone forward at the invitation, and also to the other men God had been dealing with during the Advance. I was among the first to go forward, kneeling down at the altar seeking peace for my troubled soul. The Lord spoke to me through a prophetic word that He desired to have FGBMFI in all of the State prisons. I was assured that He would open the doors for me in every State and Federal prison in N.Y.S., and that the ministry would be His and not mine. I didn't know it then, but God was also speaking the very same way to a brother from Western New York.

During the following week, I received a letter from a young inmate in Auburn State Prison. He asked me to visit him on the following Sunday afternoon, and I said I would do it. When I first met Ronny Stecker, it was difficult for me to believe that he was doing time in a maximum-security prison for a very serious crime. He loved the Lord, and had committed his life to Christ while he was in a County jail, awaiting sentencing for his crime.

During my visit to Ronny that day, I knew beyond any shadow of a doubt that this was truly a DIVINE APPOINT-MENT. I began working with Ronny to actually start a FGBMFI Chapter in the Prison. I obtained permission from the prison officials to meet with Ronny and a number of other Christian inmates who indicated an interest in FGBMFI. They had been reading VOICE magazines and Demos and Rose Shakarian's book, The Happiest People on Earth, provided for them by the Chaplain, a wonderful Spirit-filled minister. These brothers really enjoyed the testimonies of men they could usually relate to in one way or another. Each week after that, I met with those men. I soon realized that I was being helped more by them than they were being helped by me, although we were all blessed by the wonderful anointing that always accompanied our meetings.

Our fellowship and prayers together led us to a time when we received permission from the Warden and the Chaplain to open the first Prison Chapter of FGBMFI in NY and perhaps anywhere. It was exciting, and the number of men in the group grew to more than 25 men. The name of the new chapter was Auburn Convicts For Christ.

Our charter arrived and we scheduled our Charter presentation for March 1978. We had 26 charter members on that memorable evening. By that time, Steve Roblee, Syracuse Chapter President, had become involved and was committed to oversee the work of the new chapter. Each Prison Chapter had to be sponsored by a Chapter outside the prison. One of the men who attended the charter meeting sat in the back with his arms folded, looking at the floor throughout the meeting. He was a "lifer," but he was also a Believer who had graduated from five different correspondence Bible Schools while he was incarcerated. He had become a licensed minister. While I was making my presentation remarks, I felt strongly led of the Lord to remove my FGBMFI tie, a green tie with fish and scripture on it, and to give it to him. (Months later, he would write me that he wore his beautiful tie proudly each day for Jesus and me.)

When the meeting ended he came forward, head still bowed, and obviously very troubled. He had put the tie on and it matched his green prison clothes nicely. He told me ashamedly that he had a deep bitter hatred for white men, including me. These feelings went back a number of years when he was incarcerated in Florida chain gangs. He had been tortured and mistreated by white prison guards all during his sixteen years in that system. Later he told me how movies like "Cool Hand Luke" quite accurately portrayed life in the chain gangs. After that, he was an inmate in Attica Prison until the now famous uprising there in 1973. He had good reasons to be bitter toward white men, having done nearly thirty years under their repeatedly cruel thumbs.

How do you respond when you don't know what to do? Pray fervently "GOD, PLEASE HELP ME!!!" As I put my arms around my new brother, Curtis Marshall, his tears began to flow and so did mine. He resisted me for a few moments, but I hugged him all the harder. Then he relaxed, and I felt his arms coming up my back, returning my embrace. I remembered the scripture: *"The anointing shall break the yoke."* The spirit of hatred lifted, and God replaced it with a beautiful spirit of love. What a moment! Another DIVINE APPOINTMENT! One of the guards interrupted us, telling Curtis the time had expired and he had to leave for his cell. When that glorious spirit of love came upon Curtis, it also came upon me and gave me a special love for prison inmates and an even more special love for Curt. We began to correspond between my visits. I looked forward to receiving his letters, one of which I will include here:

"Our Great eternal God. Oh Thou who can awake the stars, and turn the shadows of death into a glorious morning light; Come out on the balcony of Zion and take notice of my brother Fred, his kind wife, Shirley, and his sweet little daughter, Becky, and all of us here behind the walls. The Lord support us all, all the day long of this troublesome life, 'till our shadows lengthen, our evening comes, our busy world is hushed, our fever of life is over, and our works on earth are done. Then of your great love and mercy, grant unto us all a safe lodging, a Holy Rest, and peace at last, where the flowers never fade and our day shall never end. Amen, amen, and Amen!"

(When you become a servant/disciple of Jesus Christ and you follow Him, the things that touch His heart also touch your heart. Wherever downtrodden, sick, lonely people are, that is where you will be led as you follow Him.)

* * * * *

By this time, I already was very busy working with the sixty new chapters I had chartered across New York State. Now I was to spearhead another 35 to 40 new "Set Free" Prison Chapters. I began to request the men in every chapter where I was invited to speak to obtain permission for me to also speak to the inmates in a nearby prison. Together we visited and ministered in more than fifty prisons.

I would then request the men of the host chapter to accompany me to the prison meeting. I would share the wonderful vision God had given to Brother Demos Shakarian, and that his vision also included prisoners like them. That vision held a universal calling and appeal to men wherever they were, or whatever they called themselves. Then with Shirley usually at my side, I would ask them to observe as God, through us, ministered to the men in marvelous ways. The chapter men would be hooked on prison ministry almost every time.

This ministry that God had led me into eventually became larger than I physically could do alone. Leaving home with enough clean clothes to last me a few weeks, I would return home only when there was a break in my work. Oftentimes, I stayed in the homes of the men of the chapters. Much like a father, I came to know and love them, their kids, their likes and dislikes, and their ministry outreach to the men of their towns or cities. There wasn't anything I wouldn't do for them, because of the great love my Master had for them and for those people He and His new chapter would reach for Christ. He was loving them through me. Especially gratifying were those times when I found myself really loving someone whom I never could have loved before. But at the same time, I realize that I needed some new direction from the Lord to ease my work-load. It was at about the same time that our Board of Directors implemented the Field Representative system, whereby I could appoint men to help me with my work.

One day during this time, Curtis wrote me that he had to return to Attica Correctional Facility to finish out his sentence. His thirty-year sentence would be completed soon. We had often talked about the day when Curt would be able to attend his first Advance, now being held at the beautiful Silver Bay Conference Center. How he looked forward to having a thousand brothers hug his neck, and to seeing the mountains and beautiful Lake George. He could hardly wait.

I began working to find him a good place to go and live while he became adjusted to life "on the outside." Out of all the places I knew in this world, my hometown of Lake Placid seemed most like heaven to me.

I knew a dear couple there who had a beautiful Christian retreat center known as "White Chimneys." There would be a very pleasant furnished apartment for him over their big garage. Curt not only would be ideally suited to live there, but also to be involved in its many Christian activities, and to take care of their maintenance chores. Those folks would also have the love and sensitivity required to de-institution-alize Curt. After all, for thirty years he had been told when, or when not to make practically every move he made. He would have to learn to be his own man again. Surely this was God's provision for Curtis.

Everything came together perfectly for Curtis. He would be discharged from Attica two days before our Men's Advance. Chaplain Jeff Carter, a very precious black brother who was the head chaplain at Attica, would take

Curt to Silver Bay. Some of the Lake Placid Chapter men and I would be there to take him to Lake Placid after the Advance. Perfect!

The Advance began on Friday morning. Jeff would arrive sometime during the first meeting. I wasn't as concerned about the meeting that was in progress as I was about Jeff and Curt. Eventually Jeff came in the back door, but he was alone. My heart sank. I ran back to greet him, and to inquire about Curtis. Jeff said, "Fred, you'd better come outside with me, if you can get away for a few minutes." So out we went!

We sat down on the stone wall surrounding the auditorium and Jeff said, "Fred, we buried Curtis yesterday. He had a heart attack and died instantly the day he was discharged. I didn't let you know then because Shirley and I decided it would be better for you to wait until today so I could tell you personally." I wanted to die too. I can't remember anything hurting that bad. I began to cry like a baby.

"This isn't right, Jeff. Curtis was looking forward to this day for so long. Why couldn't God have let him have just this **one** Advance? He waited so long—thirty years—just to have a moment of joy here at Silver Bay. He served his time in *this vale of sorrows*, as he put it. Why Jeff, why?"

Then Jeff put his hand on my shoulder and told me that "God knew what He was doing, Fred." He went on to say that Curtis had met a woman from a Buffalo church singing group that had been visiting the men in Attica. He was to marry her yesterday. I had to call your friends in Lake Placid and tell them about Curtis's marriage plans. Fred, Curtis had every reason to want to have some married life, after all these years. But the folks in Lake Placid did not bargain for anyone except Curtis—especially a wife, seven kids, and only the Lord knows how many other family members. All of them were excited about relocating to Lake Placid with their new Daddy. "Don't you see, Fred? God did the only thing he could have done. The Lake Placid plans had all fallen through. By the way, Brother Fred, don't you think that heaven is as nice as Silver Bay. It might even be better!"

In a few moments, I returned to reality. As Jeff explained things to me, I could understand them clearly. I repented before the Lord for accusing Him before I heard the whole story. I really was sorry.

I realized that God had brought Curtis Marshall into my life to teach me the plight of so many men in our prisons today. He knew that I had seen hundreds of men come to Jesus in FGBMFI meetings across New York State. Now I needed to learn how to assist these fine men who lived in the prisons make their adjustment back into society again. God knew what my love for Curtis and his own special brand of Christian wisdom had instilled in me, namely the motivation and courage to go way beyond myself in order to help business and professional men get involved not only in the lives of Christian inmates, but also their families and peers outside the walls. (We all need to be Proverbs 17:17 and Proverbs 27:6 type of men and to have someone like Curtis in our own lives.)

I developed a simple program that I taught our men who got involved in Prison Ministry, one part of which came from a 1996 psychiatry journal. It stated that the greatest factor in Christian Counseling is: "THE COUNSELOR IS A TRUSTED FRIEND." It's not degrees, not intelligence, not techniques, not pills nor drugs. All true solutions to problems COME FROM WITHIN THE PERSON THEM-SELVES! You are unique! God speaks to you! He is no respecter of persons. You already know the answer within yourself. What is needed is a trusted friend who will LISTEN, ask honest questions, tell the TRUTH, and hold you ACCOUNTABLE. Humble yourself. "Confess your faults one to another, and pray for one another, that you may be healed." Most men seek their own glory—a true man seeks the Glory of Him who sent him.

* * * * *

As a former Veterans Hospital patient with considerable experience with disabled veterans, I've always had a strong burden for those men as well. Whenever I spoke in a chapter, I would ask the people at some point in my talk, "How many of you have visited the sick veterans in your local VA Hospital lately?" Then I would ask them not to raise their hands one way or the other. My experience was that very few if any could say they had done that. I had been in the Syracuse VA Hospital as a patient for eight months, and in all that time I never had a visitor. More than 500 Churches exist in the Syracuse area, but the veterans in that big hospital were apparently the furthest thing from their minds.

So naturally, I developed an instruction sheet that I would give anyone who desired to know exactly what they could do to get official permission to visit sick veterans. My instructions were that they be: 1. cheerful but not boisterous; 2. interested in the veteran and his family; 3. prepared to read a special scripture and pray an anointed prayer over him; and 4. willing to listen carefully to his comments, and then move on. The sheet also included a few cautions of what not to say! Men from many parts of the country have commented to me how blessed they were by going to minister to disabled vets. Today, the need for such ministry may be greater than ever. Why not try it? You'll be glad you did.

14

JESUS LOVES
UP-AND-OUTERS, TOO

When you enroll in the School of the Spirit, you soon will discover that each lesson you learn will be followed by a test on every aspect of the subject matter; just like in any other school. So, whether it is God or your professor doing the testing, you must pass or you'll have to re-study the subject matter—or possibly repeat the course and keep taking the test until you've got it right.

On the subject of soul-winning, we learn from Jesus that The Master Teacher reached out to each one of the people he led to Himself in a little different way. So as we fishers of men try to emulate Jesus, we must wholly lean on Jesus to say the right things and do the right things that will attract each one to Christ. Of one thing you may be assured, Jesus can teach you more about soul-winning than anyone else. Fishermen also learn to use the right bait for each type of fish. And each type of bait must be presented to the fish in just the right manner if you expect to catch anything.

Is it Chinese businessmen you're after? Then expect to find yourself in a Chinese banquet facility, with Chinese food, and probably a Chinese-speaking businessman doing the ministry. In our major metropolitan cities today, we must adapt the basic BMFUSA meeting format to the customs of those ethnic or societal groups we wish to reach. (In Chapter 27, I share my experiences opening chapters in Central Africa and elsewhere to illustrate my point.)

So I was in Soul-winning 401 when I had to travel to Texas to get part of the training. I was spending a weekend speaking in the Dallas area chapters, and was being hosted by our late Executive Vice-President, Tommy Ashcraft, a man who would rather lead men to Jesus than anything else he did. He also was among those who enjoyed talking and doing other things late at night when others would be sound asleep. So on Friday evening, Tommy and I were sharing things that were on our minds. We both felt that we needed a strategy to really make an impact in New York City, something that we may have overlooked in the past.

Tommy's theory was that we needed to reach out to the upper levels of the business world. Then they, in turn, could reach everyone else within their spheres of influence. While the men in the New York City chapters had been blessed with outstanding meetings in the past, we just weren't doing it presently. Tommy's son lived in New York, so he was thinking of ways that might be used to reach out to him. As we talked about successful outreach meetings held around the world, the Holy Spirit began to open my mind to some new ideas. We agreed that if we could come up with the right plan, it should work in any segment of society in any given city. We prayed about it, and left it in God's hands to show us exactly what to do in New York City.

I was almost asleep as soon as my head hit the pillow that morning, and my alarm was set to go off in an hour. But the Holy Spirit wasn't finished with me! The Lord gave me a spiritual dream that I wouldn't soon forget. In my dream, I saw a large banquet being held in a luxurious setting. Everyone appeared to be very prosperous. All were dressed in formal attire, including the waiters who were wearing tuxedos. Everyone was enjoying the occasion enormously. At the head table, I saw Demos Shakarian, Mr. and Mrs. Lee Buck, Mr. and Mrs. Charlie Duke, Rev. and Mrs. Everett Fullam, Tommy, Shirley, and me along with other very important looking people whom I did not recognize. My dream changed scenes, and I found myself seated in Lee Buck's office. Lee was a Senior Vice President for New York Life Insurance Co. In my dream, Lee invited me to be seated in his very beautiful executive office. I began to share with him my burden for the businessmen in the City, and then the dream I had while in Dallas. At the end of the dream Lee said to me, "Fred, I'll help you." The rest of the dream provided certain other details pertaining to this important outreach. Then God showed me how the story of Levi's call to follow Jesus (Matthew 9:9-13) was the scriptural setting for this soul-winning plan.

The next week, I went to New York City to meet Lee and tell him about what God had shown me in Dallas. Lee's office was on the seventh floor of the New York Life building on Park Avenue. I had never seen such an array of beautiful offices, so I had to remind myself several times to keep my mind on my mission and not on my surroundings. Lee invited me to his office, and then showed me around the seventh floor. All the Vice President's offices were located on the outside walls, with the secretarial and other staff member's desks and files occupying the center of that large space. Lee had his own chef and private dining room where we enjoyed our lunch in real style. I was so impressed with everything I was experiencing that I couldn't eat! Then we returned to his beautiful office.

I shared with Lee my burden for the great City of New

York. Then I talked with him about how I felt we should reach out to the top level of business and professional men, and about how they would have the kind of influence and capabilities we would need to reach out to the rest of the population there. I also shared my dream with Lee. His response to my entire proposal was, "Fred, I'll help you!" precisely what he had told me in my dream.

While Lee and I had only met a few times in FGBMFI functions, we became true spiritual brothers that day. We then went over an outline of the preparations needed for a banquet that would reach out to the top levels of New York City society. Lee had a man on his staff who made the arrangements for out-of-town guests of New York Life. These important clients required the finest accommodations. He also reserved the banquet facilities for all their important meetings. So, here was the man who could put together the appropriate meal with the perfect facilities and ambiance for this unique outreach.

Lee counseled me, "Fred, most of these people have been adversely affected by religious money-raising schemes. We must show them the real Jesus. We must avoid doing anything that would make it appear that we have one hand out to welcome them to our meeting, and the other one for their money." (For some reason, I already knew that!) We decided to finance the whole affair ahead of time by donations from the members and friends of the Fellowship, along with some spare funds in our Men's Advance account. We joined in fervent prayer for the whole event, and agreed to keep everything on a very professional, yet spiritual, basis.

From there everything began to fall into place beautifully. Lee put together a mailing list of persons that would be household names for most people. He and his assistant made arrangements to hold our banquet at the famous Helmsley Palace. I couldn't have dreamed of a better place! This would be one place where any of our guests would be very comfortable. I talked to Tommy about what had transpired, and he called Demos, who, with great enthusiasm, agreed to participate fully in this important outreach.

I spoke to some of the Christian businessmen I knew, and received mixed reactions. Many wanted to participate with hardly a second thought. Others said that this would be a big waste of money. Several told me that the Holy Spirit did not witness to them that this was of God because those wealthy people could easily afford to pay for their own dinners! (I must confess that those brothers just didn't get it!)

The money came together from many sources, most of whom I never even approached for money. We also had excellent credit references from our Convention Hotels for the Helmsley group. (Money never seems to be a problem when you are operating in God's perfect will.)

We selected as our speakers Charlie Duke, the famous astronaut who drove the vehicle on the moon, and Demos Shakarian, our beloved founder and President—an unbeatable team. Our singer was a famous opera star, and the Rev. Everett Fullam was selected to pray over the meal and the meeting.

* * * * *

When we arrived at the Helmsley Palace, we were ushered into a beautiful reception room where everyone got to meet our honored guests. An abundance of hors d'oeuvres and non-alcoholic drinks were served. Shirley and I kept as low a profile as possible while still meeting many of the famous people who were there.

Among our guests that night were members of the Colgate family. Another guest was the owner of numerous upscale properties in the N.Y.C. area as well as Gardiners Island, located off the Eastern shore of Long Island and the only remaining Fiefdom on this continent! He had flown up from West Palm Beach to be with us. I believe he asked the question a dozen times, "Who is paying for all this?" But no one seemed to know except Shirley and me, the Bucks, and Tommy Ashcraft, and we weren't telling! After a brief period of making acquaintances, we were directed into the sumptuously beautiful Dining Room.

Rev. Fullam opened the meeting with a prayer so anointed that most were visibly moved. The strong presence of the Lord was very obvious. Lee did a masterful job of emceeing the meeting, making the proper introductions and announcing the next items on the program. The meal was pure gourmet and was appreciated by all. One could gauge just how much everyone was enjoying the evening by the high decibel level of conversation and laughter around the tables. Everything was moving along exactly as planned. (No wonder that Jesus nearly always chose to eat with those he wanted to lead to Himself!) After dessert, the tables were cleared, chairs were rearranged so everyone was comfortably facing the podium, and the meeting began.

Lee introduced the singer and her accompanist. Her very simple, anointed rendition of two Holy Spirit inspired songs brought an even more beautiful presence of the Lord Jesus into that place. Then Lee introduced Demos. After an enthusiastic round of applause, Demos gave one of the most anointed presentations of his testimony that those of us who had heard it before had ever experienced.

Demos took us back to his Armenian roots that began when Jesus was still ministering here on earth. He talked about the King of Armenia who sent an envoy to Israel requesting Jesus to come and heal a member of his family. Demos concluded his remarks by sharing the vision God gave him in 1952, the vision that became the foundational basis for FGBMFI. When he finished about twenty-five minutes later, the aroused gathering of 128 guests gave him a ten-minute standing ovation. (Later, while recapping the night's highlights, Tommy Ashcraft said he had never seen a group give such enthusiastic and appreciative applause as they did that night for Demos. Those dear people wanted Demos to do an encore!)

Then Charlie Duke and his wife, Dottie, were introduced. Charlie began by saying that he wanted to share with us the two most important things that had ever happened to him in his life. He said he wanted to save the best until last, so he started with his trip to the moon.

Under the conditions that existed in the room that night, Charlie was at liberty to share many of the most humorous and personal aspects of his memorable trip—things you would never hear about except from him personally. He told us how, in his excitement of walking on the moon, he did a little jump for joy. For lack of gravity, His "little jump" produced a very high leap! And he had no control over his descent! All he would have had to do was to land on one of the sharp stones with some unprotected part of his space suit, and with even the slightest puncture he'd have died instantly! He related how an immediate word of admonition from Mission Control in Houston was essentially redundant, but nevertheless, that was what he got! Charlie stirred the audience to the edge of their seats, as he brought us all back to earth from that fantastic adventure to the moon.

Then Charlie moved on to the most important thing that he had ever experienced. He began by telling how he had resigned from the space program after his return to earth. Thinking nothing could ever equal that flight for excitement, he decided to pursue other things as a civilian. His first venture was in the beer distribution business, which although it went quite well, certainly could never equal his space ventures. Everything seemed to be anti-climactic for the Dukes after that.

Charlie's wife, Dotty, who also was having difficulties, began to search for answers at a neighborhood Bible study.

One evening Dotty was born again in her Bible study group. She instantly became a new creation in Christ, something Charlie could not understand. One morning as he was entering the Interstate on his way to work, Jesus saved and filled Charlie with the Holy Spirit, including his gift of tongues. The joy that filled Charlie that morning made his trip to the moon seem almost inconsequential, because there on the Interstate his whole life was changed by the loving power of Jesus Christ. You could have heard a pin drop in the Helmsley's historic banquet facility. Nothing as important as this had ever happened in that place.

Charlie told the people that he would slowly say the prayer that he said prior to his rebirth in Jesus Christ, and that He would pause after each sentence so that anyone who wanted to have this fantastic experience, could just follow along with him as he prayed. By now, most had their handkerchiefs out, either wiping away tears or blowing their noses as they repented and invited Jesus to come into their hearts and lives.

(I was glad that someone had taught me to <u>watch</u> and pray when everyone was asked to bow their heads in prayer, or I would have missed this DIVINE APPOINTMENT altogether. I closely observed everything, and didn't see one person who was not following Charlie in that prayer.)

Only God knows precisely who was converted that night and who wasn't, but my estimation was that almost everyone there was ushered into the Kingdom of God on that incredible evening. Praise the Lord!!!

As I made out the check to pay for that entire program, including suites for Demos and the Dukes, all I could do was praise the Lord for what He alone accomplished. He provided the funds, the speakers and musicians, the meal, the anointing of the Holy Spirit, and all the guests. It was His precious nail-scarred hand that reached out and beckoned those precious people into His Kingdom—an experience we'll always remember with grateful hearts.

We hadn't reached the end of the episode yet, however. After the formal part of the meeting came to a close, a Vice President of one of the banks approached me. He had been active in a FGBMFI Chapter in London before recently being transferred to the bank's home office in NY. That conversation resulted in the first Executive Luncheon Chapter in New York City. That new chapter met regularly at The Tavern -On -The- Green, and successfully reached out to the executive community for a number of years.

One day as Lee and I talked about the banquet and all God had done there, I felt led to ask Lee if he would like to continue his soul-winning activity on a larger scale as an International Director for the Fellowship. He readily accepted, and was well received by the rest of the International Board. No one was better prepared to take on such an important task than Lee Buck. He served the Lord faithfully for many years, speaking at Full Gospel meetings around the world. Often he and Demos Shakarian would travel together. He became one of the most effective soul-winners among those of high social standing we had ever seen. Praise the Lord! How about that for a DIVINE APPOINTMENT or two?

15

" AND THE LORD WORKED WITH THEM... Mark 16: 20

After we became known throughout the Fellowship we began to get invitations to speak in many Chapter meetings and churches. As a Director I would usually get together with the men in the chapter for an informational type seminar, either before or after the Fellowship Meeting. Sometimes the wives of the members would have a nice little tea with Shirley, which helped us to know the people better. We nearly always spoke at a Friday night or Saturday morning meeting in one chapter, and usually at another nearby chapter meeting during the same weekend. Then on Sundays we usually spoke in a Church in that city , either Sunday morning or evening, or both. Our list of friends grew enormously. Sometimes we would stay in the home of a member or in a nearby motel, which would be up to the men in the chapters. These weekend meetings went on almost weekly from 1974 for more than 20 years. During the 1980's our work began to reach out to various parts of the world, which I will tell about later.

When Becky was 5,6, and 7 years old she usually went with us, except when she remained at home with her big sister. She had a pet turtle named Myrtle which always went with us when she did. Even he began to get a good reputation. Sometimes I called her Sister Myrtle, although we never found out if it was a he or a she. We never ceased to be amazed at the unique personality that little painted turtle developed.

We kept a calendar and a "Daytimer" showing all the speaking engagement so we could make plans for each meeting, and keep a diary/journal of our travels for ourselves and Uncle Sam. We kept a record of some of the outstanding miracles God did on most of our trips. So I'll list a few of them here.

Getting started on one of our trips didn't require a lot of planning. During the week we would spend a lot of time praying and fasting in preparation for our upcoming ministry. Of course, we were "happy homeowners" and had our usual chores to do, along with my office work and correspondence . Much of what we took with us remained the same from week to week.. We'd pack our bags the night before we left , Shirley would have her weekly trip to her hair dresser in the morning, we'd notify the paper boy not to leave papers until further notice, maybe stop at the cleaners , collect Sister Myrtle, pray about the journey ahead, and we'd be on our way, rejoicing for another opportunity to serve the Lord..

We had a CB Radio in our car that usually gave us some laughs as we traveled, talking with our fellow travelers. Our CB "handle" was "The Holy Rollers", which we were happy to explain the meaning of to anyone who asked. Sometimes we'd sing choruses that helped pass the time. The truckers enjoyed our renditions about Jesus in 3-part harmony , and usually loved Becky's funny little comments, and Shirley's giggles. Loving people as we did we made a number of friends along the way, and even witnessed to some of them about Jesus.

PITTSFIELD, MA. - We had looked forward to going back to the Pittsfield area because we had some very dear friends around there. One couple, Ken and Ruth Koepp, lived nearby, and planned to attend our meeting. She had been suffering with some kind of Neuropathy for several years. Kenny had set up an elevator that took her up and down stairs in her wheelchair. She got around very slowly and painfully leaning on a walker, but usually was confined to bed or the wheelchair.

When we arrived at the restaurant for the meeting there was no sign of them. After we ate and the meeting began Shirley wondered if she should call them. But I knew that if it would be possible they'd be there. I was introduced to speak and had been speaking for about ten minutes when Ken and Ruthie came slowly into the room. We were so happy to see them. When I had given my testimony . I gave my usual invitation for salvation and prayed for several people to be born again. When we invited people to come forward who needed to be healed, Shirley joined me at the front. Ruth and Ken were the first ones in line. She looked so pitiful our hearts just about broke.

I generally anointed people with oil who needed healing, then Shirley and I would lay hands on them and pray as the Lord led us. The anointing of God was so powerful that Ruth fell over backwards - slain in the Spirit - people call it. I don't know how long she laid there but it was at least twenty minutes before she began to wake up. Kenny helped pick her up, and immediately began to praise the Lord that Ruthie was able to do things she hadn't been able to do in a long time. It was a joyful time for everyone, and the last time we saw them that night they were walking out to their car, hand in hand, and Kenny had the walker up in the air.

The next morning I was scheduled to speak at the Assembly Of God Church in Bennington, VT. Ken and Ruth were there with smiles from ear to ear. We didn't know then that Ruthie's healing didn't seem to be complete, so they came forward for prayer again that morning. Again Ruth fell over onto the floor under the power of the Holy Spirit. When she got up this time she had a great testimony of how God had healed most of her problems the night before, but then she got the rest of her healing that morning. It was a very exciting time for everyone, Praise the Lord for His wonderful blessings. We gave God all the glory and honor, then and now. Yes, more DIVINE APPOINTMENTS!

CORNWALL, ONTARIO

Shirley and I spoke a number of times in the Ontario and Quebec chapters in Canada. One of our favorite memories was of a meeting we did in Cornwall, Ontario, and then the next morning a meeting in one of the churches there. Soon after I began to speak an emergency squad came in pushing a gurney with a very sick lady on it. She was a cancer patient in a local hospital, and was said to be very close to death. This church service was a last resort for her and her husband.

After I finished speaking we immediately went to pray with the sick lady who was pushed forward for ministry. Her husband explained to everyone just how very sick she was. She looked to be just skin and bones from a long bout with cancer. I anointed her with oil, we laid hands on her and began to pray. She began to sort of squirm around and was trying to say something which we couldn't understand because she spoke in French.

A considerable period of time went by while we prayed with quite a few other people, and gave an invitation for salvation.

The lady asked a friend if she could borrow her coat. Her husband helped her put it on and she got up off that gurney and was walking around the church barefooted. God had healed that dear Sister of the cancer. When we got home we got a call from them telling us that she had been helping her husband with his farm work that day, and was feeling fine. All of us were deeply moved by what the Lord did for that lady .

Lord Jesus, thank you again for what you did for that Sister. We give you all the glory and honor for that DIVINE APPOINTMENT.

WAYNE, NEW JERSEY

One night Shirley and I were ministering in The Wayne, N.J. Chapter. It was especially important because Shirley's brother attended the meeting. We hadn't seen him for several years, and we had been praying that he's be there to attend his first Business Men's Fellowship Meeting. Several people responded to the invitation for salvation. Then I asked if anyone needed to be healed.

The first gal that responded to the invitation was the pianist. Then two other ladies came and stood next to her. She told us that she had a tipped pelvis - had had it all her life, and that it caused her clothes to not fit her or look right on her. We had never ever heard of such a thing but we could easily see her deformity after she told us about it. I anointed her with oil and as Shirley began to pray she was slain in the Spirit. All three gals went down together. When she hit the floor we could hear a loud snap. I thought someone's head had hit the floor, but it turned out to be that gal's pelvis snapping into perfect alignment. When she finally got up she gave a beautiful testimony of how embarrassed she had been all her life about her problem, then she spun around for everyone to see how nice she looked. It was a glorious experience for her and everyone gave her a big hand-clap. Then the other ladies testified of what God had done for them. After we finished ministering to them we prayed for many others under a very special anointing of the Holy Spirit. So, that night we had a lot to praise the Lord for and to give Him all the glory for. DIVINE APPOINT-MENTS one after the other.

We nearly always enjoyed our work among Full Gospel Business Men's Fellowship Chapters. Sometimes the chapter president would do just about everything wrong - just the opposite of what our National Guidelines instructed them to do. But rarely did we find that God hadn't been able to somehow redeem what the men had done as long as they had a few unsaved men and sick folks there. I would just keep my cool and wait to see what God would do

NORWICH, CT.

We went to Norwich, Ct. to speak in a Chapter Meeting at one of the local hotels. When we got there on Saturday morning the Ballroom where we were supposed to meet had been taken over by a Post Masters Convention. The only other room they had available was the lounge, a large enough room for our meeting, with a bar at one end near the lounge entrance. The manager warned us that at 11:00 am sharp the Post Masters meeting would be breaking up and many of the men would be heading for the bar. So we had to be completely out of there by 11. The microphone was at the end of the bar where I would be speaking, facing away from the bar and toward the lounge. All of the bottles of liquor were neatly covered with linen table clothes. We had the piano over close to the mic and the room was set up quite well, all things considered. There were about a hundred people in attendance. I still recall a lady came to me during breakfast wondering if God could do anything in a bar. I said, "Sister, Is anything too hard for God? You and your friends just pray and we'll see what God will do."

Everyone had their breakfasts, the meeting was opened, and a lively worship group led the singing. It seemed like everything was going to be OK, until a young man was asked to give a testimony. He took much longer than he should have, so I was introduced with the explanation for our having to be out of the room by 11 - just about a half hour later. I prayed, "Dear Heavenly Father, Jesus could tell people to Follow Him and they would rise up and follow Him. He could change the world with two words. Today we have a limited time so give me precisely the words to say. Thank you Lord, Amen"

Just before I got started I noticed some ladies coming into the lounge when they heard the singing. They were the Post Masters wives who came in while they were waiting for their husbands - maybe 10 or 12 of them. The Lord graciously gave me just the words I needed. I began to explain the plan of salvation at the same time I heard some activity going on around the bar behind me. Then the cash register rang and I knew that there were two meetings going on in that room at the same time. Since no one told me to quit I finished explaining the plan of salvation and asked anyone who would like to receive Jesus as their Lord and Savior to raise their hands. I believe there were 21 or 22 hands held up, when the Chapter President whispered to me to turn around and see what was taking place at the bar. I turned to find men lined up at the bar , at least 6 of them with their hands up. So I led them all in a sinner's prayer. We sang one chorus of "Thank You Lord For Saving My Soul." and I closed the meeting. Everyone clapped and started leaving the lounge. Some of those Post Masters wives came over to tell me how much they enjoyed the meeting and they had been praying for their husbands at the bar who raised their hands. It was a DIVINE APPOINTMENT of very significant proportions. Praise the Lord! He never fails! Try doing something like that in your church sometime

UTICA, NY

Actually this event began on a Friday evening in Norwich, NY. It was a good meeting and several people come to Christ that night. There were two men whom we hadn't met before, and with whom I spoke briefly before we left. They asked me about the FGBMF meeting we'd be speaking at the next morning, that had been announced for the next morning in Utica -where, when, etc.

The next morning they were back to our meeting. Only this time they were seated at a table in the front. . They had been given name tags and one of them was a black fellow named Charlie Booth. When I gave the invitation for salvation Charlie came forward along with some others. While he was still there he asked for prayer for his heart and other very serious conditions. When we prayed for his healing he was "slain in the Spirit" and laid there for quite some time. Then we helped him to his feet and he told us some of his testimony. He had been a chef at some famous restaurants, and had served for three years at the White House, in Washington, D.C as the head chef. He had been retired because of his heart trouble. He showed us his oxygen bottle and a whole pocket full of various kinds of medications he was taking. Then he happily demonstrated his ability to breath deeply and a few other things he hadn't been able to do for years. He told us that when we gave the invitation for salvation in Norwich that he wanted to go forward, but for some reason couldn't seem to do it. All night long he had been excited about the meeting the next morning.

A couple days later Charlie sent us a picture of numerous medicine bottles he had been using but no longer needed, as well as a picture of him in his chef's uniform at the White House.

Soon after that Charlie opened up a Restaurant on Rte. 20 East of Syracuse, where people could go and partake of Charlie's fantastic dishes without having to pay anything except what they felt led to pay him. People came from miles around, often by the bus loads, for some of Charlie Booth's famous dishes. Shirley and I enjoyed ourselves there several times. Later he founded a very successful Church in Syracuse.

A few years later I was being treated for a heart attack in Intensive Care at the Cortland Memorial Hospital. When Charlie heard about that he headed for our hospital to pray for me. Only my wife and our pastor were permitted to visit me for only brief periods of time. Charlie had a big lectern Bible, and explained that he was a clergyman and that it was very important that he see me because he was my brother (a next-of-kin). But even that didn't sway those diligent nurses, although they seemed to have a good laugh. When his attempts failed he went out and entered by another path around the nurses center where they caught him again and made him return to the waiting room. No one could ever accuse him of not trying desperately to visit his sick brother-in-Christ.

By then quite a few friends had gathered in the waiting room hoping to see me. So Charlie led them in a prayer and praise meeting right there. My room wasn't that far that I couldn't hear them singing and worshipping the Lord. It was absolutely beautiful - a genuine DIVINE APPOINTMENT that I'll always remember.

CORINTH, N.Y.

Shirley had been brought up in a Catholic Church. All of her family had come to have a personal relationship with Jesus Christ , either in their homes or in our meetings in the

Saranac Lake area. We had also ministered in a number of the churches in that area, including Catholic Churches. Denominations didn't matter to us. If the Lord opened a door for us to enter we went through it.

Perhaps in the future we will talk about an amazing relationship we developed with a beautiful group of Carmelite nuns in Saranac Lake, some of whom we still keep in touch with.

One day a Priest from the Catholic Church in Corinth called us, inviting us to come to his church for a Healing Service. It was to be held on a Saturday night. We were going to be in Indian Lake (just north of Corinth) that day for an FGBMFI Meeting so we accepted his invitation. Our dear friends, the Kluins, in Indian Lake drove us to the meeting. By the time we arrived there we had trouble finding a place to park and were late arriving for the Service. That church was packed out, with people seated and standing in the aisles. They had begun before we arrived with a very anointed and lively worship service, which probably continued for more than an hour. The Priest welcomed us warmly and introduced us, and turned the service over to Shirley and I.

I don't recall the exact message I gave that night, but I believe I spoke about the love God has for us, His children, and His faithfulness to His Words regarding healing for His people. I led the people in a prayer of repentance and acceptance of our salvation through faith in the Lord Jesus Christ. Then I prayed that God would heal all of those folks for any physical or emotional conditions they might have.

The two Priests who were in charge of the meeting were the first in line for prayer. One of them was instantly healed of a shoulder condition while the other one was healed of something else, which they happily demonstrated and testified to. Then, one by one people began to come forward for prayer for their physical needs. The presence of the Holy

Spirit was so strong that each person was being "slain in the Spirit" and were healed as we prayed for them. That went on until after two o'clock the next morning. Shirley was laying hands on each one of them, as the Priest stood next to her on the altar. She always was somewhat amazed to find herself ministering "on the altar", since such a thing would never have happened in her Church when she was young.

At some point I went to a mic and gave a teaching on the Baptism in The Holy Spirit. I invited those who desired that experience to come forward for ministry. I believe about a dozen people came forward and stood in front of me. After prayer each of them began to worship God in their new prayer language. It all seemed so simple that it appeared to have been rehearsed.

Then a beautiful thing happened. When I looked at the audience (more than two hundred) they had all heard my teaching and had also joined in our Spirit-filled worship. That included five or six visiting priests who were sitting in a front row pew. We had seen many outstanding outpourings of the Holy Spirit, but I doubt if any of them exceeded what we experienced that night. The Church was electrified with the power of the Holy Spirit. Whatever anyone needed God was just giving it to them, in abundance.

Shirley and the Priest had prayed for everyone, when he told Shirley that he wanted her to pray for his overweight problem. He added, "I'd like to have that experience of being "slain in the Spirit" too. But I'm not sure I want it for the right reasons." She reassured him that if God did that for him that God would decide if his request was appropriate. Several times that evening he told her that she reminded him of Kathryn Kuhlman. That was another of those things that happened during our ministry that I wish had been recorded on a movie camera. Shirley and the Priest standing on the altar with her laying hands on his hands, and seeing him being caught by the young man who was catching the people as they were being overcome by the anointing of the Holy Spirit. Tears were pouring down his cheeks and his hands went straight up in the air before he collapsed into the waiting arms of the "catcher". We didn't see him losing weight instantly but were quite certain that the answer to his request was on the way. When he was helped to his feet he was beaming with the glory of God all over him. Everyone rejoiced with him as he shared what had just happened.

The "catcher" had caught that overweight Priest in such a way that his own back was sprained. So we took out time to pray for him so he too could be healed. Then he returned to his duties, feeling fine again. A lot of things happened that night , but that is about the gist of it all. Then they took up a very generous love offering for us, pouring it all into a big paper bag and handing it to us on the way out the door. They hadn't bothered to count it. That Healing Service was truly a huge DIVINE APPONTMENT that had literally changed the life of that Church. Praise the Lord! He gets all the glory and honor for these things.

I could write a whole book about the experiences we had ministering in Chapter Meetings and Church Services, each one a DIVINE APPOINTMENT. I have a file drawer almost full of letters and cards people sent us after being blessed in our meetings. But these will give you some idea why we loved our work so much. Perhaps we will write about some of the other marvelous things we experienced in meetings in another book in the future. Each of them were exceptional, but would require more space than we have here. Each meeting was pure joy and excitement for us. Thank you, Jesus!!!!

16

DELIVERANCE
Mark 14:8

We had just returned from our Divine Appointment in Elmira (see Chap. 5), where Shirley and I had received the Baptism in The Holy Spirit. We knew that we had received a powerful infilling of the Holy Spirit, but only the experiences we had after we returned home would reveal just how much power we had received to minister in the Name of The Lord Jesus Christ.

After we had gone to bed, I began to feel very uncomfortable in my spirit. We prayed about it, and then I went to our daughter's room where the discomfort was quite intense. The only thing I knew about deliverance at that point was what Jesus said to the demons inhabiting the Gadarene in Mark 5:8, *"Come out of the man thou unclean spirit!"* and the man was set free. So, with all my might I spoke those same words. Out of the closet flew three demons—out of the closet and out of our house! At the same time, a ouija board fell out of the pile of games in the closet and onto the floor. I gathered it up and got rid of it by throwing it off our property. The peace of God remarkably came upon our girls, although they didn't have any idea what had happened. This marked our introduction to deliverance. (I might add that Christians should never have a ouija board in their home. They are not games, but are demonic tools of the enemy meant to deceive us into thinking that those little finger things move around by themselves, and are really great fun. Get rid of them!)

A careful study of the New Testament shows us that during His three years of Spirit-filled ministry in Israel, Jesus did as much deliverance as He did healing. Yet somehow we shy away from anything that even sounds like involvement with demons. It seems distasteful to most people, and perhaps even scary to some. Many have seen Hollywood's version of deliverance in movies such as 'Rosemary's Baby." These, however, are not accurate portrayals of Holy Spirit deliverance. If you are one in whom demons have taken up residence, then you need to know that there is hope and help for you, just as there was in Jesus' day.

Where do you look for this kind of help? Our experience has been that you look for a Spirit-filled Christian who speaks in tongues. The chances are that they will know of someone who can help, even though they may not feel led of the Lord to do it themselves. Many very authoritative books have been written on this subject, including one by my dear friend and Brother, Frank Hummel, whose book is entitled <u>A Soldier In God's Army, A Manual On Spiritual Warfare</u>. Another one we recommend is by Frank Hammond, entitled, <u>Demons and Deliverance in the Ministry of Jesus</u>. You probably will need to look in a Charismatic bookstore to find these books. The Bible, itself, is by far the most authoritative book ever written on the subject, and is the standard against which all other books on the subject should be judged.

Another thing we began to learn about the Holy Spirit

was that when He fills your life, He protects you in a number of ways. You will either be repelled or attracted to things or people around you. When you enter a place where people are worshipping the Lord in Spirit and in Truth, your spirit will be uplifted and you will join in with the others. But if there is something going on there that is not of God, you will sense that as well. It's called discernment, and is one of the most important gifts of the Spirit available to us! *"To one person the Spirit gives the ability to give wise advice. . . . He gives someone else the power to know whether evil spirits are speaking through those who claim to be giving God's messages or whether it is really the Spirit of God who is speaking. . . ."* (1 Cor. 12:8-10)

Thus, we began to learn some of the rudimentary lessons about spiritual warfare the same night we received the Baptism in the Holy Spirit. Looking back on things now, I don't wonder why the devil hates having God's people receive the Baptism in the Holy Spirit. Satan is a master of deceit until he comes face to face with someone Jesus has Baptized in the Holy Spirit and who is closely following Him. There he meets his match.

One of my Full Gospel brothers called me one day to inform me of a serious problem they were having with one of the leaders of their Charismatic prayer group. She had experienced a wonderful salvation, and had been baptized by Jesus in the Holy Spirit. Nevertheless, at times as she would be talking with a friend on the phone about spiritual matters, she uncontrollably would break forth into a whole litany of profanity, screaming and calling her friend all kinds of filthy names. After hanging up, she eventually would be able to calm herself down from the emotional outburst. She asked my brother Mike if he and I would minister to her. With some reluctance we agreed. After all we had heard about Christians being unable to be demonized, we felt that this would be a waste of time.

That was the beginning of a deliverance ministry for Mike and me that continued for several years. That woman was completely set free from a spirit of murder and twelve or thirteen other demons. During her deliverance, she had a friend who was sitting behind me to sort of give some moral support. Part of the way through the process, this friend began to cough and make strange sounds as she also was being delivered by the Name of Jesus.

I should add that woman #1 was a habitual smoker. One part of her deliverance was being set free from her smoking habit. When she got home and told her husband about all that had happened, he was very interested in the smoking deliverance. He told her that if she was really rid of her smoking habit, then she could smoke and it wouldn't bother her. She didn't want to smoke and held out for several days while he continued to taunt her about it. One day she decided to get him off her case and lit up another cigarette. That was all it took for her to have her full-blown habit back again. The last I heard, she was still a habitual smoker. Don't fool around with either the Lord or the devil. Neither one will play games with you.

Another thing I learned during that deliverance was that those evil spirits manifest themselves in different ways. At times they would speak in voices that didn't even resemble the person's voice. When they spoke like that, they would nearly always be lying, so you should never carry on a conversation with them. They put on a great show at times, looking at you with fierce looks, or will cry trying to make you feel sorry for them. During deliverance, they will manifest just about any emotion except love or truth. A spirit of hate or murder will make a person's face look like the devil himself. But they can't hurt a Spirit-baptized believer who is truly ministering in the love of Christ.

For some time my wife, Shirley, wanted absolutely nothing to do with deliverance, even though she had a prophetic word spoken over her that she would be used of the Lord in healing and deliverance. She responded to that word with a "That's what you think! I'll never do that! Only over my dead body will I ever be involved with deliverance." She was of the firm opinion that deliverance ministry should be done only by men— or anyone else except her!

* * * * *

One night as she and I were ministering after I had spoken at a Full Gospel meeting, I noticed that Shirley's right hand was trembling quite noticeably. The power of God was so forceful that I could feel the power of God emanating from her. Almost every time I anointed one of the people with oil for their healing, and Shirley touched their heads with that hand, they would fall over backwards "slain in the Spirit!" We had seen this happen before, but not in our ministry. These people were being assisted up off the floor and declaring they had been healed or delivered of all kinds of maladies, or perhaps had just had a very pleasant experience with the Lord.

I whispered to Shirley, "What's going on, Shirley? Why all this shaking and people falling onto the floor?" "God spoke to me during the meeting," she answered, "and He said He was putting the gift of healing in my right hand!" I just couldn't seem to relate to what she was saying. I thought that if God were going to anoint someone, He would do both hands! I reached out to take her trembling hand to help her get herself under control. Fortunately for me, there was a wall behind us that prevented me from landing on the floor. However, I bounced off that wall like I'd been hit by Joe Lewis. Frankly, I had thought that these things were not being done "decently and in order" as we had learned to do in our church. But after that, I kept my reservations to myself, and we continued to minister to the people in a more powerful way than ever before. Plus, I got what was coming to me for trying to quench the Holy Spirit!

* * * * *

A few days later, we were ministering in a FGBMFI Meeting in northern New Jersey. One of the men in the chapter who had been asked to give a 3 to 5 minute testimony, proceeded to give one that lasted more than a half hour. As a result, I gave a very abbreviated testimony and then invited those who needed ministry to come forward. A long line of people formed, but I only recall the third person in that line. As she started to tell us about her sore gums, her voice changed dramatically to a man's voice that began to speak to us through her. It was a sneering, sort of "Brooklynese" twang that said, "Ahh, git outta heah. Ya' can't have her. We live heah." My response was, 'That's what you think, devil. She belongs to God. She is a temple of the Holy Spirit, and you can't live here any longer. She doesn't belong to you, she belongs to God. I command you demon spirit, come out of her now, in the Name of Jesus Christ." So the battle was on and old "slewfoot "was on the run! But he put up quite a struggle that took hours to complete before he left along with eight or nine other evil spirits.

This testimony would not be complete without relating some of what that young lady later wrote to us in a very nice, eight-page letter, describing in detail what happened to her that night: *"Dear Fred and Shirley: I wanted to thank you for all your help. I know it must have been quite an ordeal for both of you, as well as for me. Praise God! I really feel like a new creation. Jesus is totally Lord of my life now. And you can be sure that I'm going to keep myself filled with the Holy Spirit* (Matt 12:43-45), *so nothing will ever be able to enter me again. Praise God!"*

"It is wonderful how Jesus prepared me for my deliverance. I had read the book, <u>Pigs in the Parlor</u>" by Frank and Ida Mae Hammond, about six months ago. I felt that I needed deliverance in certain areas of my life, but it seemed like everyone I talked to about it thought I was crazy, and that the book had gone to my head. My pastor told me that no way could I need deliverance because Christians can't have demons. So I began thinking that I was wrong. Boy! That's just what the devil wanted me to think. So I continued praying about my constant tiredness and bad temper. Just when I thought I was getting better, I would get very lazy and would get angry over the smallest things.

"I then re-read <u>Pigs in the Parlor</u>, finishing it in one day. By then I was positive I needed deliverance no matter what anyone said. I prayed 'Lord, if you want me to be delivered, I'm asking you to send someone to help me this week. If you don't do that, then I'll know, Lord, that I don't need deliverance.'"

The letter continues, *"God was so good to me that week. I needed financial help, and He met my need, miraculously. I found myself helping other people instead of only thinking about myself. The Lord was rewarding me with so much joy and peace. In fact, when Thursday evening came, I was going to the Full Gospel Meeting because the girl I was with was having marital problems, and I thought the meeting would help her.*

*"When I went forward for prayer, it was for healing of my sore gums. But I found myself telling you about my bondages, instead of my gums. (*She didn't seem to recall the man's voice speaking through her.*) I remember that night very vividly, and I knew what was going on the whole time. But I was helpless to do anything about it— like having a dream, knowing what was going on but helpless to do anything about it.*

At one point it seemed like the spirits were going to

leave me, when, for some reason, suddenly I felt them getting stronger. A couple days later I was talking to a woman who attended the meeting and saw what was happening to me. She told me that she and a couple other people in the prayer line had put their scapulas and medals and crosses on my back and even in my pockets. They seemed to think there was some sort of spiritual power in the medals that would expel the demons. But the Lord showed me that those demons got their strength from the medals, which is a form of idolatry, although some people don't know it. I believe the Lord wants me to share it with my brothers and sisters in our prayer community. (People from the audience did a similar thing one night while Mike and I were attempting to minister deliverance in the Wayne chapter—with little success. Finally, I asked the men of the chapter to take all the people, along with their medals, out to another room. After they left, we once again regained full authority over those demons, and cast them out.)

*"I also remember opening my eyes two times for a minute or so. The hatred was so intense that I couldn't keep my eyes open. It was horrible! (*We thought the same thing!)

I'm glad the Lord let me remember. I now know the hate that satan has, and how he deceives us; and all the poor people who are struggling and don't know why. All these years I had put myself down and actually hated myself, but now I am free and saved out of all that darkness.

That night I felt love coming right out of your eyes, Brother Lawrence. And that is what kept me going. I thank the Lord for preparing both of you for that night. The Chapter President told me that Sister Lawrence had also just read <u>Pigs In The Parlor.</u> *The Lord knew she was going to be used in my deliverance and He prepared her with that book.* [This is partially true.] *Praise God!"*

Over the period of the next year or more, we were doing deliverances several times a week. People from many miles away would come to our home, usually at night. We didn't know how to say "No!" to them. Often the morning sun would appear on the horizon before the people would go their way rejoicing, but leaving us exhausted to carry on our regular duties.

Eventually the deliverance work became too overwhelming for us. Sometimes it would require as much energy to minister deliverance to one person as it would to minister salvation and healing to hundreds. We prayed, "Lord, please deliver us from deliverance. Please raise up others who can share this load." Gradually the Lord answered our prayers, starting with an area Episcopal Church that had invited us to be on their staff as the deliverance team. After a while, the folks in that church began shying away from us, and at the same time, our deliverance ministry began to subside. (Obviously, we highly admire those who continue faithfully to do this important ministry.)

The deliverance experience Shirley and I received has been invaluable to us, not as a separate kind of ministry, but in the daily ministry of Jesus Christ wherever we've gone around the world. Jesus always took care of the needs of the people, no matter what the problem. At the same time, we needed to be well-versed and experienced in every kind of ministry. My work among the Africans took my deliverance work to a whole new level, often having to do deliverances to whole groups of people at the same time .The same situation was prevalent in South and Central America, the Caribbean, among the gypsies in Serbia, and wherever the people did voodoo or similar demonic practices.

Don't think for a minute, however, that all demonized people live in the dark parts of the earth. Late one night, we received a visit from a man who belonged to a Baptist Church in a nearby town where they had very strict rules against any practice that might be charismatic or Pentecostal. Before joining the church, he had to sign a form forbidding his being associated in any way with Pentecostals or such practices as speaking in tongues. Our visitor was a business-man and an elder in the church, and had been one of the strongest opponents of Spirit-filled people. The reason he visited "by night" (like Nicodemus in John:3) was because he knew of our charismatic affiliations, and because he was concerned that being seen with us would hurt his business. His coat collar was turned up and his hat down over his face. (We had been referred to him by a Syracuse area bookseller who had told him that we might be able to help his demo-nized sister (whom I will call "Agnes").

Agnes had spent many years of her life in the State Mental Hospital, but when the State decided to "de-institu-tionalize " people like her, she had had to move in with her brother and his family. Her strange aberrations were "driv-ing them up the walls!" He had read some books about people like her, and determined that she was "demon possessed," as he put it. Further study had convinced him that it would have to be Spirit-filled people like us who would be able to help her, so here he was on our doorstep, looking for help. The poor guy was "firmly" standing with his two feet straddling opposite sides of a religious fence. His only other alternative was to put her in a private institu-tion in a Mid-western state. Since we had just pleaded to the Lord to deliver us from deliverance, I must admit I was a bit impatient with him.

We listened to his sad story. Our extreme dislike for the devil and his evil spirits, and our built-in compassion for people like her balanced things out in her favor. But I doubt if I'd have raised a finger to help him. In a few days, we went to visit this poor unfortunate victim of the devil. Her hair stood up in all directions, she drooled all over the place, and was unable to hold a conversation. A single word of command caused her to sit down and remain quiet. Turning to the elder and his wife, we then shared our wonderful experience of being saved and baptized in the Holy Spirit, with the evidence of speaking in tongues. We explained that the anointing of the Holy Spirit accompanied the Baptism, and that we had the same power promised to every believer to cast out demons, and that "every believer" included even them if they desired this experience. Then they would be empowered to minister to their sister equally as well as us.

It took Shirley and I a couple hours to set Agnes "free as a bird" from all the demons that had tormented her for so long in the State Mental Hospital. What the Lord did after that would bring tears of laughter to your eyes. Since repeating the whole episode would identify the couple, I will simply say that Agnes came over to our side of her brother's religious fence after being set free from the darkness in which satan had imprisoned her for so long. (Again, I must admit that I asked the Lord to please forgive me if I enjoyed this part of the ministry too much.) Walking with the Lord goes much easier if you can find a little humor in some of it. Such humor allows you to more fully enjoy the byproducts of DIVINE APPOINTMENTS like ours that accompany deliverances or any other answers to prayer you might experience.

* * * * *

A friend asked, "Fred, Why don't you just eliminate this chapter? It is controversial in some ways, and the subject is not one most people like to think about." I simply responded that our deliverance experiences give a measure of hope to all the people out there who need deliverance, especially those who don't know it or who inappropriately have been referred to a psychiatrist or psychologist. These professionals simply cannot cure patients who need deliverance, unless they too have the discernment and the necessary power of the

Holy Spirit operating in their own lives to set these "prisoners" free. Not only that, but Jesus also commanded us to cast out demons: *"Go and announce to them that the Kingdom of Heaven is near. Heal the sick, cure the lepers, and cast out demons. Give as freely as you have received."* (Matt. 10:1-8) We have been faithful to Jesus' command.

*Note: If after reading this you feel you need deliverance, please DO NOT CALL US. For health reasons, we have had to discontinue the deliverance part of our ministry. Instead, obtain the books by Hammond and Hummel mentioned at the beginning of this chapter to help you in acquiring the information you need.

17

DRIVING BY FAITH

The first few days—and even months—of walking and living totally by faith provided some of the most awesome, and occasionally some the most frightening times of our lives. Nothing in life, either in the natural or the material world, prepares one for it. Certainly this former engineer found it a bit unsettling at times, to say the least. Shirley was equally on edge about the whole process. She was especially conscious of the desirability of financial security, perhaps because of her childhood experiences.

We both had worked hard to get through college, working day and night in order to eke out a living. We each wanted to be certain that we would enjoy a secure future. I also had worked hard to build a solid experience in construction, engineering, and architecture to further ensure our future. Now then, it looked like we would be back to pinching pennies, shopping in second-time-around stores, and eating leftovers to make a go of it. A common comment made during those exciting days was, "If God can get us out of this situation, I'll never doubt Him again." He never let us down—not even once.

One Friday morning just before going to have her hair done at the Beauty Salon, Shirley had a talk with the Lord about things. "Does this faith business mean that I must stop seeing my beautician each week?" The Lord replied that He wasn't poor, nor was it necessary for his children to be poor. Hadn't He promised to *"meet all of our needs according to His riches in glory, by Christ Jesus?"* (Phil 4:19) So, she never missed an appointment nor failed to be faithful to this heavenly vision. Nor has she ever failed to share her love for Jesus whenever the occasion presented itself at the beauty parlor. Her weekly appointment with her beautician became a part of her ministry to the community.

Another disconcerting aspect of seeming to be out on a financial limb all the time was that we had nothing in reserve, no nest eggs, nothing for a rainy day. God wanted to be our nest egg, and the one we always would fall back on. The future can look pretty bleak with no savings, no retirement plan, and no insurance. But, as God's always provided day by day, we became less and less apprehensive about being on the edge of financial disaster. Time and experience has further lessened the anxieties of just simply trusting our Lord Jesus for all our needs.

Our daughter Becky got with the faith program very quickly. She became very fond of telling her friends that she had a wealthy Father. They always wondered about her beautiful wardrobe. She always joined with us in our daily Bible study, worship, and prayers for all of our needs, leaving behind any concerns she may have had before she left for school.

One day our neighbor's big malamute dog knocked Becky down and had her by the throat by the time its master got to him. It was a very scary situation that none of us easily forgot. Eventually, we felt she should start walking back and forth to school each day with her friends. At the same time, we encouraged her to never allow fear to rule her life. *"There is no fear in love; but perfect love casts out fear . . . ."* (1 John 4:18)

Another dog, a big lanky red setter, lived four houses down the street from us. He was a friendly fellow, but he liked to put his paws on, and slobber all over you. Unfortunately for Becky, he was just a bit more than she could handle, considering her previous experience with dogs.

We prayed regularly with Becky about the situation, and counseled her to trust the Lord to keep the dog away from her. I prayed, "Dear Lord Jesus, please walk back and forth to school with Becky and keep that red dog away from her." When it was time for her to come around the corner where he lived, I also made it a point to be out front of our house waiting for her.

One day the dog was untied when she came around the corner. He barked at her and looked like he wanted to lick her face. Becky put her hand up in the air and walked right by that big pest. When she got home my first question was, "Becky, you did very well coming by the dog. But I was wondering why you had your hand up in the air?" She replied, "I was holding Jesus' hand." Whatever or whomever God assigned to walk Becky home must have been that dog's biggest nightmare, because he never bothered her again.

* * * * *

Most of the men on the FGBMFI Board of Directors with whom I now associated as an International Director were very successful and prosperous business and professional men. Eventually, I became accustomed to fellowshipping with these men whom God had blessed financially so He could finance the work of the Fellowship around the world. They lived and walked by faith every bit as much as I did, and I was very honored to be associated with them. They didn't know, at least for a long time, about my financial situation.

One day I was attending one of our Board Meetings in Chicago when an amazing spirit of giving came upon us. Funds were needed to purchase land in Costa Mesa for a new Headquarters Building. The sizes of the offerings the men were donating was almost staggering to me. They started at $1000 and grew to more than $50,000. In a very short time, all the money for the land had been raised. One Brother donated all the structural steel and trusses for the new building, while another donated all the plywood that would be required for the job. Two brothers donated the entire cost of the beautiful auditorium that had been designed into the building.

I recalled with some feelings of embarrassment how earlier in my life I could have written a check along with the best of them. No one will ever know how much I wished I could do that. God saw my agony of spirit, and clearly said to me, "All I want from you is you." And that was that! For whatever I was worth, He had me—all of me—lock, stock and barrel.

Although the Board always met in fine hotels across the country and beyond (Rio de Janeiro, etc.), I missed only one of the more than forty of those meetings, and that one was not due to a lack of funds. God was always faithful to us!

A few weeks after my Chicago experience, I was called on to visit one of our chapters in the Finger Lakes area. It seemed that a problem had caused a rift among the men that they couldn't seem to straighten out. They needed an arbitrator, so I was ready to go, except I didn't have enough money to make the 115-mile trip. If I could just get there and straighten out their problem, I figured they would "pass the hat" for a little love offering to help with my expenses. As far from home as I was, I also expected that one of them would put me up somewhere for the night. So, away I went rejoicing in the Lord that I could serve Him in this way. He had promised that He would never leave me nor forsake me. So I had the greatest One in the world in my passenger seat. (Actually He was the Captain of my little ship, but He let me think I was. What a Savior!)

I arrived at my destination prepared spiritually for just about anything that might occur. However, as I drove into the parking lot, I did notice that my gas gauge showed empty! But I was there on time, trusting the Lord to solve their problem and my empty gas tank. Twenty-five men had gathered in a church fellowship hall, the first procedural "no, no" for the meeting. After some prayer and worship, the President introduced me as "Our new International Director, a successful architect from Homer. He travels at his own expense. Let's thank him for being with us and give him a nice welcome." Then he turned the meeting over to me.

This kind of meeting can get a bit sticky, but just having each man share things as he saw them went a long way toward helping me understand the problem. A few anointed questions from some of the Brothers revealed that the root of the problem was un-forgiveness. The Lord dealt beautifully with each man's confession, and after everyone had forgiven everyone, we all laughed and hugged each other's necks—the problem having been solved. Praise the Lord! (I soon learned that just being an interested, neutral person goes a long way in these situations. Jesus is still the Eternal Prince of Peace.)

After the reconciliation (and while I still had the floor), I called on a young Nazarene pastor to share his testimony. I had met him just before the meeting started, and had learned that only very recently had he received the prayer language that normally accompanies the Baptism in the Holy Spirit. He related that he had been invited to one of their Fellowship Meetings where a Nazarene Navy Commander was the speaker. The Commander's testimony had lovingly challenged his theology, and as the Commander prayed with him, the Holy Spirit had opened his heart to receive His precious Baptism. But perhaps because of some lingering denominational inhibitions, he didn't receive his prayer language.

Several years had passed, problems had developed in his church, and he couldn't get that Nazarene Commander's testimony off his mind. Finally, he became so desperate to receive God's power in his life and his ministry, that he told the Lord: "Tomorrow morning I am going downtown to the First National Bank at the four corners in the center of town. I'm going to kneel down and wait for God to fill me and give me my prayer language. I won't move from that spot until I've received with the evidence of speaking in tongues." (Now that is what I call determination! He meant business with God. It's too bad that more young pastors don't have that kind of desire for all God has for them until their ministry nearly fails for lack of the anointing. *"Blessed are those who hunger and thirst after righteousness, for they shall be filled." Matt. 5:6.*)

While driving as fast as he could to the bank for his appointment with God, he started speaking fluently in tongues. That was it! He had it! God saw his hungry heart and met his need without requiring him to kneel down in front of the bank.

For a long time his attitude had been, "Lord if you want me to have this gift, then please just give it to me." But God says, *"Ask, and it shall be given to you; seek, and ye shall find; knock, and it shall be opened to you."* (Matt 7:7) I was thinking about these things one day when the Lord said that there are basically two kinds of people: those who hunger and thirst after righteousness, and those who don't.

Because this young man received this spiritual gift, he lost his job as pastor and had been out of work for several months. So I suggested that the men "pass the hat" and help this Brother's family with a love offering. They joyfully did that, said "Good night" and "Thanks for coming," and disappeared—every last one of them! I turned off the lights and locked the door on my way out.

My car, obviously, was still sitting there with an empty gas tank. I reminded God that He was my employer (or maybe He reminded me of that) and that I wasn't especially looking forward to spending the cold night in that car. I turned the key in my ignition and my engine started up perfectly. I drove through town, noticing that all the gas stations had already closed. So, I drove up the ramp onto Rte. 17S and headed for home.

When driving at night on a super highway type road, I usually get very sleepy. But that night, the further I went, the more wide awake I became. I was having a DIVINE APPOINTMENT that I wish everyone could experience at least once in their lives. I traveled the 118 or so miles through Corning, Elmira, and Ithaca, and finally right into my garage in Homer. The moment my car stopped in my garage, the engine also stopped. I sat there a few moments thinking, "Wow Lord, I loved the way you did that! I'm glad one of those fellows didn't invite me to spend the night with him, and I'm glad that you had my car run so well without gas. Thank you, Thank you, Thank you!

* * * * *

You may be one of those who would ask: "If God really did that, why doesn't He just go ahead and do it all the while?" That's almost a good question! But God learned a long time ago when He supplied the Israelites with their daily manna (the most perfect food ever created), that they soon took their manna for granted and began to murmur and complain, and ask why they couldn't also have some meat!

We humans seem to take God's provisions for us for granted, and He doesn't like that trait in us. *"Blessed be the Lord, who <u>daily</u> loadeth us with benefits, even the God of our salvation."* So, I learned to be thankful for all of our provisions that we received day by day, because He was the source of all of them." DIVINE APPOINTMENTS just seem to get better and better!

18

THEY SHALL FLY AS THE EAGLE
Jeremiah 48:22

"If we live in the Spirit, let us also walk in the Spirit." Galations 5:25

As one who often found his abilities to reason at odds with his ability to totally trust the Lord, my scientifically-oriented mind found walking in the Spirit a difficult adjustment to make. However, the Lord is very gracious and patient as He brings us step by step into conformity with His image, and to a state of perfect trust in Him in all things. We know that our Lord said, *".....I do nothing on my own initiative, but I speak these things that are pleasing to him."* (John 8:28-29). After we are baptized in the Holy Spirit, we begin to understand these principles as God demonstrates them to us through personal experiences.

So it was with excitement and anticipation that I daily attended my spiritual classroom. I began early in the morning by just communing with the Lord Jesus, reading His Word and receiving many beautiful truths directly from the Master Teacher. Then I could expect a personal lesson on the subject to follow very soon after that.

One morning while in prayer I heard the Holy Spirit softly say, "Take the earlier flight this morning as you travel to Chicago." I had scheduled my 2 1/2 hour flight so I wouldn't have so much time on my hands before my evening meeting. I started to tell God that I had already considered His plan, but I preferred the later flight. Once more I heard a gentle voice tell me to take the earlier morning flight. (I don't think I have ever expected the Lord to repeat Himself more than once.)

The Airline people gladly rearranged my flight plans to just before lunch, and their computer assigned me to a center row seat on the big DC-10 leaving Syracuse for Chicago. I looked for signs of God's providence, wondering if the later flight would crash or what. But when I took my assigned place one seat from the aisle, with open seats on both sides of me, I thought how sweet the Lord had been to give me all of this extra space to stretch out my long legs to read and rest..

The other folks in my row were an attractive young lady and her five-year old son. I nodded my head with a casual greeting as they were seated, and then returned to my airline magazine. I watched my new neighbors out of the corner of my eye. I knew instinctively that the little boy would have to check out the plumbing and other matters of great interest in the toilet room as soon as we took off. Any frequent flyer knows that about little boys! And sure enough, as soon as the seat belt light went off they were on their way to the bathroom.

After putting down her purse, some books, and something else on the seat next to me, she said in an almost off-handed way, "Brother, would you please watch these things for me while I take my son to the bathroom? To which I readily replied, "Why yes, of course."

As they moved down the aisle, I began checking myself for any signs she might have seen to lead her to assume that I was her brother. I had no lapel pin on my sweater, no bumper sticker on my brief case nor Bible in my hand. "Could this be yet another DIVINE APPOINTMENT?" I would soon find out.

My two new neighbors soon returned. She put the boy in the aisle seat and took the seat adjacent to the empty seat next to me. She moved her belongings into the empty seat and began a friendly conversation with me. It wasn't long before I was able to ask her why she had spoken to me earlier as, "brother." (By now my extraordinary powers of observation and discernment had noticed a Bible among her belongings. What developed from there turned into one of the most exciting experiences I'd ever had.)

Joan began, "I have been a Christian nearly all my life, but it wasn't until last night that God ever spoke to me audibly—I think! At least to me it was audible, but no one else in the house heard Him. May I tell you how it all happened.?" She didn't need any permission or coaxing from me before she launched into a rather lengthy explanation. By now I was all ears.

About three weeks earlier, she and her sister were sitting in her new home in a Los Angeles suburb, just chatting and drinking iced tea. Someone rang the doorbell, and it was a nicely dressed couple who wanted to speak with them about important spiritual matters. "Could they come in for a few moments?" Joan couldn't think of a good reason to refuse them, so she invited them in. They soon revealed that they were Jehovah's Witnesses and began a demonstration of their well-rehearsed monologues. Although Joan and her sister, Jane, had been brought up in a Christian church, and Joan was a Bible teacher in her Episcopal Church, she became painfully aware of her lack of any biblical reasons to disprove the things these visitors were saying. Joan eventually accepted their magazine and saw them out.

Soon Jane had to be on her way, and Joan was left alone with extreme feelings of guilt. She wondered why with all her Christian life and upbringing, she had never heard of any of the things her visitors spoke about. And when they said things with which she didn't quite agree, she didn't have enough first-hand knowledge of the Bible to dispute their claims.

Being a serious believer, as soon as she was alone again, she went to her knees in prayer and repentance for her ignorance of the scriptures. " Please, God, forgive me for these things and please help me learn Your Bible." Then as she continued in prayer, she began to experience herself speaking in a language she had never learned. She had no idea what was happening, but whatever it was, it seemed to her to be an answer to her prayer. Since it seemed to be something good, she continued the speaking until it stopped about four minutes later.

Jane began to wonder all sorts of things that might explain her experience, but she couldn't figure it out. Perhaps those people had done something to her. Perhaps this, and perhaps that, but nothing satisfied her curiosity. She began to wonder if she was losing her mind. And there was no one she felt comfortable with that she thought could help her. What to do?

Jane got a call later that day from her Mother in Syracuse. Serious family problems had arisen. Jane's Mother needed an understanding shoulder to lean on, and could she get away for a few days to return home. The next day Jane and her son were on their way to Syracuse for a short visit. During their two-week visit, she devoted much of her time to helping solve situations involving her family. But when she was alone, she would wonder about her strange experience at home. She even tried to talk that way again, but couldn't. On the final night before her return to Los Angeles she was praying fervently, asking God what was happening to her, and was she "losing it".

God's reply was what startled her the most. He said aloud, "Joan, the man who will be sitting next to you on the plane tomorrow will answer your questions." She absolutely knew that it was God, even though He had never spoken to her that way before. It was both reassuring and unnerving at the same time. But she relaxed, and had a good night's rest for the first time since her strange experience.

When she saw me, she said that she knew without a doubt that I was a man of God. She didn't know why she felt that way, she just knew that I was the man whom God had promised would sit next to her on the plane. Hence she knew I was her Brother in the Lord. Fortunately for both of us, I knew exactly what had happened to her. The Lord Jesus had Baptized her in the Holy Spirit even as He promised every Christian before her, all the way back to the events on the day of Pentecost. The language she got was the confirmation she needed to assure her that God had indeed heard her desperate heart's cry. Now the words of God were opened up to her in a marvelous new way— speaking in tongues—a universal evidence that God has filled you with the Holy Spirit (Acts 2:4).

During the next few moments, either one or the other of us moved over into the empty seat between us. By that time, I would guess we were perhaps a half-hour outside of Chicago. I spoke to her in calm and reassuring tones, and let God speak to her through his Word. A ready learner, she took notes and highlighted in her Bible every passage of scripture I shared with her. I told her that God had prepared a special prayer language that she could use at any time. It was to be her direct line to the Father and His Son Jesus. Never again would she be ashamed of, nor be without an answer for the faith she had. Then I asked if she was ready to try her new prayer language. She said, "I'm ready. I'm ready!"

We joined hands and I prayed that God would give her a new prayer language. Her faith was such that she immediately began to speak in this new language. As she did, a look of joy and adoration for Jesus slowly enveloped her face. (At that point I told the Lord that I was real glad that she was a nice dignified Episcopalian and that her strong voice would not get much stronger.) But Joan, having become lost in the glory of her experience, began praising the Lord with her arms straight up in the air and with ever increasing volume. She was oblivious to everybody else on that plane, even those who had come running from all directions to find out what her problem was!

I eased myself back into my own seat, trying to be as inconspicuous as possible, while Joan, caught up in her charismatic blessing, continued to ignore the questions of the attendants. One of the Flight Attendants even asked me if I had done something to her, to which I replied that of course I hadn't. (Thank the Lord the plane was now descending into Chicago O'Hare and I'd soon be out of there!) I prayed, "Lord, can't you get her under control? These people think I've done something terrible to her. She's really your problem, Lord. Please!!" Help!!!" Thankfully God has his people everywhere, and He sent a Spirit-filled flight attendant from the First Class section to the rescue. She explained to everyone's satisfaction that everything was OK and that she would handle things. Which she did! And that was the end of my lesson in the School of The Spirit for that day.

* * * * *

I have often pondered about the multitude of things God had to arrange for both Joan and I to be on that plane, on that particular day, and in those particular seats! It helped me realize once again that nothing is too hard for our God. I also learned why Paul admonished us to *"Preach the Word. Be instant in season and out of season (2 Tim. 4:2),* and that we must keep ourselves constantly in an attitude of spiritual readiness for any DIVINE APPOINTMENT that arises.

19

OPEN THY MOUTH WIDE AND I WILL FILL IT
Psalm 81:10

Our adventure in living by the faith of the Son of God brought about a number of living adjustments Shirley and I hadn't fully anticipated. We did know that our financial budget would have to be adjusted to the Father's budget, a totally different thing. We learned that we must pay very close attention to the voice of the Holy Spirit, and always keep our line of communication unhindered by anything that would cut us off from God. 1 Peter 3:7 gives an illustration of this principle, "Husbands, live with your wives in an understanding way . . . so that your prayers be not hindered." Shirley and I had to learn to live together 24/7, every day, "in an understanding way." Or else!

One item that we always seemed to let come last on God's new financial plan for us was our teeth—until we got a toothache! We discussed this with each other and with the Lord. We even suggested to the Lord what we thought would be an excellent plan—having Him keep our teeth perpetually healed. Not that we didn't appreciate the ministry of dentists, but you know how it is! Somehow we didn't associate dental work with the things of God, that is, until we traveled to Rochester to speak.

We had speaking engagements for Saturday morning and Saturday evening in the Rochester area. As we finished up the morning meeting, the Chapter President, Roy Libby, invited us to return home with them for lunch. As we drove to his home, I asked Shirley to pray for my toothache. Following her prayer, I kept putting my tongue in the large cavity to see if it was being filled, all to no avail.

When we arrived at Roy's home and met his lovely family, I was shown to an easy chair by the fireplace. While sitting there and listening to the chatter in the kitchen as lunch was being prepared, I reminded the Lord that I was still waiting for Him to fill my tooth. Because I am among those who cannot sit and do nothing, I looked for something to read among a stack of newspapers by the fireplace. I picked up the top paper to see what the Rochester folks were doing to make news.

As I was reading the B Section of the Rochester Daily News, a story caught my eye about a local dentist who was on trial in Federal Court. The story was accompanied by a picture of the Dentist's family gathered together in a circle, praying before the trial opened for the day—a truly amazing and beautiful story.

"Roy, have you seen this story about this dentist and his family? This is amazing!" I remarked. Roy took a closer look at the article and said, "Fred, this paper is over a year old. I just brought these newspapers up from the basement yesterday to start my fires. That story is about the Roncone family. They all came to know the Lord through that trial, and now he serves as book chairman for our chapter."

"Roy, I just spoke in your chapter and I bought a book

from your book table, but I didn't see any doctor there. His name tag only said, PAT." I replied.

Lights began to go off in my head. This has got to be more than a coincidence. Is there a possibility I might be able to see him today? My tooth had become more like an emergency. So I told Roy about my predicament..

The next thing I knew, he was on the phone talking to Dr. Patrick Roncone, DDS, who was still in his office at 1:30 PM on a Saturday afternoon, even though his office hours on Saturday were usually from 9:00 to noon. He was running a little late and was getting ready to go home for the day when our call came in. He told Roy to bring me right over. One way or the other he would take care of my toothache so I wouldn't be in pain for the evening meeting. Toothache and all, my "acutely accurate(?)" spirit of discernment just about went off the scale! A DIVINE APPOINTMENT? No, a DIVINE DENTAL APPOINTMENT, when I least expected it!

Roy didn't spare the horses getting me across town to Pat's office. A quick introduction, and the next thing I knew, my new dentist was drilling away like crazy. Soon my old tooth was feeling like new. Praise the Lord!

After he finished, we sat in Pat's office going over the details of how I happened to be there. This was God's amazing providence, no question about it. .

Pat said, "Fred can you come back in a few days so I can take another look at it, and put in a permanent filling? I'd also like to do a few fillings for you, and take a look at that old upper partial plate which no longer had any clips on it to hold it in place. I told him that it stayed in place "by faith," but that I certainly would welcome and be most appreciative for anything he could do for me.

When the day came for my next DIVINE DENTAL APPOINTMENT, Shirley and I traveled the one hundred or so miles from our home to Rochester, just praising the Lord all the way. My tooth soon had a new filling, and my dear

Brother Pat was telling us that he wanted to be certain that the fillings were in good and solid. His prescription was one large steak, medium rare, for me, and smaller steaks for his beautiful wife, Marilyn, and Shirley.

Several times during dinner Dr. Pat asked me if I was chewing on the new filling real hard so he could be sure it was OK before we made the long drive back to Homer. That evening was one of the most enjoyable we could ever remember. Pat and Marilyn shared their remarkable testimony with us—one of the most incredible we had ever heard. Pat had indeed been on trial. He and his family, with hands and hearts joined together, prayed each day in the front of the courtroom before the trial started. Not only were they praying for Pat, but for the prosecuting attorney who was doing his best to not only convict Pat, but to put him away forever.

I don't want to share all of Pat's testimony, which belongs to him and his family. But I can tell you some of the "rest of the story." As a result of this trial, Pat and Marilyn, their son Patrick, their daughters Wendy and Joanne, and nearly all of their families on both sides of the family became on-fire, born-again, Spirit-filled Christians. But that wasn't all! God also blessed the Roncone family with the most powerful fruit of the Spirit of love we ever encountered. Each member of the family loved each other and everyone else so much that, at first, we wondered if some of it might be "put on" for our benefit. But they had the real thing!

(Shirley and I still are returning for our dental work to the Roncone Family Center Dental Clinic where son Dr. Patrick, Jr. is the chief, and Pat, Sr. is his faithful partner. We never cease to marvel at the testimony of this precious family, whose love reaches out so powerfully to their neighbors, friends, and family wherever they may be. Since our first miraculous visit so long ago, each of their children has married and has children of their own. All are now spreading the love of Christ in ever widening circles. Their cup and ours truly "runneth over" because of the loving relationship we have with all of them. Shirley and I are the first ones to get hugs and kisses when we go for our semi-annual DIVINE DENTAL APPOINTMENT.

20

ELZEOR, MY DEAR
BROTHER IN CHRIST

"Hey Fred, wanna go fishin' ?" It was a childhood buddy, Elzeor Vinette from Lake Placid, on the phone.

You talk about music to my ears! That invitation sounded like Chopin, Mozart, and Beethoven all put together to me. It had been many years since Elzeor and I last fished the famous Ausable River together. With our special, secret methods, we never failed to catch our limit of the most colorful, beautifully speckled trout ever caught, anywhere. This would be an unforgettable day.

"You say, 'Do I wanna' go fishin?' Are you kidding me, Elzie? Do I want to go to heaven some day? Of course, I do. How soon do you want to get started?" I replied.

"Let's get an early start in the morning, Fred. Those fish are just layin' around down there waiting for us. We don't want them to get tired of waiting. OK?"

" OK!" I agreed.

Nice and early the next morning (the five-hour drive for me during the night wasn't even noticed!) we were off "like a dirty shirt" to our favorite fishing holes along the Ausable River.

"You get a good nights sleep, Elzie?" I asked

"Sleep, what's that? I hardly closed my eyes. What else is new? Have we ever slept the night before a fishing trip?"

"I thought maybe that now you got saved you didn't get so excited about these things!" I kidded my brother. "Well you thought wrong, Ol' Buddy. Sure I love Jesus now, but He makes me love everything else more than ever. Remember, Jesus also stayed awake a lot before special days. Right?" Elzie's eyes were twinkling.

"Right Elz! You're always right!" was all I could think of to say..

By sun-up we were casting dry flies into some of the best fishing water God ever made— just for us! We filled our lungs with the pure mountain air. We were serenaded by the birds singing their greetings to us and an old squirrel scolding us for intruding on his domain, all to the accompaniment of the water gurgling happily along as I suppose it had done for eons before. And for us to be there together with our best friend, Jesus, made the moments almost enchanting. The sounds, the smells, the sights all around us were more vivid than I could ever remember. The whole rhapsodic episode just about brought tears to my eyes. We didn't have to say anything! What could we have said?

About ten o'clock we crawled up and onto a bank between a couple of big white birches, and opened up our thermoses and donuts. That particular spot on the Ausable will always be my choice of the prettiest place in the world. The sweet presence of Jesus made that place into a sanctuary. Even our coffee tasted like pure gourmet blend.

"How many did you catch?" I wondered.

"Well, no keepers so far, Freddie? We're just getting

started. What do ya' expect? All this and fish too? Come on!"

Somehow, fish didn't seem to matter much. The joy of the Lord that flooded our hearts was more than enough. Were we discovering why Jesus always seemed to be so partial toward fishermen?

Then I saw big tears beginning to stream down my buddy Elzeor's cheeks. I waited for him to tell me about it if he wanted to. In a few moments, he began to tell me about a great burden he had for all of his relatives who lived within a few miles radius of him. There were probably more than a hundred, and only one cousin and his sister had accepted Jesus as their personal Savior. Maybe they thought he was a bit fanatical or something when he tried to witness to them. He prayed daily for each one of them by name, and thought of them constantly—even this day when he just wanted to forget anything and everything except being there with Jesus and me.

Everyone had seen the remarkable change in Elzeor since he came to know Christ. He had been a chronic depressive for years. If anyone passed him on the street, he wouldn't acknowledge them. He was in his own world of pain over the utter hopelessness of his condition. He had wondered many times if life was worth living anymore.

But now, with Jesus Christ living in His heart, everything was brand new. 2 Corinthians 5:17 says, *"If any man be in Christ he is a new creature. Old things have passed away, and behold, all things have become new."* Elzeor now had a big happy grin on his face most of the time. The depression had given way to the love of Christ Jesus in his life.

In addition, his short leg had grown out more than five inches—not all at once, but about one thickness of shoe leather each time he attended the Preston's Bible study/prayer meeting. Every time his friends there would pray for him, his leg would grow a little more, and Paul (Preston) would remove another layer of leather from his built-up shoe.

Nearly everyone in town could see that Elzeor wasn't the same man since my Brother, Don Morgan, had led him to the Lord. "Why don't my folks see what God has done for me, Fred? I'm a living, walking miracle."

"Let's pray for them, Elzie. I doubt if we'll ever be any closer to Jesus on this side of eternity than we are right now." "OK Fred, let's do it!" We joined hands and began to worship Jesus, and then prayed for Elzeor's family, one by one. Suddenly we became aware of the sweetest, most powerful presence of the Lord we had ever experienced. He was sitting right there on that bank with us. We could feel his precious nail-scarred hands encompassing ours. He was agreeing with us in prayer! His mighty power flowed through us like warm, liquid love. The scripture found in Matthew 18:19, *"Again I say to you, that if two of you agree on earth about anything that they may ask, it shall be done for them by my Father who is in heaven. For where two or three have gathered together in my name, there I am in their midst"* became totally real to both of us simultaneously. If two would be enough for God, what would three including Jesus Himself, be worth? We didn't know for sure how much of that we could stand, but we didn't want it to ever stop, either!

Nothing would ever compare to the experience we had shared that day. It was such a holy moment we couldn't talk about it. We returned home to our separate lives with a new joy and renewed strength. I wondered a lot about just how the Lord would answer our prayer. We didn't have long to wait. Not even a month passed until Elzeor's sister, called me.

With great sadness she said, "Brother Fred, Elzeor has gone home to be with the Lord. He was just sitting here in his recliner by the window with his Bible in his lap. He gave a big sigh and was gone. He didn't suffer and he wasn't sick. There were no warnings. He just went to be with Jesus."

The funeral was set for a couple days later. I fulfilled a

speaking engagement downstate on that day, and then left immediately for the funeral parlor in Lake Placid. I arrived just as the service was getting underway. Elzeor's sister came over to me and asked me to do the eulogy. I hesitated a moment or two, thinking I hadn't prepared anything. Then the Holy Spirit said, "You've been preparing for this almost all your life." "Oh," I responded, "I'd be happy to do that," and took my seat near my buddy Elzeor's casket.

As I arose to deliver the eulogy, I looked out over the hundred or more people in attendance, and found I recognized only a few of them. I assumed the rest were the ones Elzie had been praying for. My voice shook a little as I got started, but the peace of God settled on me. As close as I can remember, the Lord caused me to speak these words:

"About thirty years ago, my family and I moved a few doors down the street from Elzeor, and we became the best of friends. One day he came by our house, and said, "Hey Fred, Wanna' go fishin'?" I replied, " OK! Be with you in a second." And we were off to a lifetime of adventures that few boys ever experience. God put the Chubb Pond (we called it the Millpond) right behind our houses, because He knew we loved to fish and stuff.

We fished on the millpond, we swam in it, we had a boat in it, and in the wintertime we skated and skied on it, and fished through the ice. We would always cross over on it if we wanted to go downtown. Only the imagination of boys could fully take advantage of such a treasure. We weren't the only ones who lived along the Millpond either. There were muskrats, frogs, turtles, and ducks, and other birds of every description, and even beavers, who loved that little river. We could regularly catch three-pound rainbow trout right in our backyard.

Then I joined the Navy, got married and started a family, and graduated from R.P.I. in Troy. We lived in various places, but I seldom got back to Lake Placid for many years. When I was thirty years old, I had the wonderful experience of being born again into the Kingdom of God. Jesus Christ forgave my sin and came into my life. I was a new man. I joined a wonderful organization for Christian businessmen called Full Gospel Business Men. Soon, I was sharing my testimony everywhere I could around the world. I became an officer in the group, and one of my duties was to organize new chapters of FGBMFI.

I headed to Lake Placid, my hometown, as my first assignment. I met some really great guys, Dean Wykoff, Bill Vigne, Art Dick, Paul Preston and others. These were the men who were deeply interested in sharing their faith in Jesus Christ with other men. They became the new chapter officers. And we met monthly at the Mirror Lake Inn. We got good publicity and many other men joined us as they too received Christ.

But one man who sort of "fell through the cracks" was Elzeor. I've kicked myself for years that I didn't invite Elzie to come to one of our meetings. I just plain got too busy.

One day, after I had been to speak for the Lake Placid Chapter, I got a letter from Elzie telling me that he had seen in the newspaper that I had been there again, and hadn't come to see him. He said, "Freddy, when I read you had been here again and hadn't called me, I just cried." I immediately called my friend, Don Morgan, from Saranac Lake and told him about the situation. He knew Elzeor, and assured me that he would go right over to talk with him. Don was knocking on Elzie's door within the hour.

Later that day, Don called me back to tell me how Elzeor had received Jesus Christ as his personal Savior during their visit. What a day! Never had anyone's testimony of salvation touched my heart as his had. Two days later, Elzie was sitting in his favorite chair by the windows and one of his neighbors walked by—something that had

*happened thousands of times before. But this time was
totally different. He had this strange feeling that he loved
that person who was walking by. He went to his door and
called out to the person, just to say, "Hi". He sat on his
porch to see if this strange feeling would happen again
when someone else went by. The same thing happened again
and again. He loved everyone he saw, and wanted to talk to
them and tell them what was happening to him. Elzeor had
been invaded by the loving Spirit of the Lord Jesus Christ.*

During the eulogy I shared the whole story of our lifelong friendship, as well as our recent fishing trip, including
the amazing prayer we experienced. I told those dear folks a
little of how much Elzeor loved them and prayed for them,
each and every one, by name, each day. I shared how the
Lord Jesus sat on the riverbank with us as we prayed for
them. Tears were coming to some of the eyes of my listeners, as well as to mine.

As I brought my remarks to a close. I told them about
Elzeor's prayer for them—word for word. So as he sat in his
chair that day, there was only one thing for him to do. He
would lay down his life just to get each and every one of
you, his beloved relatives, together, so that I, his "ol' buddy
Freddy", could be with you today, and share the wonderful,
saving love of Jesus Christ with you.

I then paused long enough to give each one time to let
those words sink in. Each of those folks was recalling inci-
dents when they had refused to take Elzeor's Christian
witness seriously. Tears began to flow freely. I closed by
saying, *"As we continue in an attitude of prayer, with our
eyes closed and our heads bowed, let us all be thankful to
Elzeor for the sacrifice he made, his very own life, so that
each of you could know the ultimate sacrifice that Jesus
made for each one of us at Calvary. Is there anyone here
who would like to raise your hand and to acknowledge that*

you would like to have Jesus forgive your sins and come into your heart today?"

No one was counting that day, but I could see hands up everywhere. Then everyone followed me in saying a sinners' prayer. All I could do was turn around and tell Elzeor that he had done it. His prayers had all been answered. Now he could just enjoy heaven with Jesus, and wait for all those relatives to join him through those gates of pearl.

The priest came forward to say Mass. Things had dramatically changed in that place. The tears dried up and people were smiling. They all wanted to shake my hand and say nice things to me. The priest met me on the porch as I was leaving. He said, "Mr. Lawrence, that was wonderful. How did you do that? I feel all clean inside, it's wonderful." I could only praise and thank the Lord for allowing me to be a part of that whole scene with Elzeor. I could safely say that that funeral was the best Business Men's Fellowship meeting I ever attended—A DIVINE APPOINTMENT to be sure!

* * * * *

P.S. Elzeor Vinette passed away in January 1982. He was born with a genetic deformity of his body, including his face. When I met him as a ten year old, I was already taller than he was. His mother had to remove him from school because the kids harassed him so much about how he looked. Later in life he had some injections that caused him to grow to more than 6' 2" in a relatively short time. One of his legs didn't grow that much. Although his body was as deformed as it was, God built into Elzie a most Christ-like character. He enriched my life and the lives of everyone he met with his steadfast love for everyone, and his enthusiasm for the Gospel of Jesus Christ. When Elzeor and I talked, we used the idiom and expressions that we had used from the time we met as little boys. In sharing this story, it just didn't seem right to correct our language deficiencies. The main thing is that what he did resulted in the salvation of his very large family at his funeral.

21

GOD LOVES SAILORS

Many persons believe that a serious Christian shouldn't concern himself with such mundane things as taking vacations. After all, did Moses go off on vacation? Well, he did try to get away from it all once by going out to do some mountain climbing. It was sort of a businessman's holiday though. He and God had to write the Ten Commandments in stone while he did his sunbathing. And Moses fasted for the entire forty days. So it wasn't all fun and games, especially when he returned home.

What about King David? He stayed home for a bit of a break while all his men went off to fight a war. (2 Samuel 11-12). In his case, he'd have been better off leading his soldiers into battle than he was watching Bathsheba. However, I do think everyone needs a break once in awhile though, from his everyday duties.

I first met Jim at a Men's Advance at Watson's Homestead. Having heard about it on the radio, he had come to see what a Men's Advance was. Jim was somewhat dismayed by the length of the trip from Southern Vermont to the New York Finger Lakes. But, thank God, he came! He was introduced to Jesus and to a whole bunch of guys who really were excited about their faith. The next year, he returned with a whole carload of men from the Bennington, Vt. area. They really got turned on to Jesus and to soul-winning

Jim and his brothers returned home to found the Bennington Chapter, which was one of the great soul-winning arms of the Kingdom of God. For many years I thought of Bennington as the place to go when I really needed some love, and to see that love reaching out to a city and really making a difference there.

Jim was blessed to have a very supportive and enthusiastic wife, Ann, who was his greatest asset. Jim and Ann are both artists by profession, but also Servants in God's Kingdom. They have a nice sailboat that they sail on Lake Champlain each summer. For several years they have graciously invited Shirley and me to spend a week or two with them on the boat. This is one of their ministries, entertaining Christian workers on their boat during the summer. (Isn't God wonderfully thoughtful to provide folks who will share their vacation time with His ministers?)

One year, Shirley had to miss the vacation trip! Traveling the five or six hours each way to get to the Vermont marina was an important time for me, because the Lord and I just seem to communicate real well when I'm alone and not under pressure to get somewhere at a specific time. On that particular weekend I talked to the Lord about the nature of sailing. You can be out on that big lake with hundreds of other boats, but you are essentially alone. Even when you anchor your boat for the night in one of the hundreds of beautiful little bays, you are still alone with your own Christian friends. On top of that, vacationing on Jim and Anne's beautiful yacht is not exactly roughing it. You have all the amenities of home except on a smaller (37 ft.) scale.

Only in the ALLELUIA (the name of their boat) you have the luxury of moving her to any place you like on that one hundred-fifty-mile-long lake. If the sun gets a bit hot, you can just take in the sails and dive in. And if you wish to visit a nice restaurant in any of the towns or cities along the Lake, either in NY or Vermont, you just sail there, drop your anchor, and they'll usually come out to meet you in a little power boat and take you ashore. Not bad, eh? But wouldn't it be even more fun to have someone to witness to while on vacation.

Arriving at the *ALLELUIA* was always great fun. I got to hug my old friends, meet new boat owners who had arrived since I was there last, have a great reunion, and go for a refreshing swim.

A small change in plans for this year already had been made by the time I went aboard the ALLELUIA. The next morning we would sail across the bay to where some of Jim and Anne's old friends lived. They would be joining us with their own sailboat, sailing along with us for a couple days. This lovely couple would have with them their son, a 25-ish young man who worked at a store in Burlington; and their daughter Cassy and her husband Chris, both Air Force Majors on leave from Wright - Patterson Air Force Base in Ohio.

After all the introductions, we all sailed off in a northerly direction together with our new friends. Not only did we have a beautiful hot summer day, but also ideal winds for sailing—like you always picture while you are day-dreaming about a vacation during those cold Northeast winters. That evening we dropped anchor in a beautiful little bay on the Vermont side of the Lake.

Jim charcoal-broiled some steaks that were so tender you could cut them with a fork (everything tastes twice as good when you're sailing!). The conversation was lively, much of it about their families since they had last seen each

other. At one point, the discussion turned to the son who
was having some job difficulties; and then to the mother
who was having severe back pains that required her to get
out of the boat as often as possible to take a walk. But even
these difficulties could not mar what was a thoroughly
enjoyable evening.

The next day was another beauty. We stopped at a
favorite spot on the New York side, close to an old Railroad
trestle. It carried the trains over a nice little brook that had
wound its way through the woods before cascading down
the side of a rocky mountain. This picturesque setting also
included a naturally sandy beach for swimming, which we
all enjoyed immensely. That evening we weighed anchor in
Willsboro Bay, a favorite spot for sailors of all description.
Again, we enjoyed dinner together, and the conversation got
around to me and what I did for a living. (It is always a
highlight for me when folks want to know that I serve the
Lord, 100%.) After a brief discussion, we took Jim and
Anne's dog for a walk, and then all took another swim and
walk before dark. Before we said goodnight, I offered the
lovely young pair of Majors a copy or two of VOICE
Magazines that I just happened to have with me.

The next morning Cassy and Chris were scheduled to
depart for home in order to return to their duty station. We
took a walk before having breakfast together. Cassy and
Chris said they had really enjoyed reading the copies of the
VOICE Magazines the night before. Anne then mentioned
to the Mother (Agnes) that "Fred prays for the sick and
often God heals them." Agnes said she indeed would like
prayers for her back, and asked that we pray also for her
son's job situation.

We gathered together on their boat. I sat across from
Agnes, while the son sat just above us on the cabin. The
others sat in sort of a circle around us. The whole scene just
screamed out DIVINE APPOINTMENT, and the presence

of the Lord was glorious. I shared some scriptures with everyone, especially geared for salvation. Everyone agreed that together they would follow me in a sinner's prayer. It seemed like everything just flowed together so naturally that everyone was totally at ease. It couldn't have been better if we had rehearsed it.

By now the air was charged with anticipation. I shared some scriptures having to do with divine healing, and offered to pray for the bad back. She readily agreed, so I took her feet in my hands, held them together so everyone could see that one leg was considerably shorter than the other one. Bill (the father) estimated the difference for us at 3/4 to one inch—being an engineer, we knew he wouldn't exaggerate! The son was looking down directly from above us so that when I prayed, and his Mother's short leg grew to the same length as the other leg, his eyes nearly popped out of his head. God is so good!

Everything about that moment was divinely arranged for a miracle. As Agnes's leg grew out, the pain in her back subsided immediately. In a minute or two, she stood up and began to try all sorts of contortions that ordinarily would have caused her intense pain. Everyone praised the Lord for His mighty power and His healing touch. (When you use God's Word, and God punctuates what you've said with a nice miracle of healing, you may be certain that they have really heard what you said!)

Before Chris and Cassy left us, I asked if I could have their address. Coincidentally (?) they lived very near some dear friends of mine, Col. and Mrs. Hank Lackey. I told them I would try to reach Hank and Lill, and if they were home, Cassy and Chris could expect a call inviting them to a Full Gospel Business Men's meeting. So off they all went into the rising sun, with the Son in their hearts. And off I went in our trusty little dingy to the nearby marina to call Hank and Lill (for some reason they always call me their "angel".) We also prayed for the younger brother and fully believed he was due for a job change of some kind.

The Lackeys were happy to hear from me. They informed me that they would be attending the large and exciting Dayton Full Gospel Chapter Meeting the coming Saturday, the only Saturday that year that they would be home. The Dayton, Ohio Chapter had more than a hundred lifetime members, all of whom were stationed at Wright-Patterson. Of course, they would love to call Cassy and Chris to invite them to attend the meeting with them. Everything went exactly as the Lord had planned it. Cassy and Chris made a public profession of their faith in Christ, received the precious Baptism In The Holy Spirit, and joined FGBMFI for life that next Saturday morning.

Jim and Anne ran into the younger brother the following week. They learned that when he returned to work the next morning, everything had turned around for him and his job situation had improved greatly. He is now active in a good Spirit-filled church in Burlington, Vermont.

Cassy and Chris also became totally involved in a Spirit-filled Church in Dayton, Ohio. Not long after that, they were transferred to an Airbase in New Hampshire. I sent them a flyer and an invitation to our next Couples Advance at Silver Bay on Lake George, which they happily attended.

We had a great reunion just about a year later. God was leading them step-by-step into His perfect plan for their lives. They had retired from the Air Force that year, and Chris had enrolled in Gordon-Conwell Seminary in Boston to prepare for the ministry. The last time they sent me one of their exciting newsletters, Chris had graduated and had become co-pastor of a new Fellowship in Eastern New Hampshire. Isn't God fantastic? That was one of the greatest vacations I had ever had!

We often use Romans 8:28 , *"And we know, that God causes all things to work together for good to those who love God, to those who are called according to His purpose,"* but we don't always see the proof of this great promise as clearly as it was demonstrated on this occasion.

22

WITH HIS STRIPES WE ARE HEALED
Isaiah 53:5

Heart Attack #1

S hirley and I arrived home after several weeks of ministry among the New England and downstate NY chapters and churches, as well as the Anaheim World Convention. We were tired, but were still excited for all the folks we had seen God touch. (We have often said that it would be terrible to reach a point in life when we would take God's miracles for granted. I doubt if we ever will.)

I mentioned to Shirley that I had experienced chest pain during the last leg of our ministry trip. I was taking nitro glycerin tablets whenever she wasn't keeping an eye on me. (She has a tendency to worry about me, and we all know that worry is a sin, so I try not to show my feelings that much.) We had been gone from home about two months by then, so my responsibilities around our home were weighing heavily on my mind.

I had begun re-roofing our house early that Spring. It was still waiting for me just as I had left it—half done! My lawn looked worse than my neighbor's hay field. If I didn't mow it soon, my neighbors would complain to the Town officials. Then, when I went to our Post Office, I had at least a bushel basket full of mail, much of which would require an immediate response. On top of all that, Shirley had been reminding me of things that needed fixing around the house.

As I deposited the mail in my living room, I began wondering which of my numerous tasks I should tackle first. Of course, no right or wrong answer could be given for such a question. Everything was way overdue. As I started to express my anxiety, I suddenly felt very faint, sweaty, and sick-to-my-stomach. Suddenly I said, "Shirley, I'm going!" To which she replied, "Where are you going?" I sat back into my lounger, and felt myself leaving my body and rising toward the ceiling.

Shirley took instant action! Rushing to my side almost as I was sitting down, she put her hands on my chest and shouted, "Fred, in the Name of Jesus Christ, come back into your body right now. I command you not to do this to me. You get back here right now.

She wasn't about to take "No" for an answer, and she kept repeating herself until I did exactly as ordered. For a moment or two, I had a view of our living room from ceiling height. I saw myself and Shirley and heard her commands. Then I fell back into my body like a high diver.

Shirley says she was watching my eyes for some sign of life. When I returned to my body she shouted, "Fred Lawrence, you stay right here. Don't you dare go anywhere while I call the ambulance!" The next thing I knew, she was on the phone to someone telling them about my condition and telling them to hurry. While she was talking, I once again "rose to the occasion," going up to the ceiling again.

We wish we had a moving picture of that whole scene. She was talking on the phone and screaming at me at the same time: "Fred Lawrence, I command you to get back here, into your body, right now". I really didn't have much of a choice in the matter, so back I came.

In a few minutes, our living room was full of people. Most of them were medical emergency squad members, but others were from the fire and police departments. They hooked me up to various kinds of wires that were transmitting my vital signs to the Hospital Urgent Care doctor. We didn't know it then, but everything that was happening was being recorded on a cassette tape recorder: EKG readings, pulse and blood pressure, as well as comments from the emergency care nurse to the doctor. Several times she repeated, "No pulse, no blood pressure!" Fortunately, they later gave us a copy of that tape.

On it you can hear Shirley telling those men that she wasn't going to stay in the kitchen, no matter what they said. Then she said, "Fred needs me! Fred Lawrence, I told you to stay right here in your body. No, you come back here, right now!" Then the monitor picked up the sound of my heart resuming its functions, and of my blood pressure starting up again. Weird? Really weird! And if we didn't have it all on tape, we would find it difficult to believe ourselves.

Soon I was on the way to the Hospital, siren screaming, with Shirley right by my side. I praise God for a wife that won't take "No" for an answer. I really had little choice about continuing to live. God and Shirley weren't yet through with me. She is a true woman of faith and power. (Doesn't it seem strange that when you need your loved one the most—like I needed her—that they always try to make them go to another room? "Please, wait in another room until we call you," they say.)

The rest of the first day in the Hospital remains a blur to

me. My doctor spent considerable time resuscitating me. I had received a shot of morphine to which I was highly allergic. Apparently it was the morphine that caused me to have so many cardiac arrests.

Shirley was being restrained outside my room. She was reassuring the nurse that I was just having a talk with Jesus, and that I'd be right back as soon as the Lord was finished with me, and not to worry. Then I became aware of a dear Brother, Jim Wolfkiel, the bearded Pastor of the Episcopal Church and a good friend of mine. He was standing at the head of my bed, anointing me with oil while the Code 5 team was doing their work. It was the faith of God in Shirley and Brother Jim that brought me back, time after time (once after a period of nine minutes, we were told). In the meantime, someone had called CBN Radio and told them of my need for prayer. This, of course, alerted all my friends around the State of my heart attack.

(If you ever find yourself with a very full schedule, with only enough energy for half of your schedule, and not enough time and strength for any schedule, then consider having a good heart attack! Your schedule is cleared for you instantly and indefinitely! Nobody even questions why you can't fulfill your obligations. There may be other ways to do it, but that way you don't have to explain things to anyone!)

My doctor told me he was inserting a "swan-ganz" catheter into my heart to monitor triglycerides and other things. As he inserted the catheter through a vein in my neck or shoulder area, I felt the tube (or whatever he was using) entering my lung! Quickly, he realized he hadn't hit the desired vein, removed the tube, and reinserted it in a vein in my right arm.

This time all went well, except that air was gurgling out through the hole he had made in my lungs. He seemed to be satisfied that everything would be fine and left me with a punctured lung! As the lung began to collapse, the pain in my chest increased accordingly. During the night I was in such agony that the nurse called in another doctor. While he was trying to figure it all out, I started dying again. This doctor then called in a surgeon, who cut a hole between my ribs and into my lung without the benefit of any anesthetic.

The way they explained it to me later was that it was a tube within a tube, one putting oxygen under pressure into my lung, and the other suctioning the space between my lung and ribs, all designed to re-inflate my lung. This procedure seemed to be working until both lungs suddenly collapsed, making things quite interesting! I passed out again! Obviously, whatever they did got my lungs going again and I regained consciousness. They also figured out an alternate pain medication that worked quite well and allowed me to get a bit of rest.

After CBN radio announced my predicament, all of my friends tried to visit me, but weren't being allowed into my room. One of my dear Brothers in Christ, Charlie Booth, who had been saved and healed of a serious heart condition in one of our meetings, tried to get in to see me. The nurses—I had two nurses, one a private nurse and one that would intermittently come and adjust the computerized machine that gave me measured doses of oxygen and medication on a continual basis—repeatedly refused to allow him to come in. So he organized a Holy Ghost prayer and praise meeting in the waiting room that I could hear all the way down the hall. It sounded like heaven to me.

After a couple days, I had a most welcome visit from my dentist, and dear friend Dr. Patrick Roncone, his wife Marilyn, and their beautiful daughter Wendy from Rochester. Because he was a doctor, they allowed them to visit me for a few minutes. These dear friends gathered around me and began to pray fervently. They spoke words of love and encouragement to me like Jesus would have if He were standing there (I wanted them to never leave me). As we joined in prayer, I watched the Shekinah glory of God filled my room in a most unusual way.

Both nurses were transfixed—they couldn't move a muscle! They, along with the rest of us were bathed in the Holy Spirit. I recall blinking my eyes a few times to see why they seemed so blurry, but they were OK. It was just that my room was filled with a golden glow. The love and power of Christ were coursing through my body in waves. For a few moments, I thought I'd be able to get up and go home after such a powerful manifestation of the Holy Spirit. But, it still wasn't God's timing for me to leave.

After my friends left for their two-and-half-hour drive back home, my nurse asked, "Mr. Lawrence, who were those people?" Now if she hadn't known who they were, they would never have gotten into my room. What she really wanted to know was about the amazing power and love of the Holy Spirit she had experienced while they were with us. ."My, what a beautiful family your friends were. We couldn't even move while they were here." There wasn't much I could say, except that they were Spirit-filled believers in Jesus Christ, and that what we all felt was the sweet presence of Jesus Christ, and the marvelous glory of God.

(I should add that while in prayer and meditation about that amazing visit, the Lord directed me to Isaiah 60:1-3 *"Arise, Shine; for your light has come, and the glory of the Lord has risen upon you. For behold, darkness will cover the earth, and deep darkness the people. But the Lord shall rise upon you, and His glory shall be seen upon you. And nations shall come to thy light, and kings to the brightness of thy rising."* The same glory the Lord spoke of through Isaiah also was upon us during the Roncone's visit.)

My doctors decided that I should be transferred to the VA Hospital in Syracuse for further examination and treatment. Often the VA gets a "bad rap" because their treatment is not always like your home Hospital. But my experiences have nearly always been positive. The night before I was transferred, the nurse told Shirley that I seemed a bit down about the pending transfer. She asked Shirley, "What could I say to him that might lift his spirits?" Shirley replied, "Just ask him what he does for a living."

When the nurse came in to get me ready for the night she said, "Mr. Lawrence, what do you do for a living?" My immediate response was, "I go everywhere telling folks how much Jesus Christ loves them, and how much He is able to do for those who put their trust in Him." She thought for a few seconds, and then told me an interesting story. As I lay there in bed listening to her, I thought what a great time and place for a DIVINE APPOINTMENT!

The nurse had two totally out-of-control kids at home. She was embarrassed to admit that she hated both of them. Her husband, a policeman, worked during the day while she slept. Then when she went to work, he took over the baby-sitting job and tried to deal with the kids. The strain on their marriage had become almost unbearable, and she didn't know which way to turn.

The Lord was very gracious and gave me some comforting and encouraging words for her. She sat back against the edge of my bed and took my hand as we prayed a sinners' prayer together. While we were praying, the night Charge Nurse came to my door and looked in. I wondered what she thought as she closed my door and left. By then the nurse was weeping profusely. The Spirit of God had come upon her to convict her of her sin and of her need for a Savior. Once again the power of God filled my room as that dear lady was born again into the Kingdom of God. All of her fear and frustration were gone, and she became a new creature in Christ. God's love for her and her family filled her being. She quickly finished her tasks and left with tears of joy in her eyes. I never saw her again, but I'm certain I'll see her again in Heaven.

One of the VA nurses on the Cardiac Care Unit at the Syracuse VA was waiting for them to push me into the room. Later she told me that while she watched me entering the room, she said to a fellow nurse, "He is a man of God." She was a very precious Sister in Christ, and the Holy Spirit bore witness to both of us that we were fellow Christians.

While I was still a patient at the VA, I had a visit from Pastor Don Yarborough and Dr. Bob Barstow from Oneonta. Only the Lord knows how much I needed their visit and ministry just then. They lived so far away from where I was, that I was just really blessed to see them. Don and Bob prayed and sang worship songs, and really had a Holy Ghost service right there. My room, not unlike all the other cardiac-care units, had a video camera by which the nurses constantly monitored my activity. The video camera captured the whole "service" for the nurses at the desk." My nurse told me later that we had a large audience in the nurse's station being blessed by one more unforgettable DIVINE APPOINTMENT. "God always has a ram in the bushes," she exclaimed. Don and Bob will always remain two of my favorite people.

The VA doctors checked me over thoroughly with all their modern equipment and numerous examinations for about a week. They concluded that my heart appeared to be perfectly fine, and that no evidence could be found that I had ever had a heart attack. No explanations were given for the difference between their findings and those of my family doctor! I leave the final analysis with my Lord.

An equally astonishing set of circumstances greeted me when I returned home: all of my hospital bills had been paid, my lawn was neatly mowed, my roof was complete, and all of my mail had been answered. Praise the Lord!

Washington For Jesus

At the time I had the heart attack, I was the New York State Chairman for "Washington For Jesus", a projected gathering of Christians on the Mall in Washington to pray for our nation. I was deeply concerned because I knew this was a very important event, yet I didn't know how to go about motivating Christians all across the State to go to Washington, D.C. to pray. My first task was to enlist one good strong Christian businessman to coordinate the work in each of the 37 Congressional Districts.

One of the first things God did to help me fulfill my responsibilities was to have my illness advertised all over the State by CBN radio. By then I was quite well known throughout most of the State, so when people heard about my problem they began to call Shirley to find out how I was. Just about everyone who called would enquire if they could do anything for us. Shirley had a map of the districts, and would find out exactly where all these well-wishers lived. She told them of the predicament I was in by being the State Chairman of an event that I was unable to fulfill. One by one she had an X in every district, with some of the finest Christian men willing to help us with the Washington For Jesus project..

Pastor John Jimenez, National Chairman for Washington For Jesus, had called all the leaders and coordinators from around the country together for a national rally to be held at his church in Virginia Beach, Va. Shirley volunteered to go in my place, assuring me that she would bring home every bit of information she could get her hands on. I thank the Lord that she has a photographic memory and good organizational skills, for when she returned from that Rally, she not only had the audio tapes, but also had remembered almost word for word everything that the speakers had said. She also recalled what they wore, including the various shades of color of the ladies dresses, and even their hair-do's. If I had been there myself, I couldn't have collected that much data. As a result, we had all the instructions and literature we needed to distribute proper information all across New York. With these materials, our program began to go forward by leaps and bounds in spite of, rather than because of me.

Thus, God brought together a statewide program that I could never have done. Whatever questions people called about, Shirley had the answers on the tip of her tongue.

The caravan of buses loaded with Christian prayer warriors provided one of the greatest sights we had ever seen as they pulled into the great Washington, DC Mall for the Washington For Jesus gathering! Not carloads, but busloads of people from every State and many foreign nations. Official estimates of the number of participants were upwards of a million people! Glory to God! We have good reason to believe that the prayers of those precious people made a very dramatic difference in the life of our great Nation. Once again God proved to us how perfect his strength can be demonstrated through the weakness of two of His servants.

I am quite certain that the first thing the average Christian would do if he were me, having just had a heart attack, would be to resign immediately from a position as important as the one I had. And who would have criticized us. But since I hadn't volunteered for the job, and the Lord knew I'd be getting sick, then what right did I have to resign? And God got all the praise for a job well done, and another DIVINE APPOINTMENT, of major proportions.

23

GOD'S ARMOR
Eph. 6:13

"**A**ll right, Anne, you may rest now and return home. The victory has been won." God was speaking to Anne Hart, a prayer intercessor. She had been praying fervently in the Spirit for more than two hours while walking up and down a dirt road outside of town, for what she didn't know, but obviously for something the Holy Spirit felt was very important. When the peace of God came, she knew her work was finished and her prayer answered. Anne returned to her home.

Later that evening after the Williamsport, Pa. Fellowship meeting, Anne was sharing her unusual experience with the Chapter President and his wife. She was still wondering what or whom she had prayed for that required such a gut-wrenching time of intercession. I was the speaker for that meeting, and after I finished praying for those who came forward for ministry, I started for the door. My gracious host and hostess, Dr. and Mrs. Ed Fenner, were chatting with

Anne as I made my way back to where they were talking. A lady approached me, with tears streaming down her cheeks. She had been seated near the back of the room, to the left of the podium. She was very hesitant about sharing her experience with me—afraid that she might not have seen what she thought she saw, thinking it might have been her imagination. I put her at ease, and told her to tell me what she saw. She was greatly relieved to learn that she wasn't the first to tell me about the phenomena that had taken place.

As I was being introduced to the gathering to speak, she saw what she thought was Jesus standing behind me. He moved with me to the podium and stood with me all the while I spoke. His arms were outstretched to the audience, with his robe sleeves touching my shoulders and his hood overshadowing his face.

I responded to her that she was only one of several people who had told me. They had all been seated in different parts of the audience. Each thought they might have been the only one to see Him, as those around them didn't see Jesus. Those who said they saw Him all saw the same thing. But what could have caused this remarkable appearance?

That lady and I then joined the others near the door and soon realized that we were all discussing the same thing, only different aspects of it. Mrs. Hart shared her experience again for us—the fervent prayer on the country road, etc.. We joined together at a restaurant for a late snack, during which I shared what I believed this whole thing had been about.

Early that morning, I was awakened by severe chest pain, was perspiring profusely, and was feeling lightheaded and nauseous. I had experienced the same symptoms on at least four previous occasions, all of which had been diagnosed at hospitals as heart attacks. This would be the fifth. But this one was different.

I was alone in the basement bedroom of my dear friends the Fenners. A bottle of nitro-glycerin tablets were in my brief case, as usual. I never knew when one of these attacks would hit me again, even though I believed with all my heart that the Lord had healed me. But I carried the nitros, just in case. An act of unbelief? Perhaps. But I believed as much as I knew how, and confessed my healing daily.

Consciously or unconsciously I had decided that, when and if the next attack came, I was not going to seek medical help. Either the Bible and its many promises concerning healing were true, or they weren't! How could I continue to travel all over the countryside declaring Jesus Christ, the same yesterday, today and forever while walking around half expecting another attack at any time. Being alone made this declaration a bit easier than it would have been if Shirley had been with me. She would have had me in that hospital before I could finish telling her about it. Furthermore, if I had told Mrs. Fenner, she too would have called the ambulance for me, and that would be the end of my ministry opportunities for that weekend.

I said, "Lord Jesus, I cannot believe that you have brought me all the way down here to Williamsport to be in the hospital. So I am going to stand firmly on your sure word from Matthew 8:17b, *'He Himself took our infirmities, and bore our sicknesses.'* If you wish to have the Fenners get involved with this, then please speak to her to knock on my door and inquire about me in some way. Also, Shirley has my phone number and she could call me. In either case I will tell the truth."

"In the meanwhile this pain is awfully uncomfortable and I'm going to ease it up a bit with nitroglycerin. But please don't delay my healing because of the pills. I need your healing touch just now more than ever. In case you choose to take me home to be with you, I sincerely pray that you will blot out all of my iniquities and forgive me of all the sins I have committed, either intentionally or unintentionally. I now believe I am ready and willing to meet You face to face, today."

The time then was about 5:30 AM. I continued to take 2 nitro tablets about every ten minutes until they were all gone. I'm sure I'm not the first person to wrestle with a heart attack before the Lord. But it was the first time I had done it. It was a struggle, the magnitude of which I cannot describe for you. About 8:00 AM the pain subsided just enough to give me hope that healing was on its way. I also ran out of nitros at that time.

As I was relating my experience with my friends that evening, I learned that Mrs. Hart had begun to pray for me with great fervency about 8:00 AM. She had willingly joined me in my intense spiritual struggle with the heart attack. At exactly 10:00 AM the pain stopped, the same time my Sister Anne was dismissed from her prayer vigil. Glory to God! How I praise the Lord that the fantastic gift of praying in tongues can allow a person to pray a perfect prayer, for something or someone they may not even know! (Romans 8:26)

I went on to relate that I was left in a very weakened condition by that event. I ate a little breakfast and returned to my bed. That afternoon I tried taking a walk to gain back some of my strength. After an hour or so, I returned to bed until time to go to the meeting. Most of us have read *II Corinthians 12:9, "And He said unto me (Paul is speaking.) My grace is sufficient for thee: for My strength is made perfect in weakness. Most gladly therefore will I rather glory in my infirmities, that the power of Christ may rest upon me."* It looked to me like I would get to see how this scripture worked its way out in my life.

When I was introduced to speak that evening, I didn't think I was strong enough to rise to the occasion. But that was when Jesus came on the scene in person. My weakness became His strength, both to stand up and then to walk to the podium and open my mouth. Jesus Christ, my Blessed

Redeemer, came to my rescue and ministered through me much like a puppet would be moved by its puppeteer.

Later I tried unsuccessfully to find out if anyone audio-taped the meeting. The reaction of everyone I spoke to said that my demeanor had been quite natural and relaxed. They said my message was very encouraging and personal, as if God were speaking directly to each one of them. I don't recall how many of those people gave their hearts and lives to Jesus that night, but I know there were several.

* * * * *

I have been examined by the doctors numerous times since that night, but never has any trace of heart damage been found. I have had a pacemaker put in my chest because my pulse rate was so slow all the while, but still no sign of heart damage. On a couple of occasions during times of stress, I have felt a certain tightness in my chest. But that only reminds me to relax and let Jesus' strength work through the stressful situation I was in.

Yes, I did think of Jacob's wrestling match with God. (Genesis 32:24). However, I never felt I was wrestling with God. And a good thing it was for me or I, too, might have been crippled for life, like Brother Jacob was. My struggle was with the heart attacks and not with God. I thank the Lord for the Holy Spirit's intervention in my situation, and for Sister Hart, who unknowingly stood in intercession for me against that powerful enemy. Isn't God wonderful! Even a heart attack can become a DIVINE APPOINTMENT if you are in God's perfect will.

A special flight to Florida

When I retuned home, I had my Doctor check me out. He suggested I take a little time off to relax from my busy schedule. I called my buddy, Hugh Bickford, in Naples, Florida, who recommended I come down there and visit him and his wife, Mary, for awhile. Shirley would remain at home and take care of things there.

One of the items in the little book they give you when you have heart problems is that you should avoid flying because of the pressure in an airplane. Only I had never read that part of the book! We had hardly left the ground when I began to have chest pain. I took my New Testament out of my pocket and asked God to please show me what to do. My Testament seemed to open up by itself to Psalm 57:7 *"My heart is fixed, Oh God, my heart is fixed: I will sing and give praise."*

With my first reading of that scripture, I thought the words weren't referring to my heart's being healed, but rather that *"My heart is steadfast, Oh God, my heart is steadfast."* But the Holy Spirit spoke clearly to me that I was to stop arguing and receive that Word from the Lord exactly as it was written. So I began to say those words, *"my heart is fixed, my heart is fixed,"* and then I began to sing those words. The more and louder I sang, the less and less my chest pain became. I didn't dare to stop even though I was attracting the attention of my fellow passengers.

The man who was seated to my left was reading a <u>Playboy Magazine</u>, and was admiring the centerfold when I began to sing from my Bible. He took one look at me, got up, and ran down the aisle, never to return. The woman on the other side wasn't lucky enough to be close to the aisle, so she turned her back to me and appeared to be looking out the window.

I said, "Dear Lord, what am I to do? The only thing that helps my pain is singing Psalm 57:7, and nobody seems to appreciate my rendition." I tried to sing more quietly, but didn't dare to stop.

During our stopover in Philadelphia, some of my audience left the plane, but a few more got on. While on the ground, the pressure in the cabin let up and my chest went back to normal. But it started right up again as soon as we took off. So I had to continually quote those blessed words, "My Heart Is Fixed" all the way to Miami. What a trip!

I had to change planes in Miami. It was specified on my ticket that I was to be taken to the next leg of my journey in a wheelchair. The lady that pushed me turned out to be a Spirit-filled Christian, who mentioned my "Heart is Fixed" song as we walked along to my next flight. She somehow understood what was happening, and stopped a moment to pray for me.

The last leg of my trip to Naples was on a small "prop" type plane that was not pressurized, so no heart pain returned. I was very happy when that little plane landed in Fort Myers and my feet were once again on the ground.

I highly recommend Psalm 57:7 to anyone experiencing heart problems. It is the best medicine I ever took, and led me to have a DIVINE APPOINTMENT at 30,000 feet.

24

DYING TO SELF

When you are forgotten, or neglected, or purposely set at naught, and you don't sting and hurt with the insult or the oversight, but your heart is happy, being counted worthy to suffer for Christ.
THAT IS DYING TO SELF!

When your good is evil spoken of, when your wishes are crossed, your advice disregarded, your opinions ridiculed, and you refuse to let anger rise in your heart, or even defend yourself, but take it all in patient, loving silence.
THAT IS DYING TO SELF!

When you lovingly and patiently bear any disorder, any irregularity, any impunctuality, or any annoyance; when you stand face to face with waste, folly, extravagance, spiritual insensibility, and endure it as Jesus endured.
THAT IS DYING TO SELF!

When you are content with any food, any offering, any climate, any society, any raiment, any interruption, by the will of God.
THAT IS DYING TO SELF!

When you never care to refer to yourself in any conversation, or record your own good words, or itch after commendations, when you can truly love to be unknown.
THAT IS DYING TO SELF!

When you can see your brother prosper, and have his needs met, and can honestly rejoice with him in spirit, and feel no envy, nor question God, while your needs are far greater, and you are in desperate circumstances.
THAT IS DYING TO SELF!

When you can receive correction or reproof from one of less stature than yourself, and can humbly submit inwardly as well as outwardly, finding no rebellion, or anger or resentment rising up within your heart.
THAT IS DYING TO SELF!

Are you dead yet? In these last days, the Spirit would bring us to the cross, "That I may know him...and being made conformable unto his death." Phil. 3:10.
THAT IS DYING TO SELF!

25

SICK UNTO DEATH
Phil 2:27

North Carolina

S hirley and I have always been quite excited about the opportunities we have had to serve the Lord as Convention speakers. So when we are invited to speak at such an auspicious occasion, we know that God has spoken to those folks who invited us. He alone has full charge of our itinerary. We had agreed to be at the Western Carolinas Convention in September of 1982. I would present the Worldwide Outreach of the Fellowship, and Shirley would speak for the Ladies Luncheon. The Convention was being held at the beautiful Ridgecrest Conference Center in Asheville, N.C.

Three weeks before the Convention, I was stricken with another heart attack. I had come to believe that these attacks were not of God and that I wasn't going to let them rob me of the joys of our ministry. Two weeks after the attack, we ignored all the doctor's orders and admonitions and spoke in a downstate chapter. If I held up OK in a chapter meeting, we believed I would be strong enough to do the meetings in Carolina.

Our ministry downstate did not go well at all. We encountered a young man (actually he was the Chapter President's son) who was addicted to drugs and alcohol. The devil told him that we were there to steal from him, so he was assigned by old slewfoot to do away with us. His attack was ferocious, but the Lord graciously delivered us from the enemy's hand. However, we were forced to return home without fulfilling our obligation there. In over twenty years of serving the Lord, we had never suffered that kind of defeat. Yet somehow having come through that incredible experience, we knew that only God could have delivered us. So it was a victory for the Lord, and not a defeat.

When we got home, North Carolina was on my mind day and night. Should we just go in faith, believing that my health would not be a factor, or should we play it safe and stay home? Our Couples Advance was only three weeks away, so staying home and making final plans for that was very tempting. I decided that if I could make it through the ordeal we went through the previous weekend, then I could handle anything that might arise. So on Thursday morning, we took off for Asheville.

When we arrived at the Washington National Airport, our connection for the next flight was all the way at the other end of the Airport. We had only a few minutes to make the second section of our flight. I was carrying my briefcase and Shirley had her carry-on. We ran the mile or so to the other end of the Airport, and arrived at the gate just as they were pulling the gate back from the plane. When we told them who we were, they put the gate back and allowed us to board. Unfortunately, our luggage didn't make the quick connecting flight. I will admit that I took several pills for my chest pain as we were running.

For most of my adult life, I would get a pain in my right side if I ran for any distance. This time was no exception. Only this time, the pain in my side didn't subside like it usually did. And when we arrived in Asheville, we found that no one was there to meet us as promised. Then when our bags failed to arrive with us, we wondered if these were indications of further trouble ahead. For lunch I ate half an egg sandwich that just didn't seem to agree with me. We wondered if I had a case of nerves. Finally someone came to take us to Ridgecrest.

On our way to the Conference Center we passed a big sign indicating the way to the VA Hospital. We both took notice of it, but the Holy Spirit told Shirley that I would be a patient there. She didn't know if my heart would become a problem again, or if my side-ache was a bigger problem than we thought. She wisely kept that information to herself until much later.

After registering and meeting the businessmen, we attended the large evening kickoff meeting in the beautiful auditorium. We had looked forward to hearing the evening speaker, an evangelist/Bible teacher from the West Coast. The audience numbered close to 2500 people. I was seated almost directly behind the speaker on the platform. About half way through the speaker's presentation, it felt like a hot poker had been driven through my belly. I kept my composure by the grace of God. My thought was that if I could hold on until the speaker finished, I could be prayed for to be healed. After his twenty-five or thirty minute talk, he began to pray for those coming forward for various needs. I went down and stood nearly in front of him. I believe he thought I was there to catch the people who were being slain in the Spirit, so he didn't pray for me!

That night was a nightmare. The pain was excruciating.

Shirley spent the night on her knees beside my bed, laying her hands on my stomach and praying. Nothing helped! At daybreak, someone knocked on our door and announced that I should prepare to speak at the morning meeting. Apparently the man who was scheduled to speak that morning had some sort of crisis and had to go home to California.

I knew that God had given me a message to share with the folks there, and it was burning inside me, just waiting to be brought forth. Ten minutes before I was scheduled to speak, the pain completely stopped. We were thinking what a miracle it was for me to receive my healing just in the nick of time.

After a quick shower, I got dressed and we went to the meeting. I spoke for about 45 minutes under a precious anointing of the Spirit, experiencing no pain whatsoever. When my message was complete, the pain again descended on me, doubling me over with its intensity.

The MC of that morning meeting was Dr. Fred Wenzel, a physician/surgeon, and a Field Representative for FGBMFI. Dr. Wenzel shared with us how he had been the Chief of Surgery at Cook County Hospital in Chicago before he and his family had moved to western North Carolina. When I finished speaking, he came to the mic and told the people that God had spoken to him while I was speaking.

He read a passage of scripture to the people from Philippians 2:25-30. How I praise God for the gifts of the Holy Spirit, especially in times like that. He read, *"But I thought it necessary to send Brother Lawrence to you* (The Holy Spirit had inserted my name in there in place of Epaphroditus.) *my brother and fellow worker and fellow soldier, who is also your messenger and minister to our need; because he was longing for you all and was distressed because you heard that he was sick* (I had called them about my heart condition before we left home). *For he [is] sick, to the point of death, but God had mercy on him, and not on him only but also on me, lest I should have sorrow upon sorrow. Therefore I have sent him all the more eagerly in order that when you see him you may rejoice. . . . Therefore receive him in the Lord with all joy, and hold men like him in high regard; because he [is] close to death for the work of Christ, risking his life to complete what was deficient in your service to me."* Brother Fred Wenzel suggested that Shirley and I sit in chairs down in front of the platform while all the people gathered around and laid hands on us for my healing.

We prayed fervently, and I believed with all the faith I had that God would heal me. We walked over to the dining room and I continued to be sick. Shirley told Dr. Wenzel about my recent illness and about my hospitalization in the VA Hospital in Syracuse. After a brief examination he volunteered to drive us to the VA Hospital. I've always been amazed how the Lord provided a Spirit-filled surgeon to be with Shirley and me during those frightful days. He was a tremendous blessing to us.

Shirley and Dr. Wenzel waited while the VA doctor examined me and did a blood test. When your appendix ruptures, your abdomen is no longer any more sensitive in one area than it is in any other area. Everything hurts! My blood test came back almost negative, so sometime on Friday afternoon they sent me back to the Conference Center.

By Saturday morning I was in critical condition. Dr. Wenzel volunteered his services to the doctors at the VA to operate on me, but they politely declined his offer. He told them that he was authorized by the State of North Carolina to do operations. However, Dr. Howe, the Doctor on duty that weekend at the VA Hospital, told Dr. Wenzel that he was fully aware of the seriousness of my case. Dr. Wenzel was about to take me to a City Hospital when Dr. Howe agreed to do an exploratory operation on me. Because I was getting worse, they returned me to the Hospital. This time my blood count had shot way up, and other signs indicated serious trouble. The VA Doctor called in his emergency surgical team and began to prepare for the surgery.

Around noontime on Saturday, the Directors of the Convention had an emergency situation on their hands. They had planned to have Shirley and I conduct the Saturday afternoon healing service, but now with me in the Hospital, what should they do? They had prayed and felt God had told them to have Shirley minister that afternoon. One thing of which we both were very conscious was that as servants of the Lord Jesus, His work came before anything else. So while I was being prepared for surgery, Shirley was holding a healing service for the 2500 people in the Conference Center Auditorium.

Now wouldn't you think that if God wanted to demonstrate His healing power through Shirley as He did, that He would make me the first one in line for that ministry? But no, my condition continued to deteriorate. The miracle healing service at the Conference Center went better than anyone ever expected. Shirley had been fasting for more than a month by that time, and the spiritual power in her life had never been stronger. The worship leader led the people into praise and worship, and as the praises of God's people ascended into heaven, God began to heal people all over the auditorium. The gift of the Word of Knowledge flowed freely, showing Shirley exactly what God was doing for the people. Dr Wenzel, working with Shirley, helped tremendously by documenting for the audience the reality of what God was doing in the lives of those He was healing.

People began coming into the auditorium for the evening meeting before Shirley and Fred Wenzel finished the afternoon healing service! When they were through, they rushed to the Hospital. I vaguely remember being wheeled into the operating room, and meeting Shirley in the hallway. They stopped only long enough for her to give me a kiss. Then Shirley and Fred went to the waiting room to pray while the operation was in progress.

Indeed, my appendix had ruptured on Thursday evening. By Saturday I had developed acute peritonitis and gangrene. When I began to come out of the anesthesia, they had me on my feet, my arms taped to I-V stands on both sides of me, and tubes coming out of me in all directions. Someone was holding me up from behind while the doctor suctioned out my lungs that had filled up during the operation. If you've ever had something in your windpipe, you know how violently it makes you cough. The suction tube was causing me great distress. Every cough made my belly scream with pain.

As I stood there with my arms outstretched, totally naked, and sicker than I had ever been in my life, I found that the Lord Jesus was sharing a very important truth to me. My entire body screamed in pain. It wasn't a natural pain. It far exceeded any pain I had ever experienced. Not only were my little toes screaming with pain, but also every little part of me including the hairs on my head were crying out in agony. I don't know how long this experience lasted, maybe three or four minutes, before I passed out.

In the midst of all that, I became aware that God was showing me a scripture from Matthew 8:16-17 *"When evening came, many who were demon-possessed were brought to Him, and he drove out the spirits with a word and healed all the sick. This was to fulfill what was spoken through the prophet Isaiah: 'He Himself took up our infirmities and carried our diseases.'"*

I'd been told that this quotation from Isaiah 53 referred only to spiritual healing. However, when our blessed Lord went to Calvary, He not only bore all the sins of the world, but He also became deathly ill, carrying on His own precious sinless body every pain and sickness experienced by man from the day of Adam and Eve until the end of this age. It is beyond our comprehension! I'll never know if God arranged these circumstances in order to show me this tremendous truth, or if I was going through the circumstances of my illness and God chose that time to reveal that truth to me. In either case, I have never been the same since.

No, I didn't receive my healing that day and walk out of the hospital! However, armed with that knowledge, Shirley and I have had the faith to walk in a ministry that has touched thousands of lives in many parts of the world with the healing virtue of the Lord Jesus Christ. I could speak for a week on the incredible truths God showed me from those verses of scripture in Isaiah 53 and Matthew 8 during those incredible days

They returned me to my bed in the intensive care unit where I stayed for the next five weeks. On the second day, I told Shirley that I had dreamed that our dear friends, the Whites, came and stood at the foot of my bed and sang me a song. Then I dreamed that they had ministered to the other men in that room. Shirley told me that I hadn't dreamed that, but that the Whites had stopped by to minister to us as they were driving through that area on their way to our Couples Advance at Silver Bay, NY, where we had invited them to minister in music. They had heard over CBN radio that I was very sick in that VA Hospital, so they came to minister to me on their way north. They then were able to share about my condition with all of our friends at the Advance, so they could pray for us. Shirley had wisely called our friend and brother, Luke Sanford, from Hartford, CT to stand in for me at the Advance.

God always knows exactly what He is doing in matters pertaining to His saints. We have always thought it was so neat that God put me in the Asheville VA Hospital, the one VA Hospital in the country devoted solely to heart conditions, and that Dr. Howe was the chief surgeon for heart by-pass operations. The problems that arose concerning my lungs and heart while recovering from a ruptured appendix were routine for Dr. Howe.

One Sunday morning after a sleepless night, and still on the critical list, the Lord ministered to me in a beautiful way. I was sitting in a chair by my bed while the nurse's aide made my bed and gave me a bath. She was a beautiful black girl, whose name I don't recall, but whose mannerisms and demeanor indicated to me that she really loved the Lord. While she washed my feet, I knew in my spirit that something more was going on than just getting my feet cleaned. Tears were streaming down the cheeks of that young lady and were falling on my feet. She washed them off. But while this foot washing was going on, I felt the love of Christ ministering to me in a powerful way. Christ's very life was being poured out on me. *"In Him was life, and that life was the light of men."* (John 1:4)

God had been using Shirley and me in a healing ministry for perhaps ten years before this hospital experience. Everywhere we went, we had shared the wonderful truths of the scriptures that promise us healing and health. Now God was giving us vivid illustrations of the things we had been teaching. If Jesus *"healed all who were sick to fulfill Isaiah's prophesy"* then, He was still doing it today.

Shirley had seen God heal so many sick persons that she almost neglected the most important truth of all, that Jesus Christ came to *"seek and to save those who are lost."* It seemed to be very important to Shirley to stay with me about ten hours a day. Much of that time I would be asleep, so Shirley would talk to the men about Jesus. Hers is a very direct approach, catching many off guard and eliciting from them an immediate and honest response. "Sir, my name is Shirley. Do you know Jesus Christ as your personal Lord and Savior? If the answer was "Yes," then she would tell them how very much Jesus loved them and how He wanted to heal their bodies, even as He had healed her so many times. And would they mind if she prayed for them?" However, if the answer was "No," or if it was very indefinite, she would simply ask if they would like to receive Him as their Lord and Savior. One after another of the men in that Hospital were coming into a personal relationship with Christ while we were there.

We normally don't keep a score card or record of what God does for people when we are ministering to them. But in this case, we took down their names and addresses with the promise that they would receive a subscription to VOICE Magazine. When we got home and counted the number of subscriptions we would have to order, we found that the fifty men we had asked God for before we ever left home, had come to the Lord Jesus in that Hospital. We have no idea how many of the patients received healings, but it was significant enough for Shirley to receive recognition from the top Hospital Administrator. Everyone in that Hospital had come to know her name, and many also came to know her Master, the Lord Jesus Christ. During the five weeks I was there, we counted four complete turnovers of the four other patients who shared my ICU room. So God was doing some wonderful things in that place while I was sick.

God also had provided us with a most precious Christian couple for Shirley to stay with while I was in the Hospital. They lived two miles down the road from the Hospital. He was a lawyer, and they provided a car for Shirley as well as a lovely room and bath. They just couldn't seem to do enough for my dear wife. Shirley's hostess, an active AGLOW member, arranged for Shirley to speak and minister in all of the area AGLOW Chapters while we were there. One young lady Shirley ministered to in her home was delivered of epilepsy. Shirley's fast lasted until we finally got back home. Only eternity will reveal the things God accomplished during those days.

* * * * *

To those of you who are suffering today, Shirley and I would like to share a few words of encouragement with you. There is no place to hide, nor such a thing as a private life in this world for a man or woman who is intimately aware of, and shares in the sufferings of Jesus Christ. God divides the private life of His saints and makes it a highway for the world on one hand, and for Himself on the other. No human being can stand that unless he is identified with Jesus Christ. We are not sanctified for ourselves. We are called into intimacy with the gospel, and things happen that appear to have nothing to do with us, but everything to do with the Kingdom of Heaven.

God is getting us into fellowship with Himself during these times of suffering. Let Him have His way. If you refuse, you will be a stumbling block and a hindrance to God in his redemptive work in the world. If God can accomplish His purposes in this world through a broken heart or a sick body, then why not thank Him for breaking yours. *"You are not your own, but His."* (1 Corinthians 6:19)

26

JESUS CRUISES THE CARIBBEAN

Shirley and I used to think that a person would have to go to church to get born again. Like us, most of our friends believed that if you wanted to learn about spiritual matters, you would have to find a Reverend to teach you. But when Jesus baptized us in the Holy Spirit, we got straightened out on that and a lot of other dumb beliefs we had. We learned that everyone was a candidate for salvation, healing, and the baptism in the Holy Spirit, and that we were the ones the Lord was referring to when He said, *"Go ye therefore, into all the world..."* We became *"ye's"* almost over night. And the whole world became our mission field. Of course, we always recommended that new believers find a good Bible-based Church, be baptized in water, and faithfully attend that Church.

Some of our evangelist friends told us that we should follow the *Sonshine* and go south during the cold winter months up north. We couldn't argue with them about that.

The Lord led the Bickfords, the Caldwells, and the Hammonds, all good FGBM men and their wives to move to the southwest part of Florida. Not long after that that, we were invited to come to Fort Myers and Naples, Florida and stay with them while ministering in the South Florida Chapters and many of the churches in that area. It didn't take us long to adjust to the change in temperature. And God certainly blessed our ministry!

Later on, the Hammonds felt the Lord calling them even further south to the Caribbean Islands. So when they asked us to accompany them and their group, we found that we could *tear* ourselves away for the work of the Lord. Our itinerary would take us from Miami to St. Thomas, then to St. Croix. From there we would fly or sail on to visit Antigua, Martinique, Barbados, and Puerto Rico. We then would return to Miami. The plan was for us to let God lead us, and to be patient and see what He would do on that huge luxury liner, the Nordic Prince cruise ship, as well as at the six islands in the Caribbean we'd be visiting. The sacrifices that some folks have to make to serve the Lord!

It was not a good place to do much fasting. When we finished one gourmet meal, they would be getting ready for the next one, twenty-four hours a day. While we were at sea, we walked along the deck a lot—five laps around the ship was just a mile. Or we could swim, or do all kinds of nice things. During our walks, we noticed a large lounge on the foreword part of the ship that wasn't being used during the mornings. So Larry (Hammond) made arrangements with the Captain for us to use that big lounge for a morning prayer-and-praise meeting. He also had called ahead to the various islands using the FGBM Directory and arranged meetings for us all along the way. We put an announcement in the ship's daily newsletter to inform everyone about the meeting.

The first morning we met for fellowship in the lounge, a lady from West Palm Beach joined us. Her friend was confined to her room because of severe pleurisy. When she saw us praying for the sick, this lady brought her friend up to the meeting. After ministry, the lady's pleurisy was completely healed. She had some friends aboard the ship that she was certain would be thrilled to attend our next meeting.

Our next "patient" was a man who had had two radical surgeries, a lobotomy for a brain tumor, and open-heart surgery to replace his diseased aorta. Two of his ribs had been removed to allow the surgeons to do their work on his aorta. This left him with a lot of pain. The Lord touched that dear man so that he was free of pain for the rest of the cruise.

We don't recall all of the things God did for the people on that ship, but a steady stream of candidates came each day for the healing touch of the Lord Jesus. Our ministry in that Lounge grew little by little until we had more than 100 people there. Only God knows all that happened.

Shirley's painful past seemed to have left her with a keen awareness of pain in other peoples bodies. One especially warm day after a walk through the shopping district in St. Croix, a number of the people headed back to the ship with painful and swollen feet. A couple of the ladies were suffering a great amount of distress, so Shirley asked if she could pray for them. So right there on the afterdeck where the people were coming and going, Shirley was on her knees praying for these ladies feet. When the precious anointing of the Spirit came on those ladies, they were blessed so much they started dancing around and praising the Lord for their healing. Another lady asked Shirley to pray for her too, having witnessed the success of the other prayers. By this time Shirley finished with this lady, a steady stream of sore-footed women had lined up for prayer. Who says God does things only in church? (I sometimes wish I had a movie camera when these things happen, but maybe the Lord doesn't want pictures, or maybe taking pictures might inhibit some from accepting ministry. We weren't there to put on a show.)

A meeting we held on St. Thomas was especially memorable. A lady of German extraction and her husband owned a very nice restaurant in town. She had a bad-looking skin cancer on her cheek. As we ministered to her, that filthy cancer fell off her face and onto the floor, and the Lord replaced the cancerous tissue with nice healthy skin. They were so happy they invited us all to have lunch at their restaurant for a celebration.

On the final night before returning to Miami, the Captain held a special black tie, tuxedo type of party in the big round auditorium. That night, the ordinary guests of the ship—the amateurs—provided the entertainment. Several of the featured entertainers were from our Christian group. They did everything from singing Amazing Grace, to giving testimonies of what God did for them in the meetings.

Sometimes I wonder if the Lord would ever lead us to have a permanent ministry aboard some beautiful big cruise ship. So far He hasn't indicated that to us, but what a ministry that would be: the sun, and the *Sonshine* every day in the Caribbean.

The men of the St. Thomas and St. Croix Chapters invited me to return to speak in their chapter meetings. My travel agent could hardly believe that I was going down there on Friday and returning on Sunday. But that was the way it was. The men in those chapters really knew how to run great meetings. The two chapter meetings went extremely well. At the end of the St. Croix chapter meeting, I met the German lady again. She was still rejoicing, and joined me in praising the Lord because more than thirty people came to Jesus that day.

Travel between those Islands is by amphibian airplanes, which are sort of fun when you fly on one for the first time. They take a bit longer to take off than regular airplanes, but once you're up there, a certain comfort comes from knowing that if the plane had to make a forced landing, it could just glide down onto the water. Only one slight problem occurred in my case. When I checked my bag at the ticket counter in St. Thomas, they neglected to put it on the plane with me. So I was forced to wait in San Juan for about three hours before my bags arrived and I could take the next flight to Atlanta.

On the Atlanta-to-Syracuse part of my flight, I was assigned to an aisle seat (which I always prefer). Next to me was a businessman from Chattanooga who was traveling to Syracuse for a business meeting on Monday morning. He, too, had encountered difficulties with his flight connections, and ended up several hours later on the flight with me.

It always seems to me when I am assigned to a certain seat, that more often than not the person next to me needs to hear about Jesus. As we chatted a bit about fortuitous meetings of people on airplanes, I shared a recent testimony of a friend of mine, Lee Buck.

Lee was traveling to Chicago for a meeting, when just before he boarded the plane, the Airline upgraded his ticket from coach to first-class seating, He was seated next to a lady with a long, foreign-looking dress, and a long walking stick. She appeared to be sound asleep. As the plane took off, Lee took his Bible out of his brief case and continued with a study he was doing on some portion of the Word. When he was finished, he put his Bible back in His bag and put his head back to meditate on the Word he had been studying. Just then, the lady next to him excused herself to ask Lee if he thought she was asleep, and therefore unaware that he was reading a Bible.

She proceeded to ask why Lee, who obviously was an intelligent businessman, would be reading a Bible. She then introduced herself as one of the foremost anthropologists in the world. She was on her way to do a lecture at the University of Chicago.

Lee shared with her how he had been born again by

putting his faith in the Lord Jesus Christ, and that he and his family had been enjoying a personal relationship with God, through faith in Jesus Christ ever since. And, yes, he was Senior Vice President of New York Life Insurance Co., and an authority in the Insurance Industry. Then, before the plane landed in Chicago, Lee shared with her how she too could have peace with God, even though she may not believe in Him.

Lee and his new friend walked off the plane, with her arm firmly leaning on Lee's arm. A delegation of dignitaries from U. of Chicago were there to greet her, but she declined their offer of an electric tram and continued walking arm in arm with Lee all the way to her limousine. There she thanked him, and promised to give more thought to the things he had shared with her. They then went their separate ways.

Several weeks later, Lee learned that this famous lady had passed away in a Boston Hospital. He hoped, of course, that she had followed his instructions to find her peace with God. One Sunday morning when Lee entered his church in Darien, Connecticut, an usher introduced him to a lady who told Lee that she was the anthropologist's private nurse. Just before the anthropologist passed away, she told the nurse about her meeting with Lee on her flight to Chicago. Then as her condition deteriorated, she told the nurse that Lee attended an Episcopal church in Darien, Connecticut. Her final instructions were for her to attend that Church and find Lee. Finally, she was to tell Lee that before she died, she had followed his instructions and had received Jesus Christ as her own personal Lord and Savior.

My businessman friend looked at me in the eye and said, "Fred, I don't think that was just a coincidence that he got transferred to the seat next to her on the plane. Do you think so?" Before I could reply, tears began welling up in his eyes and his voice was a bit unsteady. "Jim, you're right. It wasn't a coincidence. And it wasn't a coincidence that you and I are in these two seats." I replied. Jim's face was away from me looking out the window, but the fact that he was crying was quite evident.

I waited a few minutes for him to collect himself, but he continued to cry into his handkerchief. It must have been embarrassing to him, but God was doing something important in his life. As we began our descent into Syracuse, I still needed somehow to finish our conversation. I had a VOICE Magazine in my pocket. I took it out, and showed Jim what I was trying to say. The last page of that beautiful little witnessing tool always has the *Six Scriptural Steps To Salvation* in it. I showed him the page, and suggested that when he got to his motel room that night, he take the Gideon Bible out of the drawer and follow the instructions in VOICE and look up the scripture references. He replied with a positive shake of his head. We walked up the ramp, and I never saw him again. I am fully convinced that he met Jesus Christ on that plane that evening.

I never cease to be amazed at the number of details God can and will engineer to bring about the exact results of such a meeting. I pray I will always be ready when God includes me in one of His master plans for the salvation of one of His children, and allow me to have one more DIVINE APPOINTMENT

CAPE CORAL

Soon after our return from the Caribbean, Shirley was scheduled to speak for the Women's Aglow Chapter in Cape Coral, Florida. It was being held in a very nice country club banquet facility, where we and about 140 other women enjoyed the good food and fellowship immensely. Shirley shared the good things God had done in her life after she gave her life to Jesus. He had blessed us with four lovely children, and a happy marriage. The key to a happy marriage was faith in the Lord Jesus and all of the teachings about that subject in God's Marriage Manual, His Word.

An invitation for salvation was given, and the whole front of the room filled with those dear people who wanted more of God in their lives. The last couple to come forward came from the back of the room. We didn't know it then, but their neighbor had brought them to the "Club" for dinner, but failed to tell them that an AGLOW Meeting was being held that evening too. We led them in a sinner's prayer, and then prayed for each of them individually. It was a great meeting. I told them before we dismissed that I'd be meeting with the men in the Fort Myers Chapter for breakfast and fellowship on Monday morning at 6:30 am.

My buddy, Hugh, and I arrived early at the Fort Myers meeting that Monday morning. Soon after we arrived, Max from the Aglow Meeting walked in. We greeted him warmly, and ordered breakfast for him. After breakfast, we had a time of fellowship, giving each man an opportunity to share a testimony. At some point, Max shared what had happened to him and his wife Rose the previous Saturday night.

His testimony went like this: "I recently retired from my job as Senior Vice President of Marketing and Sales for a Fortune 500 Company. My work has always required me to travel most of the time. My wife, Rose, and I have homes in Bar Harbor, Maine; Vail, Colorado; and Cape Coral. While Rose and I enjoyed our various homes, we never learned to communicate with each other. When I retired, we suddenly were together all the time. Every conversation ended up in an argument, and sometimes in a "knock-down, drag-out fight!" We were discussing divorce, but we couldn't even agree on that! Our closest friend and neighbor heard our "fracases" and decided that we needed Jesus Christ in our lives. Frankly, we weren't that excited about her suggestions. So she invited us to have dinner with her at the Cape Coral Country Club last Saturday night."

"While we were eating, we noticed that the whole banquet room filled up, leaving us in the back of the room without even enough room for us to leave. The ladies sang some songs and introduced Shirley Lawrence and her husband Fred as the speakers. We enjoyed the talk she gave, how God had solidified their marriage when they gave their lives to Jesus Christ. Our neighbor had told us these things, but somehow we got really impressed when Mrs. Lawrence spoke so sincerely and right from her heart. We had heard a lot of sermons, but somehow this lady's simply sharing how Christ had changed their lives really got through to us. So, when they invited people that wanted to know Christ personally to go forward for prayer, we decided to try it. We both enjoyed the whole experience immensely, and left that place feeling like new people. Then the fun began.

We noticed that we talked about the meeting and what had happened to us all the way home. After we said good-night to our friend, we went out to our patio and continued to talk until midnight. Rose thought we should go to bed, so when we got ready for bed we were still talking, and continued to talk until morning. I think we talked more that night than we previously had during our whole lives together. We ate a little breakfast and continued to talk. We talked all day and then all night again, becoming increasingly exhausted. I came here this morning to speak with Fred, and try to learn more about what has been happening to us. We are going to die of exhaustion if God doesn't do something for us."

I said, "Brother Max, let's go outside by the pool and ask the Lord to straighten things out for you." So we went out under the palm trees and sat in the nice deck chairs. I prayed for him, and asked the Lord to bless my Brother and his wife with a good sound sleep. Before I finished praying, he was sliding down in his chair and falling asleep right there. He looked so peaceful that I rejoined the other men, and suggested that they keep an eye on him until he awakened.

And then see to it that he returned safely home. Hugh and I excused ourselves and returned home to Naples.

Shirley had spoken to the AGLOW Chapter president who had heard about Max and Rose's plight. So they went to visit her while we were in Fort Myers. Shirley said she had bags under her eyes and looked exhausted when they got there. They prayed for Rose and asked God to give her a good rest. Before they finished praying, Rose had fallen asleep in her chair. The ladies left, leaving a note that if they needed more prayer and counseling to give them a call. But the Lord had already brought things under control.

Max founded a FGBMFI Chapter in Cape Coral, and became very active in a Spirit-filled Church. The last I heard of them they had moved to Sun City, where they founded both AGLOW and FGBMFI Chapters. We just couldn't stop praising the Lord for Max and Rose, and for all He did in their lives, as well as all the others who came to know the Lord while we were there. We became good friends with Max and Rose, and just about everywhere we went to speak, they would be there. It seemed like we had DIVINE APPOINTMENTS every time we turned around while we enjoyed the Florida *Sonshine.*

27

THE UTTERMOST PART OF THE EARTH
Acts 1:8

Sooner or later every Christian is confronted with Jesus' command to *"Go into all the world and preach the gospel to every creature."* (Mark 16:15 KJV) For many, these words of Christ sound like the fulfillment of one of their worst nightmares. If they commit their lives wholly to the Lord, He will surely send them to Timbuktu or some other dreaded destination in the world where they will be faced with every fatal disease and wild animal known to man, and probably will never see their loved ones again.

But when we accept Christ as our Lord and Savior, we also acknowledge that He is well able to determine the destiny for which we were created. We are created by God to fill a role—as well as we can—that no one else can ever fulfill. And, with our creation comes a strong inner desire to accomplish that for which we were created. We can never know that strong sense of fulfillment and accomplishment until we do exactly what we were created to do. And if it means hardship, illness or even death, then so be it. The Lord promised us that he would never leave us, so we have nothing to fear.

For me, it began as a young boy with a strong interest in the stories I read in <u>National Geographic Magazines</u> about the African people. I would also read avidly from my Dad's library about men like my personal hero, David Livingston, and others whose lives on mission fields could never be explained apart from some supernatural enabling. Perhaps only they could really understand what motivated them to accomplish the amazing things they did.

When I joined Full Gospel Business Men's Fellowship (FGBMFI) in 1970, I soon learned that many of my new brothers ministered widely throughout the world, proclaiming the glorious gospel of our Lord Jesus Christ and starting new chapters of the Fellowship wherever they went. Our Founder and President, Demos Shakarian, was the greatest example any man could ever have to inspire and encourage men to attempt great things for God. I truly admired Demos and all of his men, but I believed that the things they did were way beyond my capabilities.

But what was I to do with Mark 16:15-18 (LB), *"And He (Jesus) told them, 'You are to go into all the world and preach the Good News to everyone, everywhere. Those who believe and are baptized will be saved. But those who refuse to believe shall be condemned."* That "Great Commission" repeatedly stared me in the face when I opened my Bible! My prayer became, "Lord, I get your message. Thanks. But I scarcely have money enough to travel in New York State, to say nothing of the world."

Gradually my concept of my world changed. At first, my neighborhood was my world, and even that was too big! But feeling God's calling on my life to reach out to my neighbors, I prayerfully went ahead, determined to be all I could be where ever I was. With God's help, I shared with more and more of the folks who lived in my neighborhood. Then, when my neighbors had heard the *Good News*, my neighborhood seemed to grow until it included my town, then my county, and then New York State.

A brother from South Africa who had been used mightily by the Lord in many parts of the world visited my chapter. He told us that they didn't need anyone to go to Africa unless they were making spiritual waves right where they lived. "What makes anyone think they can win souls for Jesus overseas, if they can't do it at home?" he asked. So it was that I progressed through the soul-winning ranks until the day came that I was invited by a brother from Nigeria to go there and speak at their Convention in Warri. While I can't say I felt qualified to go, I did feel that I was better prepared than I'd ever been. I responded that I would go and help him if God provided the necessary funds.

Days of preparation followed: obtaining the required shots, passport, and visas; and procuring appropriate clothing, personal effects, money, etc.. At the same time, I was fasting and praying about what God wanted me to do and say in Africa. Hopefully my experience gained from ministering in FGBMFI meetings and churches would be a great training ground for what lay ahead of me in Africa.

My first trip into the interior part of Nigeria was full of unforgettable experiences. Every minute of each day was pure culture shock. The political situation made travel there extremely difficult. The trip from the Lagos International Airport to the Lagos National Airport took me nearly one day, even though both airports were connected and shared the same runways, the two terminals being on opposite ends of the same runways. The military government suffered frequent coups, so one never knew from one day to the next when the next overthrow would take place. In addition, the Nigerian soldiers always seemed to be setting up roadblocks. They would shake down everyone they could for whatever they could get, and there was no one to hear or resolve complaints.

God heard my cry for help. He sent an angelic being to escort me when I just didn't know what to do next, because getting from Lagos to Benin City, and then by car to the little town of Warri in the southern part of Nigeria was the reason I was there.

I first realized that something was amiss in Warri when I finally located a Full Gospel Business Man. He wanted to know who I was, and what I was doing there. Believe me, no one ever just happens to be driving by and stops in to visit Warri, Nigeria. It is truly one of the uttermost parts of the earth. When I told him that I was there to speak for the FGBMFI Convention they were having, he was rather shocked—to put it mildly! He called another man to join us. And together they tried to break the news to me as gently as possible that, "Yes!" there was to be a Rally there that weekend, but "No!" they had plenty of speakers and they wouldn't be requiring my services.

I showed them my letter of invitation from their International Director that seemed to complicate the situation rather than to help it. Didn't I know that that man had packed up his family and had gone to the U.S. to attend Bible School, and in fact that he had taken the whole treasury of their Fellowship in Nigeria to pay his way? No, I hadn't heard. But I would spend the night there somewhere and return home the next day. That night I stayed in the old River Valley Hotel (It may have been new about the turn of the century, but I doubt it!), and the place where the Rally supposedly was to be held.As I poured out my heart to the Lord that night, all I seemed to get were words of encouragement and peace. God was still on His throne, even if I had so many doubts. I began to learn that, while the trip may not be exactly as I had anticipated, the destination would be exactly right when I am in His will.

The next morning, I went to the hotel restaurant for breakfast. Soon a middle aged, rather stocky lady—the manager of the hotel, whiskey in hand—sat down and began to question me. A pretty tough old gal, her name was Crystal and her nationality was German. She had great difficulty believing my story. She had never heard of anyone being so dumb as to go to Warri by mistake. Nor in her wildest dreams, could she understand why anyone would leave the comfort of their home in the USA to talk to anyone about Jesus in Africa—or anywhere else, for that matter!

Crystal and I got to know each other pretty well before she left to take care of her duties. As she was leaving I said, "Crystal, would you ask your desk clerk to help me put a telephone call through to my wife in New York?" She sat back down and said, "Haven't I made it clear to you that we have nothing here, including telephones?" To which I replied, "I told my wife that I would call her as soon as I got here. She is always anxious to know that everything is OK when I travel." "Well," Crystal replied, "this is one time you won't be doing that. Good day!" As she was leaving the room, I stated once more,

"Crystal, I never let my wife down, and I will be calling her. In the name of Jesus." She stopped short and said, "He'll have to do it because you can't. We don't have telephones."

Later that day, I was standing near the hotel entrance when Hank, a young white man from Tennessee, came walking by. We exchanged greetings and introductions. He was First Mate on a small ship that was tied up in the port on the other side of a long stone wall adjacent to the hotel. Some work was being done on his ship prior to their departure for the Nigerian oil fields in the north. After a few more pleasantries, he invited me to visit his ship and to meet the Captain and other men onboard. Being an old sailor myself, I was glad for the invitation and immediately took him up on his offer.

We walked around the wall to where two armed guards let us enter the big steel gate into the shipyard. Hank showed me around the ship, and I received warm greetings from the crew. Our final stop on the tour was the bridge, from which the Captain steered the ship. I looked at maps, at the navigation equipment, and finally at the ship's short-wave radio, about which I spoke admiringly. Hank responded, "Yes Fred, that's a nice radio. If you ever want to call home, just come down around twenty-two hundred (10:00 PM) to mid-night and you can call home by radio. There's a lady in Jacksonville who, as a service to seamen around the world, will take your radio call and plug you into a telephone line that will let you make your call home, collect." (Surprise! Surprise!) That was good news, and it was bad news. Good that I could call home, but bad because Shirley and I had decided not long before that we would stop accepting collect calls from unknown callers. Would she accept my collect call or not?

Later that day, I got another surprise—Jose Pasqua, Director of International Affairs for FGBM arrived. A seasoned traveler, he was a welcome sight. I decided to stay around another day or two to see what else might take place. After Jose and I got settled into a room together, he said, "Fred, I wonder if there is a possibility I could call home from here? I'd like to let my wife know I've arrived safely, etc.". "No problem, Jose. Just be with me tonight at 10:00 and we'll do just that. I'll tell you more about it later. Just be here." I replied.

That day Jose was busy trying to straighten out some of the problems that had arisen since his arrival, while I did a bit of sightseeing around Warri. I learned quickly to never point a camera toward a soldier or an office building, and some other life-saving tips. And I learned that anyone, including me, could be stopped for questioning at any time by the armed guards who were everywhere! If your answer didn't satisfy them, you might find yourself on your back, looking up the barrel of an AK-47 while you tried to come up with a more acceptable response. And there was no higher authority to whom you could appeal!

When 10:00 PM rolled around, Jose and I were off to the welding tender ship on the Warri River. Hank was there to meet us, introduce us to the crew, and to show us around his little ship with the big radio. When we got to the bridge, I felt that this was more than just a chance event, and that it may be a very important part of my mission, perhaps even a DIVINE APPOINTMENT.

Hank started to fiddle with the dials on his radio, and soon brought in the lady in Jacksonville. Although somewhat garbled at first, we heard her reply to Hank's radio call letters, Whiskey X-ray Whiskey, located at 10 degrees north and 10 degrees west. She put my call through to our home phone, and I faintly heard Shirley's hello. The operator told her that she had a collect call coming through from the high seas, and would she accept the charges? Shirley's reply was, "No. I don't know anyone on the high seas and I won't accept the charges." And she hung up! I told the operator that that was my wife, and could we try again? The second time wasn't much better. But the third time, I broke into the conversation, saying, "Shirley! Shirley! don't hang up. It's me, Fred! I'm here with Jose Pasqua," (a name I knew she'd recognize). This time she said, "OK, I'll accept the charges."

We had a nice conversation. Shirley was relieved and happy to hear from me, and had been praying that I would call. By the time Hank was able to put Jose's call through, the reception had improved markedly. His call went to Joyce in California with no problem. .

From hearing our phone conversations, Hank now knew that Jose and I were men who really loved the Lord and were there on His business. We asked him about his home and family in Tennessee. He said, "You guys sound like my wife. She goes to these meetings where the folks all sing and pray. As a matter of fact, she told me that they were praying for me (Hank)." I said, "Hank, before you shove off from here for your three- month stay in the North, would you like to go with Jesus in your heart and life? He loves you so much that He sent me all the way here to tell you about Him." " Why sure, that would make my wife real happy," Hank replied. So Jose, Hank and I joined hands and we led Hank in a sinner's prayer. What a joy! Hank gave me his wife's address so that when I got home, I could let her know the good news—which I did! Later, her thank-you note to me was really precious.

The next morning at breakfast, Crystal joined Jose and me at the table. She still had her glass of whiskey and didn't seem too happy. After a few minutes I said, "My, Crystal, we sure had a nice talk with our wives last night." She spoke sharply, "You did not! Don't you lie to me!" I said, "Jose, did we call home last night?" He replied, "We sure did, Fred, it was really great!" I then told Crystal how God had helped us call home. Her response was more subdued this time. She had heard that that had been done before, but she never expected me to find out about it. As she left our table she said, very sharply, "Mr. Lawrence, I must speak to you alone before this day is finished!" With my extraordinary gift of discernment, I knew that my meeting with Crystal would be another DIVINE APPOINTMENT.

It wasn't until after midnight that things quieted down enough at the River Valley so that Crystal and I could meet under the large acacia tree in the dirt courtyard fronting the hotel. She began by saying she thought I might be some kind of a *man of God* when we first met. Then, when we made the impossible call home, she became convinced that I was who I said I was. She shared with me about her life in Germany before the war. Her parents wanted to spare her from the war, and sent her to stay with friends in Ghana, West Africa. Her priest assured her that if she prayed and made the sign of the cross each day, she would be OK. Quite to the contary, life in Africa became a nightmare for this 16-year old girl. She was raped, robbed, and/or accosted numerous times following her arrival. She had escaped the war, but her life in West Africa had been insufferable. Two nights before I came, she cried out to the God she had learned about as a child, but which she had long since stopped believing in: *"GOD! GOD! ARE YOU THERE SOMEWHERE? IF YOU ARE THERE, PLEASE HELP ME! I CAN'T LIVE ANOTHER DAY HERE! PLEASE, PLEASE HELP ME!"* She added that when we met in her restaurant, it came to her that I was somehow an answer to her plea.

I explained God's wonderful plan of salvation to Crystal, that He loved her so much that He had given His only begotten Son to die on the cross so that her sins and mine would be forgiven. Then I added that *"whosoever believeth in Him shall not perish but shall have eternal life."* (John 3:16) I told her I believed that God had sent me to Warri in answer to her prayer. By then she was weeping profusely. I held her trembling hands that were perspiring in the 100 degree heat as she followed me in the prayer with great intensity. Suddenly all of the tension left her. Years of trials and tribulation became as nothing in the light of Jesus Christ shining from her every pore. Instant relief! Praise the Lord! A DIVINE APPOINTMENT for sure! I gave her a New Testament and a VOICE Magazine as she ran off to her home adjacent to the hotel, laughing, and crying, and praising God all at once.

The next morning after breakfast, I was preparing for the day when a knock came on my door. There was Crystal with her desk clerk. She introduced us and said, "He would like one of those Bibles like you gave me." Her face was shining! And for the first time since we met, she wasn't drinking whiskey. I greeted him warmly and invited him into my room. I fully explained that the plan of God's wonderful salvation is a gift to those who fully trust Him. Kneeling by the old couch with me, that precious young man wept his way to Jesus. With Jesus in his heart, a Bible in one hand and a VOICE Magazine in the other, he ran out to tell what God had done for him.

In a few minutes, he was back with the cook. "Mr. Lawrence, this is Mr.(Cook). Can he have what you gave me?" We went through the same procedure as before, and he went off praising the Lord, and looking for his two waitresses. Soon he was back with them. On their knees by my couch, they accepted Jesus as their Lord and Savior.

Just before noon, the waitress named Queenie came back to my door with two of the maids and a maintenance man. With grateful hearts, they also received their books and a blessing from Jesus. The whole staff of the River Valley Hotel, Warri, Nigeria, were safe in the arms of Jesus.

If I had shared the gospel with a throng of thousands, I doubt if I could have felt any better than I did at that moment. It was joy unspeakable and full of glory, a moment never to be forgotten, a DIVINE APPOINTMENT! God taught me many lessons on that trip, but none compared with the joy of just allowing God to use me to bless dear people in small, out-of-the-way places that most Christian evangelists never reach.

Jose Pasqua and I rented a car, and drove back to Benin City for a meeting with the Nigerian National Board. These were some of the finest Christian men I had met on the trip. Since then, I have come to know and love these brothers, and have returned several times to work with them in Chapter Workshops , Seminars, and Conventions in various parts of Nigeria. The matter of their ex-treasurer came up in one of our meetings. After we prayed about it, one of the men said that he believed God wanted them to forgive their brother and never mention it or him again. He then reached into his pocket and offered a good sum of money toward what was owed to their treasury. All of the other men agreed with him, and soon put together more than $9000 to fully restore their treasury. A joyful spirit of praise filled the room as they had cleared up this cloud that had been hanging over their heads since their brother had gone to the US. They were finally free.

Jose and I continued on together back to Lagos and then to Accra, Ghana, where we attended their first National Convention. One of the men introduced me in a meeting as "an American with an African heart."

Each day in Africa was a fulfillment of God's plan for my life. On numerous occasions since that memorable trip to Nigeria, the Lord has sent me back to various parts of Africa to assist in the great outpouring of the Holy Spirit through the Fellowship there.

Ghana

The next time I visited Ghana, I had been asked to speak at their Annual Convention in Accra, the nation's capital. A very nice young brother picked me up at the airport for the drive to the hotel where I would be staying. He told me that he had been assigned to "take care of me" and transport me to the Convention Hotel. He said, "Whatever you'd like to do while you're here just let me know." With a boldness I didn't even know I had in me I replied to him, "I would like to visit your President." He thought I meant the Chapter President, and that we would meet him soon. I told him that I'd like to meet President Rawlings, if that would be possible.

The Convention went quite well. The people were very warm and friendly, and more than a thousand were in attendance. To my total amazement, some men came running to the platform during the Saturday morning meeting to tell me to hurry and go with them to the President's castle. We would have a brief meeting with the President in about 20 minutes. (When I asked to meet him, I didn't even dream that it would happen, and had no idea what I would say to him when we met!)

I asked Jose Pasqua to join me, and soon we arrived at an old British fort where the government was located. Military coups occurred in Ghana quite regularly as well, so the President had surrounded the fort with machine gun emplacements in the turrets, each protected by sandbags built up all around them. We produced our passport/visas, and were led to a large room where we encountered a very stately lady who was in charge of protocol. (I already had met her at one of the Convention evening Sessions. I learned that it was through her that the Brothers had made my request known, that in turn had brought about this amazing meeting.) The Secretary of Protocol explained that we would enter the President's Meeting Room, and would remain standing until introductions were completed.

The President entered and introduced himself and his attendants. These included the Secretary of Interior and the Secretary of Defense, along with their attendants; some members of the Press; and a photographer. After Jose and I had met everyone, we were informed by President Rawlings that he would be unable to meet with us as planned because of some important business that had come up.

As the President left the room, the Secretary of the Interior, being the highest-level person there, took charge by personally introducing herself. She quickly looked at her information sheet that said I was a New York Architect, and then started asking me some very pointed questions. Who was I and why was I there? Before I could respond, she informed me that Ghanaians were a praying people, and what did I think I could add to their society. She also suggested that, with all the slums we had in the US cities like Chicago, St. Louis, etc., maybe I should be home helping my own people with their problems! (I later learned that she had been educated in Moscow and apparently had no great love for Americans!)

The Lord instantly gave me a response: *"Godliness exalts a nation, but sin is a reproach to any people."* I then informed her that we were a group of Christian men whose mission was to encourage businessmen and professional men to follow Christ and His teachings, and to be more responsible businessmen. These businessmen were to respect their President and his staff, to be honest and kind in their business dealings, to be better family men, and to work diligently to make Ghana a more prosperous and pleasant nation.

Without really knowing it, I had hit all the major problems her government was facing, and had addressed those things about which she personally was most concerned, namely, what we could do about the corruption and mismanagement they were facing each day? Her demeanor changed. I explained how we also shared our love for Jesus Christ and his teachings to our own U.S. businessmen. When men turned to Christ, they also became better men in every area of their lives. We were dedicated not only to reaching out to Ghanaians with the love of Christ, but we also were doing the same things at home and elsewhere around the world. Jesus Christ is the Prince of Peace! The only hope for people everywhere, as evidenced by the wonderful things He had done for us personally, was to be found in our Savior, Jesus Christ.

The meeting that had been scheduled to last ten minutes lasted forty-five minutes. When she announced the meeting was finished, I said, "You told me that you are a praying people, so wouldn't it be appropriate for us to close the meeting with prayer for Ghana, President Rawlings, and all of his government. She readily agreed, so we stood in front of our chairs that were arranged in a large circle. I said, "Let's join hands while we pray," and I suggested they follow me in the prayer. As closely as I can remember, I started by saying, "Dear Heavenly Father, in the Name of the Lord Jesus Christ . . . " I paused and recommended we agree with this prayer with more enthusiasm so that God would be able to hear us, and started over again. This time they spoke loudly and clearly, "Dear Heavenly Father, in the Name of the Lord Jesus Christ, we thank you for this gathering of people who love Ghana and President Rawlings. (response). We pray for our beloved Nation of Ghana, for its peace and prosperity. (response) We pray that you will forgive us of all of our sins and iniquities. (response) And that you will come into our lives as our Lord and Savior. (response) Thank you Lord. Amen." Someone started to clap, so they all did. With that, we started to leave. The Secretary of Defense, who was a tall (6'-6" or more) old warrior, waited until I headed for the door. As I did, he put his big hand on my back, indicating that I should stop. Then he said in a deep, sort of tremulous voice, "Mr. Lawrence, no one has ever spoken to us the way you did today. As we prayed I began to feel all clean inside. I feel so light. Please come back and see us again sometime." I thanked him, and invited him to our Convention Meeting that night.

As I left, I thought of all the times I had had similar opportunities, but had been too timid to do anything about it. I decided then and there that I would never again shy away from speaking the Word to people of high estate.

The following year we had our World Convention in Anaheim, California. When I walked into the convention lobby I noticed a group of Ghanaians, and among them was that Ghanaian Secretary of Protocol along with the Secretary of Interior. Both came over to greet me. They told me that the Defense Minister who was with us on that eventful day, had gone to be with the Lord shortly after our visit there. The Secretary of Interior Lady had attended the next FGBMFI meeting in Tema, and had gone forward when the invitation for salvation was given. Her life and the lives of her family had completely turned around. So they had joined the Ghanaian contingency at the Anaheim World Convention.

Brother Kwabena Darko, the Tema Chapter president, later confirmed all she had told me. Bro. Darko was the largest poultry producer in all of Africa, and a powerful witness for the Lord wherever he went.

P.S. Another DIVINE APPOINTMENT I will never forget is Anna, whose brother is Kofi Annan, Secretary General of the United Nations. May the Lord be praised and receive all the glory for this wonderful miracle. This and my other experiences in Zaire (The Republic of Congo) were so many and varied that I will have to hold all of that for a later book.

28

A CHANGE OF VENUE

In 1994, Demos and Rose Shakarian went to be with the Lord. I will never forget just how much they meant to Shirley and me. Under their ministry as Founder and President of Full Gospel Business Men's Fellowship, we grew immensely in the things of God. They had opened doors for us to minister throughout New York State and around the world that totally changed our lives.

Demos loved to talk with me on the phone, but being a "night person," he would always call me in the middle of the night. When I heard his voice, I would wake up very quickly. Then he would apologize for calling me so late, usually saying that he had forgotten about the time difference between California and New York. He was an encourager. I would want to get out of bed and hurry up to do whatever he was encouraging me to do. He and Rose also were two of the most gracious and loving people we ever knew. We hope that someday we might come close to being the kind of persons they were.

Someday soon you should read the book about their

lives, <u>The Happiest People on Earth</u>. It has made a tremendous impact on people around the world. It has a special place in my library, partly because of the beautiful words they wrote to us in the flyleaf of our copy. Even in their "transfer to heaven," they continue to be a blessing to us and many like us.

In 1995, several of the former members of FGBMFI felt led of the Lord to begin a new organization entitled "Business Men's Fellowship, USA." We followed Demos Shakarian's original vision for world-wide soul-winning, especially to men, but actually encompassing everyone. Demos told us on numerous occasions that when you reach a man with the gospel of Jesus Christ, you also reach his whole family. But the Fellowship continues to specialize in Men's Ministry, also known as Ministry in The Marketplace.

When the Business Men's Fellowship started in 1995, I was a founding Director. Our President has been Ronny Svenhard, a prominent baker in California, a fantastic leader of men, and a "world-class Christian Business Man". He and his wife Norma exhibit many of the fine traits of Demos and Rose Shakarian, and many more, of course, that are special with them. He is a very special person, and one whom we love with all our hearts.

I soon became Vice President of the new Fellowship, and worked very closely with Ronny and our National Board of Directors. Then I had several accidents that left me with brain damage, with headaches and some other medical problems. I felt I was not helping achieve all I should in such an important ministry to the World, so I resigned my position. The Board of Directors made me a lifetime Director Emeritus, which has been an enormous blessing to us. I still head up our Men's and Couples Advances, and I believe the greatest part of our lives and ministry is still ahead of us.

I've prayed that the Lord would use this book to encourage men to organize new chapters all over the country. If anything of the experiences that I've written in this book have caused you to have a burden to win souls in your town or State, just think how many stars you can have in your crown some day. Take out a map of your State, hang it on your wall, and each day claim a new chapter of Spirit-filled men for each place on that map. Ask God where you should go first to start a new chapter in your town or city. . Then when it gets going real well, invite people from the surrounding area to your meetings. They then will want to see a chapter in their town. You and your brothers can help them do it, and at the same time receive the greatest blessing in your life. You can obtain all the resource material you need: <u>Answer</u> magazines, chapter literature, and even manpower (including me), to reach your town and State for Jesus Christ. The address for Business Men's Fellowship is included in the last Chapter of this book. We are prepared to help you start a chapter where you live, no matter where you are in this world. Remember, we aren't starting new churches, but we're doing everything possible to make your church more successful and more effective. We train our men to be "flaming evangels" for Christ. Then we bless our pastors by bringing new sheep into his sheepfold. May your motto be "CALLING MEN BACK TO GOD." A multitude of DIVINE APPOINTMENTS are waiting for you.

29

A GOOD REPORT
THROUGH FAITH
Hebrews 11:3

"Why are you writing a book, Fred?" my friend asked me." Aren't there enough Christian books in the book stores and on Christian book shelves?" They sounded like words I had spoken to myself so many times that they echoed like the voice of a Swiss yodeler through my brain. Yet, I knew for certain that God had spoken to me through many witnesses to do exactly that, write a book.

A larger question arises once you've gotten through the "Whys," and that is, "What can be said that has not already been said about faith?" Nothing in the words of this book is a greater testimony of the grace and faithfulness of God than what already has been written many times before. But perhaps this kind of total faith in the promises of God by a common layman and his wife needs to be said over again in the 21st century and beyond.

When we read of the lives of such men as George Muller

who dared to believe God to supply his every need for seventy-three years, we are tempted to say, "But that was way back in the 1800's. In the world we live in today that could never be done." So my answer to that is, "Has God changed?"

Then we might wonder, "But hadn't God called George Muller to a ministry to orphans? That was certainly a very worthy cause in Muller's day." But the lives of the thousands of orphans whose lives were changed by the power and love of the Lord Jesus Christ then are no more precious to God than the lives of thousands of business and professional men and their families living today. Who is prepared to make such a comparison?"

"But wasn't Muller more the exception than the rule?" Yes! But can't anyone choose to launch out into a lifetime ministry in a path of utter dependence upon God alone, to give a visible proof that God would show Himself still to be the Living God?

Our God is more than able. In fact, the Word of God tells us in 2 Chronicles 16:9, that "The eyes of the Lord run to and fro throughout the whole earth, to show Himself strong in behalf of them whose heart is perfect toward Him, that He might fully support him." God is out there looking for people who will totally trust Him.

Others might add a question about 2 Thessalonians 3:16, "...if any would not work, neither should he eat." I was so conscious of this obvious truth that once when I was unable to find work for a lengthy period of time, I refused to eat. Then God spoke to me and said, "Trust Me!" (see Chapter 5) I also remember sermons my Dad preached on this subject.

So, let's look at this important scripture in its proper context. In verse 3:6, Paul is speaking to the Thessalonican churchmen about dealing with "unreasonable and wicked men". In verse 6 he continues to speak about "brothers whose walk is disorderly." In verse 10, Paul continues to address the lazy "busybodies" who refuse to work. He commands them to "work in quietness, and eat their own bread" Thus, when Paul speaks in 3:10, he is reminding these busybodies that "this we commanded you, that if any would not work he should not eat."

When you are certain that God has called you to a life of extraordinary faith, you may also be certain that He has called you to a life of back-breaking work. If you follow through on this life of faith, I can assure you God has not called you to be idle. So relax, and don't worry about your critics. They haven't "rightly divided" this truth.

The other aspect of my work with the Lord was that I never billed myself as anything but a "successful architect". And I never spoke to even one person about my "work (or walk) of faith", nor have I ever asked any man (or woman) for money, or support of any kind. Was anyone qualified to tell me to stop doing what I was doing and return to my drawing board? One of the men did suggest that they offer to pay some of my expenses, but no one responded! No one else ever brought up the subject.

I learned a lot from my many personal conversations with Tommy Ashcraft, Executive Vice President of the Fellowship. Tommy, a man who had a deep understanding of the Word of God, always made his decisions based on scriptural principles with which no man could argue. I was pleased to acknowledge him as my spiritual mentor. He told several people that there was no way I could have been employed full-time and have accomplished the things I did. When God calls you to work for Him 100% of the time and you agree with Him, then He can assign you to any kind of work He wishes to. The 81st Psalm (vs. 6) puts it like this, "I removed his (Israel's) shoulder from the burden: his hands were delivered from the pots." Then in vs. 10 "I am the Lord thy God, which brought thee out of the land of Egypt: open thy mouth wide, and I will fill it(referring to satisfying the desires of Israel completely if they would only be faithful to God). This is the testimony of this book. If you feel so led of the Lord, then just be real certain that it is God directing your path, launch out into the deep where your feet can no longer touch the bottom, and swim into God's special plan for your life.

Someone surely will ask if I think that everyone God calls to serve Him on a full-time basis is also meant to live totally by faith. In one way or another, the answer is yes! But I don't believe for a minute that it takes more faith and trust in the Lord to work full time for God and let Him furnish your income as you need it, than it does to go to work each day and bring home a paycheck. Please be clear on this subject. When you are living in God's perfect will for your life, it is also His will to "supply all your needs according to His riches in glory by Christ Jesus." (Phil. 4:19)

It is never faith for one who has no visible source of income to try to make someone who has a profitable business or profession feel guilty about any perceived or even real difference in income they may have. The one who does that short-circuits God's supply line of income to himself. In effect, he is saying, "I work for God, but He doesn't pay much so I need some outside help." Beloved, if that is your attitude, you are in trouble. God owns all the silver and gold on a thousand hills, and He uses it to further His own ends in His own inimitable fashion.

Well what about the "Name it and Claim it" folks? They are full of faith and have plenty of scripture to back up their beliefs. One of those dear ones came to meet me at the Houston Airport. He was driving a new pink Cadillac that seemed like half-a-block long and had every possible gadget you could imagine. Our discussion that day was totally about the car. The Name of Jesus just never came up. That example pretty much speaks for itself.

I am now convinced that the reason God wanted me to have the experiences I've had, and then to write about them, was to illustrate the great value there is in simply surrendering every part of ourselves to our loving Heavenly Father. He will do "exceeding abundantly above all we can ever ask or think, according to the power that worketh in us, Unto Him be glory in the church by Christ Jesus throughout all ages, world without end. Amen." (Ephesians 3:20-21.)

END

Printed in the United States
36720LVS00002B/157-165